THE GREAT ESCAPE

THE
GREAT
ESCAPE

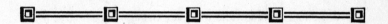

By PAUL BRICKHILL

INTRODUCTION
By GEORGE HARSH

FAWCETT COLUMBINE • NEW YORK

A Fawcett Columbine Book
Published by Ballantine Books

Copyright © 1950 by Paul Brickhill
Copyright renewed 1978 by Paul Brikhill

All rights reserved under International and Pan-American Copyright Conventions. Published in the United States by Ballantine Books, a division of Random House, Inc., New York, and distributed in Canada by Random House of Canada Limited, Toronto.

http://www.randomhouse.com

Library of Congress Catalog Card Number: 97-90866

ISBN: 0-449-00139-3

This edition published by arrangement with
W. W. Norton and Company, Inc.

Manufactured in the United States of America

First Fawcett Crest Edition: March 1961
First Ballantine Books Mass Market Edition: December 1983
First Ballantine Books Trade Edition: September 1997

10 9 8 7 6 5 4 3 2 1

TO THE FIFTY

INTRODUCTION

SEVERAL days ago I was given the manuscript of this book to read. I took it home and Eleanor and I, becoming engrossed in it, sat up all one night poring over what Paul Brickhill has written. "Whew!" she said when we had finished. "Did all this really happen?"

The manuscript was on the floor between us and I was staring out the window.

"Yeah," I murmured. "It really happened."

And that is the only introduction this book actually needs: Yes, it really happened. But because every man mentioned in this book was a friend of mine, because I have shared pitifully small rations with them, fought lice with them, baited the Germans with them and because many of them are now dead, I am grateful for this chance to point out that they did not die for a senseless reason.

This book is many, many things. It is the story of a project, a project conceived in the minds of, and carried through to success by, a group of ragged, starving scarecrows who, despite all privations, never lost sight of their sworn duty.

There is something demoralizing about being taken a prisoner of war. At first it stuns the mind and one is overwhelmed with a feeling of helplessness, and hope is only a dim, dim shadow. The new prisoner is sorely tempted to sit back quietly, co-operate with his captors and thus make life comparatively easy for himself. In fact that is the philosophy the

Germans were constantly trying to drive into our minds. They offered us many alluring inducements in the form of extra privileges and rations to "behave," to co-operate and to give up our vexing escape attempts.

But it is the duty of any officer in time of war, should he have the bad fortune to be taken prisoner, to do all in his power to escape. If escape is impossible it then becomes his duty to do everything within his means to force the enemy to employ an inordinate number of soldiers to guard him, to do all he can to harass the enemy and to convince his captors that they have caught a very large, very active and troublesome bear by a slippery tail. If the carrying out of this duty can be heavily spiced with a rollicking, ribald sense of humor and a sharp sense of the ludicrous such as is possessed by most Americans and British, then this duty becomes more a game than a duty, a game to be entered into with fiendish glee. And as such it was considered by all the thousand-odd officers whom the Germans had corralled in the North Compound of Stalag Luft III during the war.

By the time the Americans began arriving in the North Compound the escape, sabotage and harassing organizations were already well organized. There was considerable doubt in the minds of the more prison-wise British as to just how helpful the Americans would prove to be in this game of cloak and dagger with the Gestapo. The average Briton of course prides himself on being part of "perfidious Albion" and the British contingent was doubtful that the Americans, with their vaunted background of Dan Beard–Boy Scout–Fair Play training, could turn their minds from this pabulum and take an effective part in activities that required a completely Machiavellian attitude.

However, the British obviously overlooked the fact that an American only has to be sold on the idea that his cause is just and he is capable of anything. (The American Indian and the Panama Canal are two points in proof.) And it was not long before all the subversive activities of the camp were taking on a rowdy, fresh air of hubba-hubba that was leaving the Germans completely bewildered. As soon as the Americans got over the initial shock of being prisoners they started robbing the Germans blind of anything they could possibly use, lying through their teeth to their captors with all the persuasiveness of a European diplomat and, if need be, were quite capable of slipping up behind a guard with a ready loop of piano wire—to the constant terror of the reprisal-fearful British. They began showing even the wily British some new and improvised tricks in waging an undercover, unscrupulous war.

But this book is a whole lot more than a hilarious story about a group of food- and sex-starved men playing grim practical jokes on a race of square-headed people who are devoid of any sense of the ridiculous. It is the story of achievement against impossible odds. And it proves something that I believed then and know now—there is nothing that can stop a group of men, regardless of race, creed, color or nationality, from achieving a goal once they agree as to what that goal is. The aftermath may be sheer, stark tragedy—that lies with the gods—but the point is, men, working together, can accomplish anything. This book—and the episode about which this book is written—proves it.

In its essence this is the story of a group of men—and of one man, Roger Bushell, who was the colorful leader. And yet through it all runs the theme that even in death man can triumph over any obstacle. To my mind this is also the story of a Tower of Babel. The fact that this tower was in reverse and happened to be a tunnel is a minor point. What was important then—and is more so now—is that this Tower of Babel was successfully erected. It proves something important. In one magnificent gesture the seventy-six ragged, verminous men of all nationalities who climbed out of that stinking hole in the ground in Silesia on that windy March night in 1944 thumbed their collective nose at the entire Third Reich and all it stood for. They triumphed, through the only means left to them, over an idea that was rotten from the core out. And they proved for all posterity that men, working together, can dig a damned deep hole in the ground—or build a shining Tower of Babel.

George Harsh
New York

FOREWORD

PRISON camp life would not have been so bad if:

(a) It weren't such an indefinite sentence. At times you couldn't say you wouldn't still be there (or worse) in ten years.

(b) The Germans didn't keep dropping hints that if they lost, Hitler was going to shoot you anyway, just to even the score.

(c) You could get enough food to fill your belly again. Just once.

So we spent a lot of time trying to escape. It is a melancholy fact that escape is much harder in real life than in the movies, where only the heavy and second lead are killed. This time, after huge success, death came to some heroes. Later on, it caught up with some villains.

You learn to escape the hard way. It took us three years to become proficient—from the first primitive tunnels to the deep, long ones with underground railways, workshops and air pumps, forgery and compass factories, and so on. Above all we learned how to "destroy" sand and to hide everything in our little compound from the Germans constantly searching us.

The British had a start on the Americans because they were there first. Then the Yanks joined us and took to the escape business like ducks to water.

One got used to living in a microscopic world where life lay in working patiently for that brooding genius, "Big X." I sup-

pose it is romantic now. It wasn't then. Life was too real, grim and earnest.

They were all real—Rubberneck, the humorless and coldly efficient German; "Big X," the South African; Walenn, that charming Englishman; Ker-Ramsay, the dour Scot; Harsh, the rambunctious Yank; Sage, another Yank, also rambunctious; Floody, the Canadian who looked consumptive (and still does); Cornish, the baby-faced Australian; Pohe, the dark Maori; Minskewitz, the Pole with the Uncle Sam whiskers; Staubo, the handsome Norwegian; and all the others, too numerous to mention, even in the narrative that follows. No one ever noticed a nationality tag.

The Germans tried to play off the British against the Americans and vice versa, and in the end they took the Americans away and segregated them in another compound. We got along too damn well together.

Of my own part in the show—little enough to say. I am a sort of Boswell, not a hero. I was a cog in the machine, boss of a gang of "stooges" guarding the forgers, who had to work in an exposed position by windows to get enough light. Walenn, the chief forger, and I invented the "cloak and dagger" stooging system that gave them warning. It was rather complicated, but it never let us down—and that was the main thing. It just meant being on the job all the time, but there was nothing else to do anyway.

And when I finally drew a privileged position for the actual escape, "Big X" debarred me and three or four others on grounds of claustrophobia, a correct, if infuriating, decision. A few weeks later I was deeply grateful.

With the exception of the fake passport photograph of Ed Tovrea, the photographs in this book were taken by the methodical Germans. Some pictures, like the views of "Harry," formed a part of the official record. Others, including all the group pictures, were taken by the camera fans among our captors; often they gave us prints of their work—unhappily not so good as it might have been.

A couple of years after it was over, a friendly German interpreter sent prints of about half of those used in the book to our old leader in the camp, Air Commodore Massey, who kindly lent them to me. The rest of the photographs were preserved in one way or another by George Harsh, Col. A. P. Clark, Lt. Col. Jerry Sage, Capt. Donald Stine, and Ed Tovrea, to all of whom I am indebted in more ways than one.

The maps and drawings printed throughout the text are by Ley Kenyon and were made from sketches Kenyon did at the camp as a diversion from his regular work as one of Tim Walenn's star counterfeiters.

Since the war I've twice been back to Germany to dig deeper into the story, being lucky enough once to get into the forbidden Russian zone and fossick once more round the scene of the crime. After the hangman's job was done in 1948 I went through several thousand pages of unpublished reports, getting all the German side of the affair as well as a lot more of our own. And then I searched out the important survivors and filled in the few gaps left.

So here it is, as nearly the way it happened as I can make it.

Paul Brickhill

THE GREAT ESCAPE

◧ PRELUDE ◨

ROGER BUSHELL had just turned thirty when he reached Dulag Luft, the reception camp for Air Force prisoners. He was a big, tempestuous man with broad shoulders and the most chilling, pale-blue eyes I ever saw. In his early twenties he had been British ski champion, and once in an international race in Canada he had come swooping downhill like a bat out of hell and taken a bad spill over a boulder. The tip of one ski caught him in the inner corner of his right eye and gashed it wickedly. After it had been sewed up, the corner of his eye drooped permanently, and the effect on his look was strangely sinister and brooding.

It was on May 23, 1940, that he had led the twelve Spitfires of his squadron in over the coast between Dunkirk and Boulogne. Down below, men in sweaty battle dress were digging in on the beaches and spilling blood on the sand from the bombs. There weren't many R.A.F. fighters about because there weren't many R.A.F. fighters, and most of them were over on the rim of the battle trying to stop the dive-bombers from getting through.

Forty Messerschmitt 110's had slid down toward the Spitfires, and five of them picked on Bushell. He steep-turned and they overshot and pulled up. As he saw the last one sliding above, Bushell straightened out, pulled up, and was almost hanging on his propeller when his stream of bullets hit the

German. Smoke poured out of the Messerschmitt's port engine, and it turned on its back and went straight down.

Another Messerschmitt was coming at Bushell head-on. They were both firing; everything was red flashes, and then Bushell shot inches above the German and saw the German behind shoot steeply up, flick into a stall, and spin down, smoking. Bushell was on fire too, smoke pouring into his cockpit. His engine seized and the smoke cleared away.

Gliding down, he picked a field, and as he slid the Spitfire into it on its belly flame spurted under the engine cowlings. He had cracked his nose on the gunsight and scrambled out with blood pouring down his face. Watching the plane burn while he fished for a cigarette, he judged he was in British-held territory and with any luck would be back in his squadron in a couple of days.

A motorbike came pelting down a lane and turned in at the far end of the field. Bushell waited placidly for it, and then he saw that it wasn't a crash helmet that the rider was wearing but a coal-scuttle helmet, and a moment later he saw the gun pointing at him.

If the Germans had realized what a troublesome man they had caught they would possibly have shot him then. It would have paid them.

Though he was a squadron leader in the R.A.F., Roger Bushell had been born near Johannesburg, and at the age of six he could swear fluently in English, Afrikaans, and Kaffir and spit an incredible distance. Later he acquired public-school polish by being educated in England at Wellington. His housemaster when he first went there summed him up very neatly in a letter to his mother: "Don't worry about him. He has already organized the other new boys. I know the type well. He will be beaten fairly often but he will be well liked."

At Dulag Luft the Germans put him hopefully in solitary confinement to soften him up for interrogation, but that was not an enormous help because Bushell had been a barrister with a talent for suave belligerence, and they got nothing out of him except a rather acid charm. They turned him loose then in the compound, a bare patch of earth a hundred yards square with three long, low huts surrounded by mountains of barbed wire, searchlights, and machine guns, and inhabited by an unhappy band of men trained to fight but shut up behind barbed wire while their country awaited invasion.

The senior man, Wing Commander Harry Day, had been shot down five weeks after the war started, flying a Blenheim on a suicidal, lonely daylight reconnaissance over Kaiserslautern. He'd flown as a youngster in the first war, and now he was graying, a tall, stringy, vital man with a lean face (the type they call "ravaged") and a hooked nose. There was a wild streak in him, and prison camp didn't help it. He was capable of a sort of austere introspection, and then it would vanish in a mood of turbulent gaiety. He could be steely and frightening, and then sometimes that wry mouth of his would relax in a gentle smile.

"The Artful Dodger," Major Johnny Dodge, had been born an American (his mother, Mrs. Charles Stuart Dodge, was a daughter of John Bigelow, U. S. Minister to France under Abraham Lincoln). In the first week of the 1914 war, the Dodger, a smooth-cheeked youngster of twenty, sailed to England to get into the fight as soon as possible. Five years later he was a colonel with the D.S.O. and M.C. When things started again in 1939 the Dodger's friend and family kinsman, Winston Churchill, soon had him back in the army and the Dodger was trapped a few months later with the B.E.F. in France, down the coast from Dunkirk.

Now, in his forties, he swam miles out into the channel to intercept a ship, missed it, swam back, was caught, escaped, then was caught again by the Luftwaffe and always thereafter stayed in Air Force prison camps (when he wasn't es-

5

caping). Tall and courtly, the Dodger had an incredibly charitable nature and a strange insulation from fear. I don't say that extravagantly. I think fear didn't bother him. Bushell was like that and so was Wings Day.

So was Peter Fanshawe, a Fleet Air Arm lieutenant-commander, regular R.N. in character as well as fact—fair-haired Fanshawe, whom you couldn't call Peter because he was so Royal Navy, but very sound and hard to get to know. Jimmy Buckley was also a Fleet Air Arm lieutenant-commander, more hard-boiled than Fanshawe. There were the dependable Mike Casey, Paddy Byrne, and a lot of others. In the subtle hierarchy of character, independent of rank, Bushell was soon one of the leaders in the common ambition to escape. He, Wings Day, and a dozen others started digging tunnels. They had a lot to learn about it. The first one they started under Paddy Byrne's bed, cutting a trap door in the floor. The Germans had a lot to learn about finding tunnels too, so they got away with a lot they shouldn't have, burrowing into the wet earth with their hands, hauling the dirt back in basins, and dumping it under the hut. It was pitch-black down in the rat hole, and they did it all by touch, working in long woolen underclothes so that dirt stains on their uniforms wouldn't give them away.

The first tunnel was just under the wire with about eight feet to go to freedom when they ran into a spring and water gushed up and flooded them out. They started another tunnel in another direction. The Germans found it. Winter closed in and the escape season was temporarily over. You can't hike two hundred miles over snow without much food and no shelter to a friendly border.

As spring softened the country they started a fresh tunnel under a bed in Wings Day's room, and this time there were no serious hitches. By July it was eighty feet long, under and past the wire with only a couple of feet to dig up. And after all that, Roger got away the night before they made the break.

The prisoners were taken into an adjoining field for exercise, and in a corner of this field a goat lived in a tumble-down shed. A mock bullfight between the goat and the prisoners drew the guards' eyes (as it was meant to), and Roger crawled into the shed. There had been a lot of debate as to how he would get on in the shed. Buckley started the old gag by saying, "What about the smell?" and Paddy gave the stock reply, "Oh, the goat won't mind that." And, as it happened, the goat didn't mind at all. There was no fuss and after nightfall Roger crawled out and was away across the fields.

The next night there was a great din from a midnight party in one of the huts in the compound, and while the guards pondered on the merriment from behind their machine guns, Byrne dug out the last couple of feet of the tunnel and seventeen shadows emerged at the far end and snaked off into the woods under cover of the party noise.

Getting out of a camp is only half the battle; they learned this bitterly. They were all caught—most of them on the following day. The Dodger was snared trying to cross a bridge where there happened to be a guard. Wings Day stayed out three days till a couple of woodmen bailed him up with a shotgun. He had roughly tried to convert his uniform to look like civilian clothes, but you want a dark night to get away with that sort of thing.

Roger had crushing luck. He got away to the Swiss border and was within thirty yards of the frontier in a little village at night when a border guard stopped him. Roger pretended he was a slightly drunken skiing instructor going home after arranging a skiing match in the village. The guard was friendly and believed him but said he'd better come along to the station for formal check. Knowing what that would mean, Roger charmingly agreed and suddenly bolted around a corner and was away with a couple of bullets chasing him. He thought he was completely clear when he found he'd run into a cul-de-sac with high walls all around it, and back he was brought to punitive solitary confinement in a Frankfurt jail and then to Dulag.

Still, it had been valuable experience and the prisoners had tasted blood.

It was a good lesson for the Germans, too. They "purged" Roger and the Dodger and all the others who had escaped to a new camp at Barth, up by the shores of the Baltic. Within the next year, forty-eight tunnels were started there; but water lay only about four feet under the surface so the tunnels had to be very shallow, and the Germans used to collapse them all by driving heavy wagons around the compound.

Apart from the normal fervent wish to get out of prison and back home to the war, there was plenty of other motive for escaping. The Geneva Convention lays it down that captured troops are to be properly fed. The German idea of proper feeding wasn't much more than a formality; they fed us on about 1/2d. a week. If you've ever known hunger—not gnawing appetite, but real hunger—you'll understand part of the reason for P.O.W. reluctance to endure German hospitality. In his first year in the bag, Roger lost nearly forty pounds.

After a few months there, he and some others were herded into cattle trucks for transfer to another camp. Roger and some others levered up the floor boards in their truck, and bodies began to slip through into the night. One man went under the wheels, had both legs cut off, and died immediately.

At night, in a siding near Hanover, Roger and a Czech officer in the R.A.F., Jack Zafouk, slipped out, reached cover, and set off for the Czech border, where Zafouk's brother lived. Jumping a couple of goods trains, they reached the brother,

8

who gave them money and the address of a friend in Prague, who took them in and sheltered them.

For a week they both had to keep inside in the friend's flat. Zafouk didn't dare to go out because old friends might see him, and Roger had to stay in because he couldn't speak Czech. The host contacted the underground and arranged for their escape through Yugoslavia, but just as they were setting out the Gestapo broke the escape chain and executed the members.

Still shut in, Roger and Zafouk waited weeks till another underground chain arranged to pass them along to Turkey. They got to the Czech border when the Gestapo broke this chain too, and they narrowly escaped back to Prague. Czech patriots shot the Gestapo chief Heydrich about that time, and hell broke loose in Czechoslovakia. There were many executions and tortures besides Lidice.

And many spiteful betrayals. One morning the bell of the flat rang sharply. The Czech host, his son, and daughter were all out. Roger and Zafouk kept quiet and didn't answer the bell, but the door was burst open, five Germans pushed in, and in a few moments they were off to the Gestapo cells.

Zafouk was interrogated for a week and then sent to another camp. Roger was taken to Berlin, to a Gestapo cell. The Czech family was shot.

Meanwhile, other escapes were going on; that is, escapes from prison camps. No one yet had succeeded in getting back to England. At Barth, a primitive escape committee was organized to co-ordinate escape work. Wings Day nominated Jimmy Buckley as first chief. A genuine cloak-and-dagger atmosphere was creeping in. They called it the "X organization" for security reasons, and Jimmy Buckley was officially labeled "Big X."

The Germans became escape-conscious too, and "ferrets"

9

appeared in the compound—German security guards dressed in over-alls and armed with torches and steel spikes to probe for tunnels. Then they dug sound detectors into the ground around the barbed wire to pick up sounds of tunneling, and like clockwork they found tunnel after tunnel.

But there were still other ways of escape. One man dressed himself as a ferret and walked openly out of the gate at night. Others hid in trucks that brought food into the compounds. A Swiss commission (the Protecting Power) came to inspect the camp, and while they were in the compound a team dressed in makeshift civilian clothes walked out in their place. Pat Leeson dressed himself as a sweep with a dirty face and a cardboard topper like the German sweeps wear and walked out of the gate while the real sweep was in the compound.

Another reluctant captive was Douglas Bader, that phenomenal man who'd lost both his legs in an aircraft crash in the early thirties and went flying with tin legs to get a string of victories, wing commander's rank, a D.S.O. and Bar and D.F.C. and Bar. He'd collided with a German fighter in a scrap over France and had a leg trapped immovably in his damaged cockpit. So he took his leg off (the only time he ever appreciated losing his real ones) and baled out. The R.A.F. dropped a new tin leg for him and, mobile again, Bader was so intractable that the Germans took him out of the camp and put him into a prison hospital.

A few days later, Bader sneaked into a working party of British soldier prisoners being taken to a near-by airfield for labor. He stayed four days with them there looking for a chance to jump into a plane and take off for home, but before he could make it the working party was paraded one morning and a German security N.C.O. who knew Bader appeared and put the finger on him. They packed him off to Kolditz Strafelager, the punishment camp for the naughty boys.

In England, the R.A.F. air offensive was getting into full swing and a lot of good men were being shot down. Mostly they died, but some landed alive and were captured, and the number of prisoners was growing. To cope with them, the Germans built a new camp at Sagan, a town of about 25,000 in Germany's dust-bowl, Silesia, about halfway between Berlin and Breslau. It was up toward the Polish border and a long, long way from any friendly or neutral territory. The Germans called it Stalag Luft III, and by that name now it is notorious. We called it Goering's luxury camp, but that was sardonic. In the spring of 1942, a couple of hundred prisoners were purged to Stalag Luft III from Barth and other camps.

Among them was a fellow with the D.F.C., a persistent escape fiend. While crates containing equipment were being loaded on the train at Barth, a German interpreter said archly to the prisoners doing the loading, "Be careful of those crates. Maybe an escaper is nailed up in one."

The boys all dutifully said, "Ha ha, how funny that would be," knowing very well it was funny because the D.F.C. man was nailed up in one of them. He broke out on the journey and got away for a day or so but was caught and sent to Kolditz Strafelager.

When the others reached Sagan they found it about as grim as they'd expected—six low drab wooden barrack huts in a patch of sand surrounded by a double barbed-wire fence nine feet high. Spaced about a hundred yards apart just outside the barbed wire, the "goon-boxes" stood up on their stilts about fifteen feet high so that from the little huts on top the sentries behind their searchlights and machine guns could look down into the compound with clear vision and an unrestricted field of fire. (They were called goon-boxes because every prisoner in the Third Reich referred to the Germans as Goons.)

About thirty feet inside the barbed wire ran the warning

wire on its little posts about eighteen inches high. It was there to keep prisoners away from the fence, and it certainly did. If you put a foot over it, you could be reasonably sure of several bullets from the nearest trigger-happy sentry.

The night the first party arrived at Sagan, Wings Day and two others dressed up in R.A.F. uniforms they had converted to look like German Luftwaffe uniforms (all the guards were Luftwaffe) and tried to bluff their way through the gate. The guard wasn't fooled, and they were marched off by a reproachful Kommandant for fourteen days' solitary in the cooler. The cooler, like Grannie's castor oil, was the German universal remedy for intransigent P.O.W. behavior and, like Grannie's castor oil again, solitary is not funny. Even the Germans, incidentally, called it the "cooler," an expression they picked up from us.

There were many more reluctant guests in the new camp. Jimmy Buckley had been purged there too, and he started up the "X organization" again. Before long there were several tunnel syndicates worming out under various huts and a variety of other schemes too.

Bravest of them was a brilliant idea of Ken Toft and "Nick" Nichols. Nichols was a good-looking Californian with a crew cut; a cool, composed and deliberate individualist if ever I saw one. He'd been in the American Eagle Squadron, with the R.A.F., and been shot down early in 1942. Nick didn't seem to have any nerves, which was just as well for the kind of job that he and Toft pulled. They had a theory that halfway between the goon-boxes there should be a blind spot hidden from the sentries by the long line of thick, coiled wire. If they could get to that spot across the lethal area from the warning wire, they could cut their way through in safety (?). If the theory was right they had a slim chance of getting through the wire (probably to be caught soon after). If they were wrong, a probable bullet each.

Four goon-boxes had a view of the warning wire at the chosen spot, so Jimmy Buckley laid on four elaborate diversions. At a given signal, a prisoner yelled to the sentry in one box to ring up for an interview with the Kommandant. In front of the next, two men staged a spectacular (sham) fight and one of them was knocked out while the sentry gaped at them. Another prisoner hailed the sentry in the third box and asked permission to get a ball that had been tossed over the warning wire. By the fourth, a man was doused with a bucket of water while the sentry looked on and laughed.

And in the vital five seconds Toft and Nichols crossed to the fence and crouched down by it. A hundred men held their breath (including Toft and Nichols), but the theory worked. They weren't seen. Nichols had a pair of crude wire-clippers made from a couple of hunks of metal. Strand by strand they worked their way through the wire till they were through. At another signal, four more diversions were repeated in front of the sentries, and Toft and Nichols ran the few yards into the cover of the woods. It would be nice to report that they got back to England, but they were caught soon after and slung into the cooler for the punitive solitary.

The tunnelers in the new compound were soon running into complications. The Germans had built the huts in the middle of the compound and cleared the ground on the far side of the wire so there was well over a hundred yards to tunnel to get to cover outside the wire. The soil was sandy and collapsed easily, and one by one the tunnels were found. One was very shallow and a horse pulling the ration wagon stuck his hoof through it, to the grief of the diggers, the joy of the Germans, and the surprise of the horse.

"Piglet" Lamond, a slight, toothy little New Zealander, won fame with his brilliant "mole" idea which greatly shortened the distance necessary to tunnel. We had been digging a sump by the ablutions hut, only about five yards from the wire, and

13

it was Lamond's idea to tunnel from the sump. When it was about seven feet deep he tunneled a hole in the side toward the wire, covering the entrance by hanging a coat over it. After a few days he had a little tunnel about twenty feet long, and one evening he and two others crawled into it. We buried them there alive, filling up the pit with rocks and gravel. Lamond's idea was to tunnel the remaining few yards in the one night and surface just outside the wire before dawn.

They were all stark naked, carrying their clothes in bundles, and there was just room for them to lie one behind the other, with a few feet to spare behind.

Lamond in front did the tunneling; the other two shoved the sand back, filling up the tunnel behind them. They were only about four feet down and stuck pointed sticks up through the surface for breathing holes. It was pitch-dark down there and stiflingly foul. No one had done this sort of thing before, and it was just a theory that they could get enough air to keep them alive. For all they knew they might gradually lose consciousness and suffocate.

Prisoners watching from the nearest hut saw steam rising out of the air holes and prayed that the hundfuehrer and his Alsatian dog who patrolled the compound at night wouldn't notice. The "moles" lost track of time after a while. Their watches stopped because of the sand, and in any case the air was too foul for a match to light. They were thinking they might be far enough to dig up and away when Lamond saw light filtering down through an air hole. It was day.

They lay sweating in the foulness all day. The tunnel was just as wide as their shoulders, and they could hardly twitch a muscle. When no more light came down the air hole they still waited a few more hours for wandering Germans to go to bed, and then they tunneled up the few feet and found themselves just outside the wire.

After tramping through the woods to the Oder River eight

miles away, Piglet found a rowboat and they set off downstream toward the Baltic, hundreds of miles away. Within a few hours the boat was reported missing, and a policeman downstream on the watch for it picked them up at gunpoint.

To stop this sort of tunneling nonsense the Germans dug an eight-foot-deep ditch between the warning wire and the fence. Three men crawled nervously out of their hut one night, dodged the searchlight beams, snaked under the warning wire, dropped into the trench and started to dig a blitz "mole" tunnel like Lamond's. They only had about twenty feet to go to get outside the wire, but they didn't push enough sand out of their entrance hole into the trench. No matter how tightly you pack it, sand that is dug out fills up a third as much space again in its loose form. Before they reached outside the wire the sand they had passed back had filled in all the tunnel behind them and they could pass no more back. So they were trapped—couldn't go forward, couldn't go back. All they could do was to dig up, and when they surfaced it was dawn and they were caught, feeling rather foolish out there by the wire.

The Germans very quickly filled in their anti-escape trenches and took new, and much more efficient, precautions, burying microphones all around the wire, as at Barth. Over in the *Kommandantur* (the German administrative compound) men sat with headphones plugging in to each detector in day- and night-long watches.

Buckley heard about it and he and the tunneling experts, Wally Floody, "Crump" Ker-Ramsay, Johnny Marshall, Peter Fanshawe, and others had a conference at which they decided to dig two tunnels thirty feet deep to get out of the range of the microphones. If one tunnel was found, they might break out from the other. They made camouflaged trap doors in the floors of two huts, and then came the master stroke! They dug two shallow camouflage tunnels about thirty feet long and stopped them there. Halfway along each of these they made a

15

second camouflaged trap in the floor and under this sank a shaft twenty feet vertically and started the real tunnel from there. If the Germans found the shallow dummy tunnels they probably wouldn't find the secret deep shafts, and the diggers could burrow down to the real tunnel from another direction. They were learning, growing in cunning.

The ferrets did find one of the dummy tunnels, and then, by accident probably, hit upon the hidden trap door in it and that was the end of that one. The other tunnel forged ahead, the tunnelers hacking at the crumbling face in stinking darkness, passing the sand back in a metal washbasin drawn by plaited string. Special dispersers hid the sand under the hut and carefully raked it over so it did not seem obvious.

They devised a crude form of ventilation for the deep tunnel. Short sticks were fitted into sockets in each other like a fishing rod and pushed up through the soil till they broke through the top, twenty feet up. A P.O.W. sentry (always known as a stooge) lay upon the sand above to hide the stick as it pushed through, and then he camouflaged and protected the hole with a stone. Stinking air filtered up through these little holes. They made conditions just possible for working below, but only just. After a couple of hours of blind digging at the face, men crawled painfully back up with splitting heads and retched up green vomit. Pretty often it was dry retching because on German rations you didn't have much to bring up.

Johnny Travis, a dapper little Rhodesian, had been a mining engineer until he was trapped for three days 4,000 feet down a gold mine once by a fall of rock. He had bad claustrophobia from that, but he still used to go down the tunnel and work close to screaming point for a couple of hours, then come up to vomit. The sand was so crumbly there were frequent falls and there was always a number two digger close behind to haul you out by the legs if you were buried. It was grim.

Buckley noticed that Travis was a minor genius with his

hands, making baking dishes from old tins, and shaving brushes from hunks of wood and bits of string. He pulled Travis out of the tunnel and started him making escape equipment—fat lamps from old tins with fuel made from margarine boiled to extract the water, and wicks made of pajama cord. He made shovels for the diggers from bits of metal from old stoves and filed down broken table knives for chisels. (Buckley got the bits of file from bribing German guards.)

As the tunnel lengthened, the air got so bad they couldn't go on. Buckley commandeered an old accordion from one of the prisoners, and they used this to try to pump some air in. Then Marshall, Travis and some helpers designed a rough pump from a kit bag, with old boot leather for valves. It was just finished when someone fell on it and smashed it. He made another, and the Germans found it before it could be smuggled below. He made another, and it pushed just enough air into the tunnel to enable them to carry on.

The level of the dispersed sand was rising too noticeably under the hut so they dug a short tunnel back to the adjoining hut and started putting sand under there. The main tunnel was steered under the kitchen hut to disperse more sand there, but they were disappointed to find that there was no room underneath. There was a huge fall under that hut, and Wally Floody was nearly suffocated under half a ton of sand. It shook him up.

Then the Germans found the shallow dummy tunnel. All of us held our breath, but the Germans missed the secret trap door in it. They destroyed the dummy tunnel, so Floody and Crump dug a new dummy tunnel from another room and sank another secret shaft to link up with the main tunnel again. They didn't know the burrowing had undermined the hut foundations, and the weight above collapsed the new dummy tunnel as Floody was crawling naked along it. Ten feet of it came down along his body but by a miracle he had his face just over the trap door to the secret shaft and could breathe. The tunnel team dug madly for an hour and got him out. He was lucky.

They dug another shallow dummy tunnel, sank another deep shaft and at last made contact again with the main tunnel.

They'd been working for months now, and the X organization was slowly growing all the time. Tim Walenn and a couple of men who'd been artists before they became airmen started a little factory for forging papers and passports. Tommy Guest organized a tailor shop to convert uniforms into rough civvy clothes. More metal workers and carpenters joined Johnny Travis. The tunnel pushed on till it was over three hundred feet long; less than a hundred feet to go now, but the sand was rising blatantly under the new dispersal hut.

A gang of ferrets raided the hut one morning, cleared everyone out, and almost took it apart. Underneath they found fresh sand over the exit of the dispersal tunnel, dug down to the trap door, and traced it right back to the deep shaft. They blew up the lot.

Buckley, Wings Day, the Dodger and others were purged to Schubin, a camp up near Bromberg, in Poland. In the train going there the dogged Dodger prised up a floorboard in his cattle truck and jumped out. A guard saw him and a posse jumped off the train and persuaded him to come back at pistol point. Paddy Byrne got out too. Also caught.

Within a week of arriving at Schubin, Buckley, Wings and company were tunneling from one of the lavatories, and this time there was no hitch. The tunnel was 150 feet long when they surfaced outside the wire, and nearly forty men got out through it.

It wasn't discovered till *Appell* (counting parade) next day, and even then the Germans nearly missed it. Normally we

18

paraded in five ranks for appell, but that morning some sections paraded in fours. The German officer had nearly finished counting when he noticed some of the fives he was counting were not fives but fours, and his blood pressure nearly sprayed out of his ears.

Five thousand troops turned out for the search, and before long the escapees had nearly all been caught. Wings Day was out for a week till a Hitler Youth boy spotted him hiding in a barn, and the local Home Guard winkled him out with shotguns.

Two they never caught and this was tragedy. Jimmy Buckley and a Danish lad in the R.A.F. got to Denmark and started out in a little boat from the Zealand coast. Five miles across the water lay Sweden and freedom. No one ever found out exactly what happened. Maybe they were rammed, or shot, or just capsized. The Dane's body was found in the sea weeks later. They never found Buckley.

Late in 1942 Roger Bushell arrived in Sagan. The Gestapo had grilled him for several months, trying to pin charges of sabotage and spying on him, but Bushell's tough and nimble brain had kept him clear of the firing squad. They would probably have shot him in any case if Von Masse, chief censor officer at Stalag Luft III, who knew and liked Bushell, hadn't heard that the Gestapo was holding him. Von Masse's brother was a *Generaloberst* (colonel-general), and he used this influence to have Bushell handed back to the less lethal custody of the prison camp.

In Prague Bushell's Czech host had given him a smart, gray civilian suit, and it never occurred to the Gestapo, who dealt mainly with civilians, to take it from him. Roger wore a tattered old battle dress back to Sagan and carried his suit with him, wrapped in paper. Von Masse met him when he got to the camp, and Roger went for him with bald-headed fury over the way the Gestapo had treated him. Von Masse apologized.

"Don't blame us, please, for what the Gestapo do," he said. "They're not the real Germany." He added warningly: "What I particularly want to say is that you're lucky to get back this time. You won't get away with it again. I'm telling you that if you get out once more and they catch you I think they'll shoot you."

"If I get out again they won't catch me," Roger said, and went off into another tirade about the Gestapo, upsetting Von Masse so much that he forgot to search him—which was what Roger had banked on. He brought his suit into the compound, planning to use it on his next break.

This was a changed Roger—not the old boisterous soul who thought escape was good, risky sport like skiing. When he skied he used to take one course straight down at uniform, maximum speed, swearing like a trooper. Now he was moodier, and the gaze from that twisted eye was more foreboding. In Berlin he'd seen the Gestapo torturing people, and he did not tolerate Germans any more. By now he'd been behind the wire nearly three years, and his frustrated energy was focusing on the people responsible. He cursed all Germans indiscriminately (except Von Masse), but inside it was a clear, cool-headed hatred and it found sublimation in outwitting them.

With Buckley and Wings Day gone, he took over as Big X.

◻ C H A P T E R 1 ◻

IT LOOKED like a long war, and the Germans were building a new compound at Sagan. In the pine wood across the *Kommandantur*, gaunt Russian prisoners had felled some trees to clear a patch and workmen were putting up the long, wooden huts.

"You will be happier there," said Hauptmann Pieber, the lageroffizier, who had stopped by the wire to welcome Roger to Stalag Luft III. Pieber, who had known Bushell at Barth, was a kindly little man with dueling scars on his cheeks and a sentimental heart. If he'd been lageroffizier in hell and had seen you brought in screaming he'd have blinked tenderly behind his glasses and wished you a felicitous sojourn.

"Most of you will be going to the new compound," he added. "It will be a happier new year for you. You will have taps in your huts and even lavatories."

"A change," said Roger sacastically, "is as good as a holiday. When are we moving?"

"I think March," Pieber said, and Roger, eyeing the snow that hung on the ugly wire, was thinking of summer, the escape season.

He called on Wally Floody, and they collected Fanshawe, Crump Ker-Ramsay, and the others.

"If the bloody Goons don't rupture themselves, we'll be in the new compound by spring," he said. "We're going to get cracking on schemes now. My idea is to dig three major tunnels simultaneously and get about five hundred men on the job. The Goons might find a couple of them but we ought to make it with at least one. What d'you think?"

The conference lasted two hours with all of them shooting out ideas, some wild, some good. When it broke up they had the basic points decided—three tunnels thirty feet deep with underground railways and workshops, mass forging of passes, a tailor shop, mass-produced compasses and maps, and a huge intelligence and security organization. A year ago it would have seemed impossible, but they had been learning the hard way for a long time and now they knew what they could do.

Roger took the details to Massey, the senior British officer, and the group captain, resting his game leg on his bunk and drawing on a pipe, listened with satisfaction but made a disturbing suggestion.

"Look, Bushell," he said. "You've been out twice now and nearly made it. The Gestapo think you're a saboteur and would be happy to get something more on you. Lie low for a while and leave it to the others. I don't want you getting a bullet in the back of the head."

"I won't, Sir," said Bushell. "This is going to be a long job, and if we get out they'll have forgotten about me. I'll worry about that when the time comes if you don't mind."

"You'll be worrying before then if they think you're working on tunnels. You'll be off to Kolditz," Massey said.

"They're not catching me this time." Roger was quite confident. "We're flat out for security, and I don't think there'll be any slips."

Massey looked at him doubtfully and then said, "Well for God's sake be careful. I think you'd better keep in the background as much as you can and try and look like a reformed character. Stick to the brains part of it, and as far as the actual work is concerned I'll see you have the whole camp behind you. Let me know of anything or anyone you want, and I'll make it an order."

He said it a little wistfully, resigned to the fact that he had no chance of escaping himself. He'd won his M.C. flying in the first war, but had smashed his foot when he'd been shot down then. The same foot had been damaged again when he got his D.S.O. in Palestine in the thirties, and he'd bent it a third time when he bailed out over the Ruhr in this war. He shouldn't have been flying really, but he wanted to make one last trip before they made him an Air Commodore. Now, when he could move, he hobbled with a stick, his foot swaddled in an old flying boot.

Roger collected his specialists, and one by one he walked them miles around the circuit while he told them what he wanted. The circuit was a beaten track around the compound just inside the warning wire. You could walk there for hours till you were numb and didn't worry about home or the war or even the more important things like sex or liquor. You could also talk there without being overheard. The ferrets had a habit of hiding under the huts or in the roofs or outside the walls at night with ears agape.

Pounding the circuit Roger told Tim Walenn he wanted two hundred forged passes, and Tim, who never swore and was the politest man I ever met, pulled on his great long mustache and said, "Jesus!"

"Maybe he'll help you," said Roger ruthlessly. Walenn said earnestly he didn't really think it could be done, as all the printing on every pass had to be hand-lettered, but Roger said flatly he wanted them and wouldn't argue.

He told Tommy Guest they would need eventually two hundred full outfits of civilian clothes, and Guest, appalled, said it was impossible. Apart from the materials and manufacturing, there would be nowhere to hide them till a tunnel was ready.

"Make your own materials," Roger said. "Most of the boys

who get out will have to convert their own duds to civvies. I want you to co-ordinate the thing; make some yourself and show the rest how."

"And how do we hide all this stuff?" Guest asked, resisting to the last.

"We'll fix that when the time comes," Roger said.

Al Hake, phlegmatic Australian, lifted his thick black eyebrows when Roger told him he wanted two hundred compasses. He said he'd see if he could get a mass-production line going.

Roger told Des Plunkett he wanted a thousand maps, and Plunkett said he'd be quietly confident if he could get some jellies to make a mimeograph.

Travis nearly had a fit when Bushell described all the railways, air pumps, pipe lines, and underground workshops he had in mind. He said he'd start tooling up.

Roger had another conference with Massey, and Massey went to the Kommandant and suggested a few P.O.W. working parties might go over and help in the new compound. A good co-operative spirit, thought the Kommandant, and benignly agreed. So the working parties were marched over, and with them, in the guise of innocence, marched Roger, Floody, Crump, and "Hornblower" Fanshawe. They mapped the layout of the new camp, tramped out distances, measured angles and more distances by rough trig, and surveyed the area outside the wire. Back in their own compound they put it all together and worked out where to dig the tunnels and how long they would have to be.

One of them showed such interest that a kind German surveyor showed him most of the plans, and the prisoner limped back to the old camp stiff-legged and thoughtful. Down the leg of his pants he had a stolen copy of the underground

24

sewage system. They looked it over back in the compound, and there were two beautiful, tailor-made tunnels leading out to near-by drainage areas. If only the pipes were big enough, it looked like happy days. Roger didn't take anything for granted, and the tunnel chiefs carried on their planning.

Wally Valenta was training men who spoke German for the intelligence branch. Day after day, "Junior" Clark, George Harsh and Tom Kirby-Green padded around the circuit devising security on a scale they'd never tried before. Security was going to be one of the keys to the whole thing. Clark was chief of security and known as "Big S."

On the face of it, proper security looked impossible. There were going to be half a dozen Germans in the compound all the time wandering around with torches and probes. We had to hide the proposed forgery and map factories, compass and clothing factories, metalwork and carpentry shops, the sand we dug out and the tunnel traps. . . . We even had to hide the security stooges themselves because nothing stuck out to the ferrets' eyes more than some character self-consciously sitting around in the same spot every day and all day trying to watch, give signs of approaching ferrets, and look innocent all at the same time.

Junior Clark and George Harsh were both Yanks of totally different types. The Yanks were just getting going in Europe, and a lot of them were being chopped down as they experimented with the dangerous business of daylight bombing. The ones who didn't die were being trundled dolorously behind the wire to join us, and there were about a hundred of them with us at that time. Clark was a gangling red-headed youngster in his twenties and already a lieutenant colonel. George Harsh was well into his thirties and as gray as a badger. He looked like a Kentucky colonel and was a wild, wild man with a rambunctious soul. He'd joined the R.A.F. a couple of years earlier

25

and had been shot down as a rear gunner over Berlin. Tom Kirby-Green was a big, black-haired Englishman who looked like an overgrown Spaniard.

Roger controlled every phase of the growing organization, holding daily conferences with the departmental chiefs, presiding over them as charmingly incisive but slightly sinister chairman. He had a mind like a filing cabinet, and that was one of the reasons he was so brilliant at organization. Once he'd chosen his man for a job, he never roughly interfered with him. He listened to his problems, made suggestions, and when they'd thrashed it out and a decision had been made, he gave the man concerned full brief to carry it out. With that twisted eye taking everything in, he was a potent influence enveloping every detail of the planning. He wandered around in a battered old R.A.F. tunic, scarf around his neck and hands in pockets, a tall, brooding figure, with that steady and disconcerting gaze. Every day he went to Massey, and they talked over the master plan.

By the end of March, the new compound was ready. So was the X organization.

We moved on April Fool's Day, a straggling line of seven hundred scruffy prisoners carrying all our worldly possessions. Most of us wore all our clothes, festooned ourselves with cooking pots, plates and mugs, and the gadgets made out of old tins, and carried cardboard Red Cross boxes with what food we had and a few beloved personal things like photographs and nails and bits of string. Mother wouldn't have known us. There weren't enough razor blades to shave every day so some of us were shaven, some had felonious stubbles, and a few had beards ranging from the farcical to the flamboyant. Here and there a bottom peeped pale and unashamed out of obsolete pants, and the air was blue to the noise of happy

26

cursing. A change, as Roger had observed, was as good as a holiday.

Henceforth the old home was known as east compound and the new one was north compound. First the Germans searched us, but no more efficiently than usual. People clustered around and harried them, passed articles from one to another, and the result was mildly chaotic. No one lost anything of importance. Roger, amazingly enough, got his gray suit through. Travis brought all his tools, and Walenn had no trouble with his forging pens and inks. Then the screen of tommy-gunners ranged up on each side and escorted us the four hundred yards to the new home.

North compound was as innocent of luxury as we'd expected. There were fifteen bare wooden huts in three rows in the northern half, and the rest was a patch of stump-studded, loose gray dirt for recreation and appell.

The compound was about three hundred yards square and right around it ran two fences about nine feet high and five feet apart, each strung with about twenty close strands of rusting barbed wire. In between them great coils of barbed wire had been laid, so thickly in parts that you could hardly see through it. Some thirty feet inside the main fence ran the warning wire. Just outside the northern wire lay the Vorlager, containing the sick quarters and the long, gray concrete cooler with its barred windows. Another double fence of spiked wire sealed off the other side of the vorlager. The entrance to the compound was on the north side, so there had to be a gate in each fence and each was guarded.

Every 150 yards behind the fences the "goon-boxes" stood up with their watchful sentries, and at night more sentries patrolled the fences and another hundfuehrer prowled inside the camp with his dog trained to go for a man's throat if necessary.

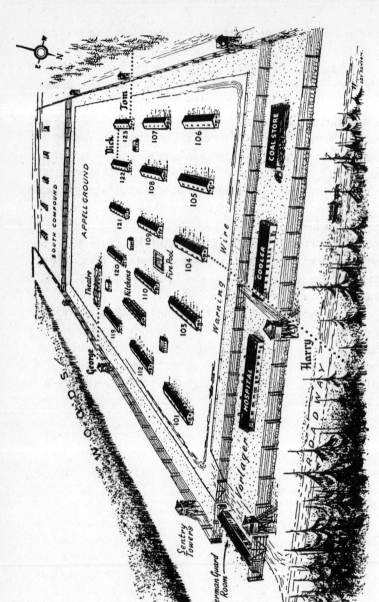

THE NORTH COMPOUND OF STALAG LUFT III

Woods completely encircled the compound; not pleasant green woods but gaunt pines with skinny, naked trunks, packed close together in the dry, gray earth. They were everywhere you looked, monotonous barriers that shut out the world and increased the sense of Godforsaken isolation. Just outside the wire the Germans had cut the trees back for about thirty yards so there would be no cover for escapers and so that any tunnels would have to reach a hundred feet beyond the wire.

The huts were divided into eighteen rooms about fifteen feet square, each to be bedroom, dining room, and living room for eight people, and three little rooms for two, reserved for those who could pull enough rank to deserve them. Furniture was elementary—double-decker bunks, a deal table, stools, lockers, and a stove in one corner on a tiled base. The bunks consisted of four corner posts with planks screwed along the sides and across the ends at two levels. Short, flat boards rested across the side planks, and on these one laid one's paillasse—a bag of woven paper that looked like hessian, and stuffed with wood shavings.

These flat bedboards were about thirty inches long and six inches wide. If they'd been specially designed for shoring tunnels they'd have been just that shape and size!

Each block had a washroom with a concrete floor, a lavatory, and a tiny kitchen with a coal stove that had two burners on top and a little oven. There were to be over a hundred men in the block, and they had to do all their cooking on that little stove. Actually there was a kitchen block in the compound, but that could just cope with boiling water for the brews and sometimes boiling potatoes (if there were any) or making soup.

We got by with cooking on the little block stove because there wasn't much to cook. German rations allowed a very thin slice of bread, margarine, and ersatz jam for breakfast, a couple of slices for lunch, and a couple for dinner, probably with neither margarine nor jam. Usually there were a few potatoes and once every three weeks a little minced horsemeat. Occasionally there were some vegetables or barley or sauerkraut. If Red Cross parcels were coming in (thank God they mostly did after the first couple of years), there would be an evening meal of bully beef or Spam and extra luxuries like chocolate, coffee, cheese, and jam.

There was a mad rush for rooms, and as there weren't enough prisoners to fill the huts yet, there was a wonderful lot of space, almost enough to swing a stunted cat. That day and the next three days were chaos—on the German side too —while everyone was getting organized, and the X organization took advantage of it. Escape fever hit the camp.

ROGER first settled the question of the drainage
pipes. Within an hour a willing bunch of prisoners gathered
for an open-air meeting as a diversion, and in the middle of
them someone whipped off a manhole noted on the stolen
drainage chart and Shag Rees, a nuggety little Welshman,
slipped into it. He was up again in a minute with a dirt-
streaked face.

"The bastards," he said. "You couldn't pull a greasy piglet
through them." He indicated with his hands a circumference
of about six inches, and there was a low moan. Roger cut it
short.

"Can't expect the Goons to be stupid all the time," he said.
"Let's get on with the other things."

There were a few hungry Russian prisoners still in the compound under guard clearing away the last of the spindly pine
trees they'd cut down, and trucks loaded high over the cab
were taking the branches and foilage away. The road out
went past three of the huts, and before you could say "Hitler
is a *Schweinhund*," furtive shapes were crawling up on the
roofs of those huts under cover of the near-by trees. As the
trucks rolled past, shapes hurtled through the air and crashed
down out of sight into the loaded branches. There were so
many trying it that a man about to jump had to look carefully
to see there wasn't already a man who had jumped from the

previous hut looking up from the branches, making frantic signs for him to wait for the next truck and not brain him with his boots as he came down.

But every truck was searched at the gates, and one by one the prisoners were winkled out, and with much show of jovial regret from the Germans locked in the cooler for the traditional two weeks' solitary. A couple, however, burrowed deep into the branches and got away (to be caught soon after). The Goons took to probing the branches with pitchforks, and when a would-be escaper caught a couple of prongs in the bottom, the rest turned to other methods.

Ian Cross climbed under one of the trucks and hung on to the chassis. A few moments later, the chief German ferret, *Oberfeldwebel* (staff sergeant) Glemnitz, had a word with the driver, and the truck shot off like a rocket across a patch of the compound studded with tree stumps. We held our breath waiting for Cross to be mashed to pulp, and then the truck stopped and Glemnitz walked up and leaned under.

"You can come out now, Mr. Cross," he called. "We have your room ready in the cooler."

"You see," said Roger, watching Cross marching lugubriously off, "how bloody careful we've got to be. Secrecy is the key."

Glemnitz was the archenemy. We didn't exactly like him, but we certainly respected him. He was a droll fellow in a sardonic way, with a leathery face you could crack rocks on. He didn't wear overalls like the other ferrets but was always in uniform complete with peaked cap and the dignity of rank. A good soldier, Glemnitz, efficient and incorruptible, too good for our liking.

Griese, his second in charge, was the other dangerous ferret, a lean *Unteroffizier* (corporal), with a long thin neck and known, naturally, as "Rubberneck." He was smart but he didn't have Glemnitz's sense of humor.

"Cherub" Cornish, an angelic little Australian, didn't shave for two days, borrowed an old Polish greatcoat that reached to the ground, rubbed dirt into his face, and slipped among the last group of Russian prisoners leaving the camp. At the gate a bovine guard counted them and scratched his head. Fifteen had come in and sixteen were going out. He reported this phenomenon to the Herr *Hauptmann* (captain), and Pieber, more in sorrow than in anger, plucked Cherub from the tattered ranks despite the truthless but virtuous vows of a gaunt Russian who claimed that Cornish was an old pal from Smolensk.

As the cooler door closed on Cornish, the escape fever was over and the organization settled down to the real stuff.

Roger appointed a "Little X" and "Little S" in every block to co-ordinate the work in their blocks. Conk Canton, built like a pocket battleship with a great aggressive jaw, became Roger's adjutant; Crump, Johnny Marshall, and Johnny Bull were the tunnel committee under Floody. Fanshawe was sand dispersal chief. George Harsh had charge of tunnel security. They all met in conference nearly every day.

One tunnel, Roger had decided, was to go from Block 123 out under the western wire to the woods beyond—an obvious choice as it was as near the wire as any hut. It was also on the far side of the compound to the German camp and the farthest hut from the gate, which meant more seclusion and more warning of any snap search. It also meant it was going to be a hut the Germans would suspect, but you can't have everything.

"We're going to call this one 'Tom,'" Roger told the attentive committee. "They're all to be known by their names, and by their names only. If any bastard in this camp ever utters the word tunnel carelessly I'll have him court-martialed."

The second tunnel was to go from 122 because it was an

inside hut and not likely to be so much suspected. It was to be known as "Dick." The third one was to go from Hut 104 by the northern wire. This meant an extra hundred feet to go under the second boundary wire, but that also meant the Germans wouldn't regard it as a likely site. Roger named it "Harry."

Roger, Floody, and the other tunnel kings surveyed the three huts to find sites for the trap doors, a most important part of the business because it was usually the traps that gave tunnels away. So the traps had to be perfect, and this was a headache because the Germans had built the hut floors about two feet above the ground so they could crawl underneath to see if anyone was tampering with the soil of the Fatherland. They made one mistake, though, because they made solid brick and concrete foundation walls right around under the washrooms in the huts and also under a little square of each living room where the stove stood. The ferrets couldn't crawl into these areas, so they were the logical spots for the traps.

By April 11, Roger and Floody had picked all trap sites. "Tom" was to be in a dark corner of the concrete floor by a chimney of 123. "Dick" was to start from the washroom of 122, and "Harry" was to drop under a stove in one of the end big rooms of 104.

Minskewitz, who was the trap expert, was a short, wiry little Polish officer in the R.A.F., with a little gray goatee beard which he was always tugging lovingly. The German workmen had left some cement in the compound, and Minskewitz used some to cast a concrete slab about two feet square in a wooden mold. He reinforced it with bits of barbed wire left lying around and sank a couple of lugs in the sides, almost flush but protruding just enough for a couple of pieces of fine wire to be looped around them. He hid it under a paillasse to dry while he chipped a slab out of the concrete floor of 123, exactly the same size as the slab he'd made.

Stooges kept watch for ferrets outside while he handled his chisel like a surgeon and, when he'd finished, his home-made slab fitted the hole perfectly and could be lifted on and off with the wires on the lugs. The wires themselves folded down into the cracks when the trap was in position, but you could fish them up in a moment with a knife blade. In position, the slab rested on a padded frame beneath, and the cracks all around were lined with cement paste and dusted with dirt.

It was such an extraordinary precision job that Roger and Floody took Massey over to see the site for "Tom" and Massey examined the corner and said, "Seems a good spot, Bushell, but how are you going to camouflage it when you've chipped a hole there?"

"We have, Sir," Roger said, and Massey got down, holding his game foot out, and peering hard could just see the outline. He shook his head in wonder.

"It's just extraordinary," he said.

I wouldn't have believed it possible myself if I hadn't been taken in the same way.

Minskewitz, tugging on his beard, said cautiously, "I seenk it will do."

For "Dick," Minskewitz devised one of the most cunning trap doors in the history of prison camps. In the middle of the concrete floor of 122 block's washroom was an iron grating about eighteen inches square through which overflow water ran into a concrete well about three feet deep. A foot up from the bottom a pipe led off to carry the water away so there was always a foot of water in the well up to the edge of the pipe.

Minskewitz took off the iron grating while the stooges watched outside, bailed out the water, and mopped the well dry with old rags. He chipped away one wall of the concrete well laying bare the soft earth behind just ripe for tunneling. He cast a new slab to fit where the broken wall had been, slipped it in, sealed the cracks with soap and sand, put the grating back on top, and sloshed water down till the well was again full to the outlet pipe. The ferrets didn't have a hope of finding "Dick" unless they had second sight, and they didn't have that.

With practice it took only a minute or two to take the grating off, bail out the well and lift out the slab. Later on, when the shaft was dug beneath, the diggers would vanish into it, the slab and grating would be replaced, and water poured into the well so they could work happily below for hours without a stooge on top.

Floody, Canton, Crump, and Marshall had already started to sink the shaft under "Tom's" trap. It was to go straight down for thirty feet so that when the tunnel was burrowed out at the bottom it would be out of range of the sound detectors around the wire.

Then Crump started "Harry's" trap. In Room 23 of Block 104, he heaved the stove off the square of tiles on which it stood, took up the tiles one by one, and recemented them on a wooden frame that Travis' carpenters had made. He hinged this on as a trap door in place of the former solid tile foundation.

Under it he found solid brick and concrete to get through to reach the earth. Someone had souvenired an old pick head which the Russian workmen had used, and Crump fitted a baseball bat in it for a handle and bashed into the brick and concrete. It kicked up a hell of a ringing noise, exactly like a pick biting into brick and concrete; and it was obvious Glemnitz and Rubberneck and every ferret within half a mile would be galloping up inquisitively at any moment.

Half a dozen diversionists gathered outside the window hammering at bits of tin and wood making innocent things like baking dishes as noisily as they could for a couple of days while Crump sweated with the pick until he had cleared a

36

way to the earth. Crump was a good man with a pick, a wiry stocky character with a square red face and red hair.

Half a dozen of the tiles on the trap had been cracked, and it wasn't good enough for him.

"It looks too suspicious," he said at a meeting of the committee, and they searched the camp till they found some spare

Sunken lifting Lugs

"HARRY'S" TRAP DOOR

tiles in the kitchen block and replaced the cracked ones. To muffle some of the hollow sound if the ferrets should tap on the trap, he fitted a removable grill that covered the top of the shaft just underneath and piled blankets in the little space. Minskewitz put the same sort of grill under "Tom's" trap and, as "Tom's" concrete slab sounded more hollow than "Harry," he made little bags of sand to stow on the grill.

It was a good moment when Floody reported to Roger that the last of the traps was finished. It had been the riskiest part of the scheme because if he'd seen chunks of flooring torn up, even Dopey, the dimmest of the ferrets, would have guessed that something was wrong. When Crump was making "Harry's" trap, the floor was up for about ten days and covered with spare paillasse when a ferret wandered near by. It would never have passed undetected in later days, but in the first weeks of the north camp occupation the ferrets were not well organized and the gamble came off.

Only a few dozen people in the whole camp knew where the trap doors were. A lot of the rest didn't even know what huts they were in. That was how good the security was. Yet nearly everyone was working in some way on the X organization. A couple of days after we moved into the compound, blank sheets of paper had been pinned up in all huts with such headings as "Volunteers for cricket or softball teams will please put their names down here." Little X in every block went around interviewing everyone who signed to see if he had any useful skill, from languages to mining and needlework.

Anyone who could sew went to join Tommy Guest's tailoring section. Artists went to Tim Walenn's forgery factory, miners into the tunnels, engineers to Johnny Travis' department, and so on. The rest became stooges or penguins, the penguins being the people who dispersed the sand from the tunnels. Most, of course, became stooges, doomed to hour after hour of skulking and spying on ferrets and warning of their approach to any danger area.

Junior Clark had the compound divided into two sections, "D" for danger zone and "S" for safe. "S" was the east half of the camp where the gate was. The rest was "D" zone, where the tunnels and factories were. As soon as a ferret penetrated into "D," he was tailed, and if he got within fifty yards of an exposed tunnel or factory, work was packed up right away till he wandered off again.

Down by the gate, the "Duty Pilot" sat with his runner, watching everyone who came into the camp, noting on his list the time they came in and the time they went out. He sat there every minute of every day without a break, never moving till the next man came to relieve him. All over the camp there were warning points to relay his sign messages. Near him was a little cement incinerator, an innocent-looking Red Cross box, and a coal scuttle. If the coal scuttle alone was lying carelessly on the incinerator, it meant there were only a couple of administrative German staff (pretty harmless) wandering about. If the Red Cross box was tossed up too, it meant ferrets in. There were various combinations and positions.

Over by the back of 110, a man lounging on a stool with a book kept his eyes on the incinerator, and if the box and scuttle position flashed a danger sign he got lazily up and rearranged some shutters. Across by a corner of Block 120, a man casually blew his nose, upon which George Harsh, looking out of a window of 123, put his head around the door and said pithily, "Ferrets. Pack up." And then the trap was on in seconds, the wires folded down, and sand and cement paste smoothed into the cracks.

Every factory had its own stooges watching in case a ferret got through the general screen. There were nearly three hundred stooges altogether rostered in shifts. The organization needed them all.

The whole scheme was taking shape so smoothly that Roger one morning said thoughtfully to Floody and George Harsh, "You know, this time it might really be home for Christmas for some of us," and for once they didn't laugh.

FLOODY had dug only six inches into the dirt under "Tom's" trap when he came to the yellow sand. The gray dirt was only a thin layer over the surface of the compound, and everywhere underneath was the bright yellow subsoil. Whenever the ferrets saw it they knew there was a tunnel, and the heat was on till it was found. With three tunnels going, there would be about a hundred tons of yellow sand to disperse, about as easy as hiding a haystack in a needle. It was the worst enemy.

"You'll never get a tunnel out of here," said Glemnitz once, "till you find a way of destroying sand."

Fanshawe had been thinking solemnly about this for a long time. "You don't have to destroy it," he said (to the committee, not to Glemnitz). "You ought to be able to camouflage it."

Everyone, he said, ought to dig gardens outside the huts so the yellow sand would be turned up naturally. Glemnitz couldn't be very suspicious of that. He'd watch them, but if the level of the gardens didn't rise he wouldn't suspect any tunnel sand was being dumped there.

"We can save the gray sand of the garden topsoil and mix a bit of tunnel sand in the gardens," Fanshawe explained. "Then we can spread the rest of the tunnel sand in the compound and spinkle it with the gray stuff we've saved from the gardens."

"Sounds possible," Roger said, "but how are you going to

spread the yellow stuff without being spotted? It'll look pretty bloody obvious."

Fanshawe had done his heaviest thinking about that. "With trouser bags," he said cryptically, and out of his pockets he dragged what can only be described as a gadget. It consisted of the two legs cut off a pair of long woolen underpants, and to the tops he'd tied each end of a piece of string. He explained that you looped the string around your neck under your tunic and the underpants legs could then hang suspended down inside the legs of your trousers. He had a pin stuck in the bottom of each trouser bag and a string tied to each pin. Those strings, he explained, led up inside the trousers to the pants pockets.

"I don't usually wear these things," he said apologetically. "It's just an idea. You fill the bags with sand at the traps and you wander around the various spots and then you pull the string in your pockets; out come the pins and the sand flows out of the bottom of your pants. If you're not a complete clot the ferrets'll never see a thing."

For a conservative citizen like Fanshawe, R.N., the idea was indecently brilliant.

"By God, we try it immediately," said Roger.

"I have already," said Fanshawe. "It works."

The penguins (there were about 150 of them) made themselves trouser bags complete with pins and string, cutting up long underpants with sadistic joy. Our clothes came through the Red Cross, and they, bless their maternal hearts, thought mainly of long woolen underpants. They were the only things we had plenty of. It's bad enough rusting behind barbed wire thinking of Dorothy Lamour without the final degradation of long underpants. You feel so hopelessly celibate.

In the deepening hole under "Tom's" trap, Floody and Marshall were scraping the yellow sand into metal jugs and passing them up to Minskewitz, who acted as "trapfuehrer" for "Tom." Minskewitz had blankets spread around the hole so none of the yellow stuff would be left on the floor. He had the trap door drill down to a fine art, and whenever George Harsh stuck a warning head around the corner he had the men out of the hole and the trap back on and sealed in a shade under fifteen seconds. Beside him in the corner he kept his tin of dirt and cement paste to seal the edges. The penguins took it in shifts, walking up with their trouser bags, stopping a moment by the trap while Minskewitz filled them, and then wandering casually out into the compound.

Jerry Sage, the lanky Yank from Washington State, organized the dispersal diversions as though he were planning the invasion. A tough curly-headed fellow with a permanent ferocious grin and pointed ears, he'd been a paratroop major in North Africa, and the Germans had only cornered him after he'd been walking about behind their lines for two weeks sniping at people with a tommygun.

For his diversions he used to get about forty men having unarmed combat drill—a milling mass of bodies, dust rising in all directions, and the penguins in the middle being flung over someone's shoulder with the sand dripping out of their pants. The yellow stuff was shuffled into the sand, and the gray soil from the gardens sprinkled over any parts that showed. Sometimes Sage had volley-ball games going with a mob standing around cheering, and the sand was shuffled in among them. More sand was poured down the deep privy pits.

A curly-headed Australian called Willy Williams, who was supply chief, stripped some of the double-decker bunks and smuggled the bedposts over to 123. When Floody had sunk the shaft about five feet he stood four of these posts in the four corners of the shaft, bolted them together with cross braces, and slid bedboards in behind as a solid wall. After he'd packed sand as tightly as he could behind the lining boards, that part of the shaft framing stayed rigidly in position while he dug down another five feet and put in another section. He framed the whole shaft like that, and as they got deeper he nailed a ladder in one corner.

When it was about fifteen feet deep Johnny Marshall took over "Tom" with three or four selected diggers, and Floody went to start "Dick's" shaft with another team. It was strange that these two could work so well down tunnels; they were both so tall. Floody was lean as a beanpole with a large, rather sensitive mouth and eyes sunk back in his head making him look solemn and ill. Johnny Marshall lived a lot on his nerves, very intelligent and good-looking, a little thin on top and with perfect white teeth.

They dug fast because the sand was crumbly, but they would rather have dug through hard clay. Even in clay you could dig as much as the dispersers could handle and clay was safe. The sand wasn't. It collapsed if you winked an eye at it; and it had to be solidly shored all the way. Even so, there were a lot of nasty falls, dangerous things thirty feet down a rat hole when a couple of hundred pounds of earth slips away and can smother you.

Just before sand falls like that, it gives a faint crack and there's a shaven second to get out of the way. No one ever spoke much down below. You were too busy listening.

"Tom's" shaft was thirty feet deep in a couple of weeks. "Dick" reached the same mark a few days later, and over in "Harry," Crump was getting down to the twenty-foot level. Marshall and his gang started to excavate the working chambers at the base of "Tom." They dug a little chamber about five feet long where a shaft man could store his gear and assemble the tunnel-shoring frames. On another side they dug a similar chamber to store sand in when it came back from the tunnel until the dispersers could handle it; and on the third side they made a chamber six feet long for the air pump and pumper. The fourth side was the west side, facing the wire—the tunnel side.

Crump left "Harry" to help Floody dig the workshops at the base of "Dick." They were down there one day with Canton shoring the pumping chamber when they heard a crack in the shaft and Canton looked up and saw a broken bedboard sticking out of the frame about twenty-five feet up. Sand was pouring through the gap, and, as he shielded his eyes from the cascade, there was a rending sound up there; a frame burst out with the pressure behind it, and as the sand crashed down, the shaft framework began to twist and break up.

By some miracle the ladder held, and Canton was going up it like a rocket with the other two right behind. Canton and Crump shot out of the top and turned to grab Floody just in time. The sand had reached his waist and he was pinned and couldn't heave himself any higher while the sand mounted. They were just able to heave him free. When he'd got the sand out of his eyes, Floody swore for five solid minutes. He had an imaginative vocabulary. "Dick's" shaft was full to just below the top.

Floody found Roger out on the circuit and told him the news. Roger said one exceptionally rude word and was calm again. I've watched Roger flare up in passion over some little provocation, but when big things went wrong he had this bitter calm.

"How soon can you start digging it out?" he asked.

"Crump and Conk are on it," Floody said.

They had "Dick's" shaft dug and framed again in four days. Leaving Johnny Bull to carry on, Floody and Crump went to hack out the chambers at the base of "Harry."

Wings Day arrived at north compound that day. The Kommandant at Schubin had been severely reprimanded after the tunnel break there, and when Wings was caught the German gave him a solid stretch in the cooler and purged him to Stalag Luft III as soon as he could. Nothing could have pleased

44

Wings more. He stalked through the gates under the usual tommygun escort, looking more like a hungry and unfriendly hawk than ever, and asked the way to Roger's room.

It was on epic meeting. Roger told him briefly what was going on and, without telling him what was there, suggested he go and live in 104, Room 23. He took him across and Wings walked in and saw the open trap with Floody and Crump just climbing out.

"Oh God," he groaned, "not here," and dashed off to find a peaceful room. It wasn't that he didn't like tunnels any more, but when you live in a room with a tunnel, the tunnel is the boss. The stooges are always about, inside the room and out, and there is usually a diversion team standing by to beguile any ferret who gets too close. If you live with a tunnel, you can't walk into your own room when you want to, or out again either. You're a servant to a great ugly hole in the ground.

Crump went back down "Harry" with Johnny Bull to put the last touches to the workshop chambers, and at the bottom, with his ear cocked, he was thinking of his narrow squeak in "Dick" when he heard the sinister "crack" again. He and Johnny Bull shot out of the trap above like champagne corks with dust puffing up behind them as the sand thundered down. When it had settled, they found all the chambers and half the shaft full. Doggedly they started digging it out.

Jerry Sage had a victory that week. A few hundred yards away there was an *Arbeitskorps* camp, and every morning the good young Nazis tramped to their work along the road outside the wire with shovels over their shoulders, just like a newsreel, always smartly in step and singing Nazi marching songs. Jerry got two hundred men every morning smirking offensively through the wire singing with horrible voices the marching song from *Snow White and the Seven Dwarfs*, the one that goes, "Heigh-Ho, Heigh-Ho, it's off to work we go," and after four days the Germans changed their route.

□ CHAPTER 4 □

IN A GAGGLE of men noted for beard stubble, shaven skulls, and general spectacular scruffiness, Travis stuck out like Beau Brummel. He'd got his R.A.F. uniform through in a Red Cross parcel, and he pressed his pants every night under his bunk and ironed his tunic with a tin of hot water. He polished his boots, wore a silk scarf, brushed his hair and begged, borrowed, or stole enough razor blades to keep his pink face as smooth as a baby's bottom. He had a theory that if he went around looking immaculate the ferrets would never bale him up in the compound, as they sometimes did to people, to search for things no model prisoner should have, even to the extent of looking into embarrassing parts of the body.

The idea seemed to work because they never tackled him, which was just as well because he was in the middle of tooling up the engineer's section and usually was a walking toolshop, with pliers and chisels and hacksaw blades stuffed in his pockets. He had nearly a dozen tin bashers and woodworkers now. One of the ace carpenters, Digger McIntosh, had been shot down and badly burned on the suicide raid on the Maastricht Bridge in France in 1940 when the Germans first broke through. He was just going into his fourth year in the bag. Another, Bob Nelson, had been shot down a hundred miles behind the German lines in the desert and walked right back to the lines, keeping alive by licking the dew off rusty gasoline cans. He'd been within three hundred yards of safety in our lines when a German patrol caught him.

Valenta's intelligence men had bribed a couple of pliable guards to bring in some bits of file and hunks of apparently useless metal, and the engineers sat hour after hour filing away till they had a couple of cold chisels, a couple of wood chisels, screw drivers, wirecutters, and even an augur they filed out of a thin rod of steel. McIntosh made a winding frame for this so they had a drill for boring. They filed thin metal strips into blades and knives and fitted some of them in wooden frames so they had planes and spokeshaves.

Some of the knives were so good you couldn't tell them from the genuine article, but they didn't get that way by accident. Travis spent ninety hours filing one of the knives he made. Their fingers were getting into shreds until Guest's tailors made some gloves for them. It wasn't humanity so much as necessity, because when you don't get enough to eat, sores take a long time to heal. One of the Germans brought in a broken gramophone spring, and they filed teeth on it, strung it on a wooden frame, and made a saw.

Willy Williams got a lot of materials within the camp: bedboards and wall battens and soft metal tie-bars off the angles of the huts. He had men pulling nails and screws out of the huts till it was a wonder some of them didn't fall down.

Every second day, a gang of about thirty ferrets and guards poured into the compound after morning appell, threw everyone out of one of the blocks, put a screen of tommygun men around it, and searched the thing from top to bottom, turning everything upside down, sticking their dirty fingers into the sugar and barley to see that nothing was hidden in them, and emptying paillasses on the floor. They used to do a different hut each time and take about three hours on the search, leaving behind chaos and usually all the things they were trying to find, such as Travis' tools.

Ted Earngey, "Little S" in 110, cut out bits of the inside of books so the chisels and pliers fitted flush inside and were never noticed unless the book was opened; and the ferrets, fortunately, never went in for literature.

The outer hut walls were double, with about four inches in between, and in the little end room opposite Roger's, Digger McIntosh moved a wall out about nine inches so neatly you'd never know anything was wrong unless you measured the room dimensions (and I don't think the ferrets even knew the room dimensions, except that they were exceedingly small, which we knew a damn sight better than they did). Digger put a concealed trap door in this wall and Earngey parked a lot of material behind it. Digger did the same to another wall in 120.

He made concealed trap doors in the double walls of other rooms, so Roger Bushell had a dozen equipment hide-holes throughout the camp. One was in his own room.

Travis was always short of a good hammer till the honey wagon, a great horse-drawn cylinder on wheels like a neolithic oil tanker, trundled into the compound one day to pump out the earth latrines. A stooge sidled up to it while a couple of diversionists staged a fight on the other side to entertain the mustachioed old peasant who drove it. At the height of the battle, the stooge yanked out of its socket the great iron spike that held one of the wheels on the hub, and retreated. The fighters patched up their differences, the driver went on with the pumping, and then giddyapped his horses to take his load away.

At the first corner, down by 101, the wheel came off, the cart wobbled for a moment, and crashed on its side, spilling unspeakably.

Watching from afar, Travis balanced the iron spike in his hand. "It'll make a bloody good hammer," he said, holding a handkerchief to his well-scrubbed nose "but I'm not quite sure it was worth it."

48

It was about this time we were building the camp theater just beyond the ends of blocks 119 and 120. Under the parole system the Germans had lent tools for the work, and it was galling for Travis to see all the tools he wanted so close at hand; but the parole system was inviolate and no one ever broke it.

They didn't wait to finish tooling up before they started on the three air pumps for the tunnels, working in a room of 110 that had been set aside as a library and with stooges at the windows and doors watching for ferrets. Travis and Jens Muller, a Norwegian, had designed a new-type pump with accurate working drawings of every part, and in the library the engineers were hammering and bashing, filing and sawing at bits of tin and wood, kicking up a great racket.

There were eight of them in there one day just after appell, going hammer and tongs (literally), the floor littered with verboten tools and gadgets and wood shavings, when three ferrets heard the din and crept up under cover of 103. A stooge spotted them and relayed the alarm, and in the ten seconds it took the ferrets to get to the library window everything was out of sight in the wall panels and the shavings swept under a blanket. The ferrets looked in and saw two bored prisoners hammering out a baking dish with the heel of a boot.

It was a fairly close shave all the same. Bushell sent for Jerry Sage and that urbane and tolerant character, the Artful Dodger.

"I think, Roger," said the Dodger, "that if you want a really noisy diversion this time we ought to have music while you work."

Every day after that about a hundred prisoners gathered outside the library window and raised their voices in community song, accompanied within by the muffled anvil chorus and without by a lean and lugubrious Yank called Tex—on a leaky accordion.

The singers all thought it was part of the camp social pro-

49

gram for their benefit, and one day a squadron leader stuck his head sourly through the library window and said, "For Christ's sake, keep quiet in there. I can't hear myself sing."

With new purges, the camp was now about eight hundred strong, but only about a dozen knew everything that was going on. The rest knew little more than the job they were doing

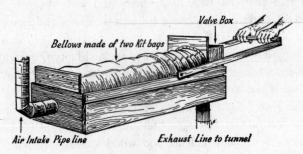

AN AIR PUMP

themselves. It was safer that way. They wouldn't talk if they couldn't talk, and it only needed a couple of words to wreck everything. Even the diversionists, most of them, knew how they were diverting and whom they were diverting, but not why they were diverting him. "X" told every new prisoner that no matter what silly sight he saw in the compound he was to ignore it and carry on as though nothing were happening.

"It's like this," Russell in 103 said to a new prisoner. "If you see me walking around with a tree trunk sticking out of my arse, don't stare. I'll be doing it for a good cause."

The three pumps were finished in about ten days and smuggled down the shafts. The bellows were kit bags ribbed with wooden frames carved out in arc sections, mortised, glued, and screwed in circles and fitting tightly inside the bags. The tops of the kit bags were sealed around a wooden disk, and they had fully automatic double inlet and outlet valves of leather-lined blades of wood working off a spring-loaded camshaft (the spring coming from a set of chest expanders).

The pumper sat in front, grabbed the handle of the pump, and pulled the kit bags in and out like a giant accordion, as though he were rowing. The bags folded in and out on runners. When the pumper pushed, air was shoved out of the exhaust valves and when he pulled, it sucked in through the inlet valve.

The pumps weren't any good without air pipe lines, but the engineers had been making these out of powdered milk tins from Red Cross parcels, collected after use by the "Little X's." The tins were about four inches in diameter, and the engineers peeled off the bottoms, leaving a clean metal cylinder. Where the lids had fitted, the tins were a shade smaller in circumference, and this section fitted very neatly into the base of the next tin. The joint was wrapped tightly with paper and was strong and airtight enough because once the pipe lines were laid they were never touched. They made yards and yards of the piping and smuggled it down the shafts.

The intake pipes for the three tunnels led from airbricks in the foundations well under the huts and camouflaged so the ferrets crawling under there wouldn't notice. To get to an airbrick for "Dick," Floody tunneled about ten feet through rubble under the washroom floor. The pipes then led down to the intake valves on the pumps, and another pipe led from each exhaust valve to the spot where each tunnel was to start. Above in the shaft an outlet pipe led off underground to the nearest chimney.

Crump and Floody tested every pump by holding a piece of smoldering rag in front of the airbrick where the inlet pipes started. The man down below kept pumping, and after a while the black fumes came puffing from the outlet pipe. They examined the piping in between but there was no trace of any leaking fumes.

From that moment on, the trapfuehrers shut the traps on top as soon as the diggers went down. They could work indefinitely below then, sealed and safe from prying eyes above. As the pumper worked, fresh cool air from under the hut flowed into the bottom of the shaft, and the stale air, rising as hot air always does, drifted up through the outlet pipe into the chimney, drawn beautifully by the chimney whenever there was a breeze on top.

Sometime about the third anniversary of the day he was shot down, Roger Bushell was sitting on his window sill, leaning against the frame with his hands in his pockets, staring moodily across the hot compound when Valenta came in.

"You're early," said Roger. "The others won't be here for half an hour."

"They'll be here in a few minutes," said Valenta. "That new ferret's in again."

"What's he doing?"

A little grimly Valenta said, "He dived straight under 122 with a torch."

"Christ!" Roger got sharply to his feet. "They're testing 'Dick's' pump."

"It's all right," said Valenta. "George got everyone in the block stamping around their rooms. There'll be so much noise underneath the ferret won't hear a thing. George signaled the boys to pack up just in case. They're coming across."

"We'll have to watch that," Roger said frowning. "You can hear the pumps under the hut sometimes through the inlet pipes. This new ferret's a pretty keen type. What's his name?"

"Don't know yet. Haven't made contact."

"He'd better go on the danger list with Glemnitz and Rubberneck," Roger said. "I'll spread the word. We might as well christen him 'Keen Type.'"

Floody and the others drifted in in twos and threes, and

after a while Block "X" stuck his head around the door, gave the all clear, and the committee was in session. Floody reported all the pumps were working.

"All set to go," he said. "We've got over thirty good underground men in three teams for each hole. Marshall's taking 'Tom,' Johnny Bull'll be on 'Dick,' and Crump and Muckle Muir will have 'Harry.' "

"How much can you do in a day?" Roger asked.

Floody said he thought they could dig ten feet in each tunnel, and Roger turned to Fanshawe.

"What can you disperse, Hornblower?" he asked.

"Not that much," Fanshawe said bluntly. "For all three we might manage six feet a day each . . . that's without too many risks."

"We don't want any risks," Roger said.

"I don't think we have to be rigid about it just yet," said Floody. "We can dig what we can and store it in the dispersal chambers. The penguins can get rid of what they can, and then we'll know how much we can dig next time."

The first shifts were down that afternoon. The traps were closed on top, and in the sooty glow of fat lamps they were gently scraping away the sand that started the tunnels themselves. A man was sitting in front of each air pump pushing and pulling rhythmically on the bellows so that cool air from under the hut panted out into the base of the shafts and the lamps flickered now and then as the draft from a powerful thrust caught them. Black fumes from the lamps rose wispily into the gloom at the top of the shaft and were sucked into the outlet pipes and out the tops of the chimneys.

Every half hour the pumper changed places with the digger so that one set of tired muscles could take a rest and another set could be brought into play on a different task.

The digger excavated a space a little larger than the tunnel was going to be, and after about nine inches of forward progress he selected four matched bedboards with tongues and slotted ends from the workshop chamber. First he laid the baseboard, about two feet long, then an upright side board leaning slightly inward. On top he held the roof board which was only about twenty-two inches long, then fitted the other side board in and packed sand tightly behind each board. As the tunnel section tapered slightly toward the roof, the weight of the earth above held the whole frame rigidly, and there was no need for nails or screws.

Under the baseboard he dug a little channel about nine inches deep, and into this he fitted the air pipe line, wrapped more tarred paper around the joint, and packed the sand in tightly around it so the pipe line was airtight and safely out of harm's way under the floor of the tunnel.

They worked steadily for several hours packing the sand they excavated in the dispersal chambers and taking things very carefully this first day so there would be no blunders. They did roughly three feet in each tunnel. The stooges reported to the trapfuehrers about half-past four, and when they had given the "all clear" the trapfuehrers opened up and the diggers scuttled up the ladders. A few minutes later, after a scrub under the tap, another brushdown and combing the sand out of their hair, they were on appell.

The next shifts reported as soon as appell was over. This was the dispersing shift, and it meant that the traps had to stay open while the sand was being hauled out. It came up in metal jugs hauled on a rope, and as the first jugs came up in each shaft the controllers signaled the first of the penguins. A penguin reported to each trap, his trouser bags already in place inside his pants. He stood on the blankets on the floor so no sand would be spilled, his bags were filled, and he strolled out into the compound where Jerry Sage and the diversionists gave him cover.

54

One by one the penguins reported, collected their sand, and disposed of it. Then they strolled back for their next turn. The controllers sent them in by several different routes to every trap door so no ferret would notice the same men doing the same thing several times in one night.

By nine o'clock nearly half a ton of yellow sand had vanished into the gray dust of the compound, the tunnelers came up from below, and the traps were shut till the morning.

Morning appell was at nine-thirty. It lasted about twenty minutes as usual, and by ten o'clock all the traps were open again and the duty shift was slipping underground. Johnny Marshall was first down "Tom" and knew there was trouble as soon as he put his foot on the bottom of the shaft and felt it squash into soft sand. He lit the fat lamp and saw the mouth of the infant tunnel nearly blocked with sand that had cascaded out into the base of the shaft.

The top boards of a couple of the first box frames had collapsed in the mouth of the tunnel, and several hundredweight of sand had crashed down. Just as well no one had been under it. Marshall felt a little dread as he realized that directly above the spot of the fall stood the chimney of the block beside the trap, a dead weight of about five tons. The crumbly sand below was so undermined that the whole thing was liable to come crashing down and wreck everything, including anyone who happened to be down there.

His number two digger joined him at the bottom of the shaft, saw the damage, and had the same thought.

"I should think," said Marshall, "that the chimney is held up just now purely by sky-hooks and the grace of God. You'd better go up on top again and give me plenty of room to clear this up."

He got a blunt refusal and the two of them set to work to patch up the damage, making nervous jokes about the glories of a martyr's death. They cleared away the mess, fitted new double-strength shoring, and through a small gap in the side of the shaft packed sand for hour after hour into the great domelike cavity left by the fall above the roof of the tunnel. When it was done, they carried on where they'd left off the previous day, burrowing into the blind face of the tunnel to win a few more feet.

After evening appell, the penguins got rid of most of the sand dug during the day, but not quite all. The Keen Type was in the compound again. He was a short man with blond hair, a long sharp nose, and a tight little mouth, and he tramped tirelessly up and down and around the huts, in one and out the other end, and then darted to the next. He had a sharp, suspicious eye, and every trap had to be closed a couple of times as he entered the area. Once he came almost at a trot out of Block 109, turned straight for 123, and walked in the door. The trapfuehrer had had about seven seconds' warning.

The penguin controller had been sitting on the ground a few yards away directing his penguins by signs. He half got to his feet as the Keen Type bowled into the hut and then he sank back, his palms sweating a little. There was nothing he could do.

Keen Type just missed his promotion. He was three paces from the alcove where the trapfuehrer was lowering the heavy concrete slab over the mouth of the shaft when a door burst open, a body came hurtling out pursued by shouts of wrath from behind and crashed headlong into him. They both went down on the floor, the Keen Type underneath. He tried to get up, but the body was lying heavily on him, groaning.

Several people came out of the room and gathered about, helping both to their feet and brushing them down. George Harsh was holding his knee, his face twisted in pain, and trying to apologize. The ferret didn't understand English, and Harsh made signs that he didn't understand German. Someone of-

56

fered to translate, and in a prolonged three-sided conversation George reviled himself for his clumsiness. The ferret was too winded to be impressively angry, and eventually, with a rather icy smile, he walked on.

The trapfuehrer had had time to replace the trap, camouflage it, and smoke a cigarette.

"Thanks, George," he said, "it was nicely timed."

Harsh was swearing too much to listen. He really had hurt his knee.

VALENTA had put Axel Zillessen on to the Keen Type. Axel wasn't his real name, but the one he'd chosen to use if he ever escaped from the compound so that he could travel as a Swede. He got everyone to call him Axel so he'd get used to answering to it. Actually he was a wool buyer from Bradford, a tall young man with a slightly hooked nose and kinky hair; and with a charming and infectious enthusiasm, Axel could talk the leg off an iron pot almost as fluently in German as in English.

The next time Keen Type came in the duty pilot's runner went and told Axel, and Axel strolled into the dusty compound where Keen Type was patrolling. He passed him a couple of times without speaking and on the third time gave him a casual greeting and they exchanged a few words about the weather. The same thing happened the next day. The third day they spoke for about five minutes.

Keen Type came in every day, and as soon as he did, the runner warned Axel. By the end of the week, Axel and the ferret were walking up and down together chatting for an hour. Gradually they got on to the war, Axel staying always on neutral ground, regretting the bombing and the suffering on both sides.

"It's ridiculous," he said. "Here are we, two ordinary people talking as civilized people, and if I put a foot over the warning wire you have to shoot me."

The Keen Type laughed.

"I have shot no one yet," he said mildly.

"But you would!"

"Only in the leg," said the Keen Type, "and with regret."

"That doesn't make it any more civilized."

"The bombing is not very civilized either"—this rather resentfully.

"We didn't start it," said Axel, and veered off what could only be a bitter subject. "What are you going to do after the war?"

The ferret laughed without humor. "Why worry now? I don't think it's ever going to end, and if it does I probably won't see it."

"Look," said Axel, "when it's over we're going to need the co-operation of Germans who weren't mad Nazis. You won't be an enemy then."

The ferret considered the delicate implication but did not answer. Neither did he think to deny, as normally he automatically would, the clear inference that Germany was going to lose.

Axel took him to his room for the first time next day for a cup of coffee. "X" gave the room a little extra ration for this, and whenever they wanted hot water for a brew they could claim time on the stove, no matter how many other pots were on it.

The others in the room, Dave, Laurie, Nellie, and Keith gave Keen Type casual welcome. He sat among them with a hot brew, a biscuit, and a cigarette. It was more comfortable than padding around the dust of the compound, and it was interesting to hear the British and American point of view. It is a soldier's privilege—his only one—to grumble, but you couldn't grumble in the German Army unless you were tired of life and wanted to go to the Russian Front. Keen Type had a lot that he hadn't been able to get off his chest, and now he had a sympathetic and safe audience, and he spoke with more and more freedom.

"What can we Germans do?" he said, after a week, sitting with his coffee and nibbling a piece of chocolate from a food parcel. "Against Hitler and the Gestapo—nothing."

"I'll tell you what you can do," Axel got up and sat down on the bunk beside him. "You can realize that the war is lost, and nothing you do can help that. The sooner it's over the better. We're not going to be enemies forever. Start regarding us as friends now." He added quietly, "We won't be forgetting our friends."

The duty pilot checked the Keen Type into the compound just after appell the next morning, and the runner slid off to warn Axel. Then he saw that the Keen Type seemed to be following him so he shied off. The ferret went straight into 105, knocked on Axel's door, and put his head around the corner. "Keen Type here," he said with a friendly grin. "Can I come in?"

He stayed a couple of hours, and then he excused himself, saying he'd better put in an appearance in the compound or Glemnitz would be wondering what he was doing. He was much more leisurely this time in his patrolling. He reported to Axel's room every day after that for a brew, and when he reluctantly went out into the compound again he had a new benevolence. After a while Roger took him off the danger list.

Valenta had detailed a German-speaking contact to every ferret and administrative German who came into the compound. The contact made friends with his man, fed him biscuits, brews, and cigarettes, and listened sympathetically to his grumbles and worries.

Funny people, the Germans. When you got them in a bunch they were all Nazis (they had to be), but when you got the little people by themselves and worked on them for a while they didn't have any morale underneath. Inside they seemed naked and defenseless. You could bribe 90 per cent of them—including the officers—with a little coffee or chocolate.

In a way, I don't think you could blame them. Valenta's contacts were like white ants, nibbling away a little at a time at the German faith in victory. Hitler had said that if you tell a big enough lie, people will believe it, but he rather over-looked the fact that once the lie is exposed, everything else you've said is also disbelieved. It wasn't hard to get a German thinking that Hitler wasn't the angel of virtue, and then the rest of his edifice of wishful faith came tumbling down.

The contacts sympathized with their Germans that they had to fight Hitler's war, lamented with them about Gestapo persecution, and poured out a stream of irresistible logic to show that Germany could never win.

"Why then," they said, "regard us as enemies? Soon, you will want us as friends."

The talking wasn't only one-way. Delicate steering had the ferrets talking about the security measures they planned, about conditions in Germany, details of the area around the camp. Dozens of little snippets were picked up, and Valenta, who had done an intelligence course at Prague Staff College, put them all together with Roger.

Soon they knew all the paths around the camp, how far the woods stretched, and the layout of Sagan town. They had timetables of all trains out of Sagan Station and the prices of all tickets. They knew what foods were ration-free, where the Swedish ships lay in Stettin and Danzig, what guards were around them, what guards covered the Swiss frontier and the Danish frontier, and a thousand other handy hints on how to get out of the Third Reich.

Some of the most useful information was gathered by Bill Webster from the German officers. Webster was an American, though born in South Africa and educated there and in England. He was always impeccably dressed and had a man-of-the-world air about him that encouraged the Germans to believe he would never do anything so vulgar as to engage in escape activities.

Bill did nothing to disabuse them of this belief. Whenever one of them dropped in on him he would graciously make his visitor welcome, and a pleasant chat would follow. Ultimately they would get around to lamenting the disruptions the war had caused—disruptions especially galling to men of the world like themselves.

"It is all so insufferable," the German would say.

Bill would give a heart-felt sigh and nod his head.

"Even I must now have a special pass to visit Berlin," the German would continue.

This, Bill would say politely, was an outrage.

And so on. By the time the tête-à-tête was over, Bill would know all about the special pass, the trains to Berlin, and conditions in the city.

Bill also interrogated all the newly-arrived prisoners to get from them every scrap of information about conditions outside that would be useful in an escape. This sort of work was going on in all the compounds, and we were pretty successful in exchanging the information.

"Why do you make such a bloody mess when you search the huts?" Axel asked the Keen Type.

"We have to be thorough," said the ferret. "Germans are always thorough. We have to take everything apart or we are in trouble with Glemnitz. And if we waste time putting everything together again, we are in more trouble with Glemnitz."

"You never find anything."

"Orders," said Keen Type virtuously, "are orders."

"Orders don't say you have to make a bloody mess wherever you go," said Axel, who'd reached the stage where he could be a little stern with the Keen Type. "Last time you people went through my room, you pinched half the wood-shavings out of my paillasse, and it was spread all over the floor. It took me half an hour to clear up."

"It wasn't me," the Keen Type said apologetically. "I will do your room myself next time." He added reproachfully, "You must not forget that you are our prisoners. Do not expect too much."

"Don't forget you'll be our prisoners one day," Axel said, with flippant menace, though the Keen Type did not need much reminding. Axel had been wedging the thought into his mind for a couple of weeks.

"It'd help us all," Axel went on, "if we knew when we were going to be searched. We could have things a little more orderly, and you wouldn't have to waste so much time going through all the mess. Be a help to you too."

"You ask too much," said Keen Type, shaking his head in fright at the thought.

Axel carefully brought up the subject again the next day, but it was a fortnight before he got Keen Type to tell him what huts were to be searched in the next few days, and after that it was easy. Roger nearly always got at least a day's notice of searches, and it was just a question of smuggling verboten stuff out of the hut next on the list, usually to the hut that was last searched. That was the safest spot of all. Once the ferrets had searched a hut it was usually immune till all the other huts had been searched and its turn came up again. It suited us.

"There's madness in their method," said Roger with satisfaction.

The contacts got more than information out of their German friends. There were a lot of things we wanted, and a prisoner's opportunities for shopping are limited. If Plunkett wanted maps or Travis wanted some tool, Roger passed it on to Valenta, and Valenta told his contact men. Once a contact had his German well trained, it wasn't difficult.

A bearded young man called Thompson worked in the kitchen block and was practically blood brothers with the little German clerk who checked the rations there. He was a nice little German who'd been a juggler in a circus before the war and traveled around the world a couple of times as a steward on boats and had no illusions about any nation, including his own.

Sitting over a brew one day Thompson had a tantrum and smashed his cup on the floor.

"I'm going nuts in this place," he moaned. "I'll be no bloody good when the war's over. I'll be wire-happy in a strait jacket."

"I would rather be here in your shoes than at the Russian Front," said the little German philosophically. "You are better off than some. There's an old Arabic proverb that says, 'I cried because I had no boots till I saw a man who had no feet.'"

"I'd rather be flying again," Thompson said dolefully, "even if I did get the chop. At least I wouldn't be sitting on my arse all day being useless and thinking too much. I want something to do."

"You can study your German," said the little clerk grinning. "Your grammar sometimes amazes me."

"Reminds me too much of being in here," said Thompson. "I'd like to take up drawing again. I used to do it at school, and it was very soothing."

The little German nodded approvingly.

"Only I haven't got any bloody thing to draw with," said Thompson plaintively. "Look, could you get me some drawing paper and nibs and Indian ink?"

The German looked doubtful. "You're not allowed to have pens," he said.

"They'll never know. I won't leave them around, and if the ferrets did find them, they'd only confiscate them. They only cost a couple of marks, and I could pay you with some coffee and chocolate."

The German promised to think it over, and Thompson prodded him for a couple of days till one day the little clerk produced three drawing nibs, a little bottle of ink, and a dozen sheets of cartridge paper. He was nervous about it but went off happily with some cigarettes and coffee stuffed in his pockets. Thompson delivered the drawing materials to Tim Walenn in his forgery factory.

"It was a piece of cake," he said. "I'll get him to bring in some more in a couple of weeks."

The first time was always the hardest, but once a man had done it, overcome his scruples, and found it easy and profitable, he did it fairly readily the next time until it became a habit.

There was a very young *Obergefreiter* (private) who was persuaded to bring in a pair of pliers and was paid very generously in chocolate. His contact explained apologetically that he had to draw the chocolate from his room mess and had to account for it. Would the obergefreiter mind signing a receipt for it. Just a formality. Why no, the obergefreiter wouldn't really mind at all, pocketed the chocolate, and signed on the dotted line.

He came to regret it. Later he brought in passes, money, files, maps, tools, and even some German uniform buttons and badges. It was much better than having his receipt handed over to the *Lageroffizier* and getting a bullet for trading with the enemy.

Bit by bit the stuff came in through all the contacts—pliers and hacksaw blades for Travis, inks and nibs and pens for the forgers, a magnet for Al Hake and his compass factory, bits of cloth and thread and buttons for the tailors, two prismatic compasses so the tunnels would go straight, German marks in dribs and drabs till "X" had quite a bank roll socked away. Also radio parts.

German news was a wee bit angled in their favor, and it was

nice to hear from home. A couple of radio operator–air gunners assembled a compact and very powerful receiver. Travis made a hide-hole for it in Hut 101 by ripping a lavatory off its base and sinking the set in the floor below. The lavatory was set back on its base and looked as respectable as any lavatory can look, but the bolt heads holding it down were dummies. A couple of shorthand writers listened to the B.B.C. every day and took it all down. With stooges posted, it was read in all huts. The B.B.C. has never had a more appreciative audience. Nor, I imagine, will they ever have again.

But you couldn't bribe all Germans. Glemnitz and Rubberneck were so obviously incorruptible that I don't think anyone ever tried them. I don't think I ever heard anyone ever refer to Glemnitz without saying "That bastard Glemnitz," but there was no hatred in the term; it was almost an expression of respect because he was a good soldier, even if he was a German. Rubberneck was always called a bastard too, but with Rubberneck we meant it. For all the sinuous length between his head and his shoulders, he was a stiffneck, rank-conscious and with a dangerous temper.

There were a lot of good Germans in the camp. They were all Luftwaffe, just ordinary *Soldaten*, with wives and families and homes, and when you take the nationality tag off ordinary people they're pretty much the same all over the world. It wasn't till later that the Gestapo and S.S. came into the picture.

The Kommandant had been wounded seven times in the 1914 war, and now he was just over sixty, still as straight as a young lad. He was an *Oberst* (colonel), and his name was Von Lindeiner. He was a lean, good-looking man with composure in his face, always immaculate in the Prussian tradition, the Iron Cross on his left pocket, tailored tunic, extravagantly cut riding breeches and black riding boots.

Within the limitations of war, he and Massey were friends.

Even if Von Lindeiner had been a petty tyrant, Massey would have tried to keep on reasonable terms for the concessions he could worm out of him for the camp; but as it was, it was an association based on mutual respect.

Von Lindeiner had once been a personal assistant to Goering, and Goering had put him in command of the camp because he knew him to be firm but humane. There wasn't much that was humane about Goering, but he had been a brilliant operational pilot in the 1914 war, and we gathered he had a soft spot in his heart for Air Force prisoners. I can't say any of us returned the feeling, and in any case Goering himself lost it when the bombing got under way.

Von Lindeiner was very correct. It is military etiquette in a prison camp for a captive officer to salute a captor officer and be saluted in return. But you must never salute without a cap on (except in the U. S.), and there were only a few caps in the whole of north camp. So whenever Von Lindeiner came into the compound, the bare-headed prisoners who passed him would nod politely, and the impeccable Prussian would salute the scruffy prisoner who, like as not, had a great hole in the seat of his pants and a two days' stubble because he'd been using the same razor blade for a month. It was an intriguing situation, a touch of ritual and civilized sanity.

And next day the Kommandant would issue a routine order emphasizing to all guards the necessity to shoot anyone who poked his nose over the warning wire. (Not many of the guards needed prompting. The bombing was hurting them too much.)

Pieber was another good German. Actually he was Austrian, but that didn't count. A lot of people said Pieber was two-faced, and perhaps he was. His brotherly love was half opportunism, but the other half was due to a kind, if not very stout, heart. He liked to be on good terms with everyone.

ROGER went in search of Travis and found him in his room filing a broken knife into a screw driver.

"Can you make me a rifle?" he asked, and Travis stared at him.

"It's for show, not for shooting," Bushell explained.

"What sort of a rifle exactly?"

"German one. Imitation. We've got a new show on. D'you remember the time just before we moved they took a mob out from East Camp to be deloused?"

"Yes," said Travis. "Someone on a new purge came in with wogs all over him."

"That's it," said Roger. "I think we can put on a couple of unofficial ones. We've got to have some Goons to go as escort. Guest is making the uniforms. You're going to make their guns."

"They'd have to be terribly good to pass the gate *Postens,* Roger," Travis said slowly. "I don't know that we can do it."

Roger swiveled his twisted eye on him. "I want them in a week," he said, and walked out.

Travis, McIntosh, and Muller tried to put on paper an accurate plan of a German military carbine and found they didn't have a clue about the detail and dimensions. Muller went and got Henri Picard out of the forgery factory. Picard, a young Belgian, was one of the best artists in the camp. Muller's idea appealed to him, and he went away and cut a rough pair of calipers out of a piece of tin.

Coming off appell that afternoon Muller started chatting to one of the guards, and Picard stood just behind very carefully measuring with his calipers the width and depth of various parts of the carbine slung over the guard's shoulder. Then he stood beside him and calculated the length of the rifle, noting where the barrel came to about the height of his head and where the butt finished by his thighs. For the next day he cautiously trailed several guards drawing in rough detail parts of the gun.

Travis had noticed that about one in every three hundred bedboards was made of beech instead of pine, and Williams toured every hut and swiped every beech board he could find. The boards weren't thick enough to make a rifle, so they sawed and carved out each rifle in two halves, glued them together, and clamped them to set in vises made out of reinforced ping pong net-posts. They carved out in wood the parts that were supposed to be metal, barrel, breech, and bolt, and rubbed and polished them with a lump of graphite brought in by a tame German till they looked like blue gun metal. The wooden parts that were really wood they stained with tan boot polish and rubbed and rubbed till it looked perfect.

The clips around the barrels Muller made from strips cut off a metal jug; he used bent nails for the sling clips and belts for the slings. Muller didn't think the polished wooden barrel looked quite perfect enough, so he melted down silver paper from cigarette packs into lead and cast a proper barrel end in a soap mold. He polished it with graphite until it was perfect.

By happy chance, the gray of Luftwaffe uniforms was almost identical with R.A.F. gray-blue, and Tommy Guest used old R.A.F. uniforms to cut out several unteroffiziers' uniforms. Six of his amateur tailors hand-sewed them.

Muller made the little eagles that went on the lapels and

the belt buckles by casting melted silver paper in soap molds, carving the eagles in the mold himself. The belt buckle was perfect. One of the contacts got his Goon to take off his tunic on a hot day while he drank his daily brew and Muller stealthily pressed the buckle into the soap to make his mold. Guest cut a bit off the tail of a terrible old shirt of Kirby-Green's to make the color patches on the uniforms.

Tim Walenn produced several beautifully forged gate passes (the originals had been brought in by a tame guard). The "unteroffiziers" would have to show the passes to get out of the camp with their party, and Walenn's staff had hand-lettered them, working nonstop on the job for about a week. He took the passes to Roger.

"Which is the real one?" he asked.

Roger peered at them for a while. "They're bloody good, Tim," he said. "I don't think I could pick them apart."

"As a matter of fact," Tim said, "they're all forgeries."

And the day it was all done and thirty-two men were getting their last briefings for the break, the German unteroffiziers came in without rifles. They all had pistols instead, in holsters on a belt. It was a new order. Unteroffiziers weren't going to carry rifles any more, and there had to be an unteroffizier on the fake delousing party. An ordinary *Gefreiter* (private) wouldn't be allowed to escort a party out of the gate.

Roger really lost his temper this time, and for two days he was quite unbearable. Travis and Muller weren't much better.

One of Tommy Guest's men had been a handbag maker in private life, and Roger put him to work making imitation pistol holsters out of cardboard. He marked the cardboard to give it a leathery grain and rubbed it with boot polish, and you couldn't tell the result from a real holster. McIntosh made a couple of dummy pistol butts out of wood and fixed them so they peeped coyly out of the holster flaps.

Roger planned the break in two phases. First, twenty-four

men escorted by two "unteroffiziers" were to march out of the gate (they hoped) ostensibly bound for the delousing showers. Ten minutes after they were clear, Bob Van Der Stok, a Dutchman in the R.A.F. who spoke perfect German, was to march out a party of five senior officers for a "special conference" with the Kommandant.

Roger, Wings Day, and the committee hand-picked the people to go, selecting men who'd been working hard for "X" and who'd been behind the wire for a couple of years or more. Roger himself toyed with the idea of going, but Wings and the others energetically talked him out of it. As Wings pointed out, there was a very fair chance of the alarm being given quite quickly, in which case many of them probably wouldn't get very far, and if Roger was caught again so soon after the last time, he knew what to expect.

"Wait till you can get out through 'Tom,'" Day said. "You'll be out of the area by train then before they wake up to it."

Roger reluctantly agreed, partly because he was banking so much on "Tom." Floody wanted to go on the delousing party too, but Roger vetoed the idea, and they had a short, sharp argument. Arguments with Roger were often sharp and always short.

"We need you here for the tunnels," he told Floody flatly.

"God, I'm sick of tunnels," Floody groaned. "I seem to spend my life down a stinking hole in the ground. I want a change."

"Look, Wally," Roger said. "We're just getting somewhere now, and everything's going like a bomb. Don't spoil it. We'll get 'Tom' out in a couple of months, and then you can go for your life, but not now. You're needed here."

"But I'd be back," said Floody, spreading his hands appealingly. "They'd catch me. Nothing surer. I'll go on the delouser now, and in two days I'll be back in the cooler. Then I can

71

have a nice rest for a fortnight and come back fit. How 'bout that?"

"No," said Roger.

It was just after two o'clock on a warm afternoon that twenty-four men fell in outside 104, carrying bundles wrapped in towels, presumably to be dumped in the steam delousers. It would be too bad if the gate guards inspected them because they contained uniform jackets and pants converted to look like civilian clothes and little packets of concentrated food cakes made from oatmeal and breadcrumbs, milk powder, chocolate, and sugar. In the pockets were maps and a little German money. Two "unteroffiziers," holsters at their waists, formed them into three ranks, and they straggled off toward the gate laughing and joking with the fake heartiness people show as they climb into the dentist's chair. The atmosphere was a little electric. Roger and the envious Floody felt it a hundred yards away where they sat by a corner of a hut, unobtrusively watching.

The party stopped at the first gate, and one of the "unteroffiziers" showed his pass. The guard hardly even looked at it, and then the big barbed-wire gates were swinging open. They marched to the next gate, the guard looked casually at the pass, and in a few moments they were walking out into the road that curved into the pine wood. It was practically an anticlimax.

Three hundred yards down the road without a German in sight they turned sharply and vanished into the trees, then broke into a run for half a mile. Deep into the woods they changed into their traveling clothes and split up into ones, twos, and threes.

At a quarter-past two, Van Der Stok walked out of 110 with the second party and headed for the gate. Goodrich, the senior, was an American colonel of about forty, with a red, rough face and barrel chest. Beside him walked Bob Tuck, slim and elegant, a Battle of Britain ace with a D.S.O. and three D.F.C.'s; then Bill Jennens, R.A.F. squadron leader and compound adjutant with a voice like a drill sergeant and a face like a lump of uncarved granite. The other two were the lanky "Nellie" Ellan, who looked after the camp radio, and a Polish wing commander.

Van Der Stok showed his pass at the first gate, and they walked through. At the next, the guard was a little more conscientious and turned the pass over and looked at the back. (We found out later it was only a week before that the Germans had put a new mark on the back of the gate passes in case they were ever copied.) Van Der Stok's pass didn't have the mark, and the guard looked suspiciously up at him. It was only then that his brain slowly grasped the fact that he had seen this man walking around the compound as a prisoner. He raised a shout and a dozen German soldiers came clumping out of the guardhouse.

Van Der Stok bowed disarmingly and raised his hands.

Broili came over from the kommandantur in response to an urgent message. He was chief security officer, a plump little major with shiny black hair, given to monumental anger when prisoners escaped and patronizing politeness when they failed to. He greeted the little group jovially.

"Mr. Van Der Stok," he said roguishly, "you are improperly dressed. Ah, it is too bad, gentlemen," (with a happy grin) . . . "the fortunes of war. Perhaps you will have better luck next time."

He congratulated the guard on recognizing Van Der Stok, and the guard put his foot right in it.

"I thought it unusual, Herr Major, that two parties should leave the camp so close together," he said smugly, and Broili looked suddenly older.

"Two parties?" he asked in a voice of doom, and the guard told him.

"*Mein Gott, sechsundzwanzig,*" shrieked Broili, and with a

73

terrible look at Van Der Stok and Goodrich he ran for the guardhouse phone.

The Kommandant reached the gate within two minutes and strode in followed by Broili (sweating), a dozen guards from the guardhouse and a screen of ferrets. The ferrets and guards ran ahead shouting, "Appell! Appell!" Pieber ran in flapping his hands. He went straight to Bill Jennens' room to get him to hurry everyone along for appell and stopped foolishly in the door when he remembered Jennens was with Goodrich, Van Der Stok, and the others in the cooler. Through the trees from the kommandantur marched nearly a hundred jackbooted and helmeted troops carrying rifles and tommyguns. They moved into the huts clearing everyone out.

Block "X's" went quietly through their huts and out in the compound telling everyone to take his time. There would be an identification parade to discover who was missing and the longer it took, the better chance the delousing party would have to get clear. The prisoners were all moving like snails, and Pieber found Wings Day.

"Please," he said. "Efferybody on appell quickly, and we will have no shooting. The Kommandant is most angry."

Von Lindeiner's face was the color of a storm cloud. He stood apart from everyone watching the eight hundred men dawdling. Glemnitz stood apart, too, his mouth shut in a hard line, and you could see the jaw muscles sticking out at the sides. Rubberneck, as usual, showed more outward signs than anyone. He was very red in the face, his forehead creased and his mouth drooping as though he'd been found in a girls' school without his pants. No one laughed because he had a pistol in his hand.

Eventually we formed up by blocks in the usual hollow square and stood there seven hours. Pieber counted us twice, and it didn't check so he counted again and then started the business of the individual photograph check.

Army and Navy officer prisoners of the rank of colonel or above, and every British or American pilot, no matter what rank, was classified as "important prisoner," and the Germans filed their photographs and fingerprints. One by one a ferret called us by name and checked our faces with our photographs. It wasn't easy. Not many looked as they were when they were shot down. Everyone was thinner and many had beards or shaven heads.

It had been hot when we went on appell, and most of us had only shorts on. About four o'clock a thunderstorm broke and the rain bucketed down for an hour. None of the Germans had topcoats. Von Lindeiner looked as though he wasn't even aware it was raining. He stood by the photographs, implacable and still, and soaking wet. You had to hand it to him. As darkness closed in about nine-thirty, it was all over, and we were allowed, shivering but satisfied, to go back to the huts.

None of the twenty-six made it back to England. Within three days they were all caught but three, Morison, Welsh, and Stower.

In the bundles they carried out of the gate Morison and Welch had fake German uniforms they'd made for themselves. They donned them in the woods and got to a near-by airfield where they sneaked into an old Junkers training plane. They were just starting the engine to fly to Sweden when a German pilot came along—quite unsuspectingly—to fly the plane. He thought Morison and Welch were ground crew. They couldn't speak a word of German but saluted madly, wound the starting handle for him and the German took off, leaving them on the ground grinding their teeth. They crawled into another plane, found it didn't have a starting handle, so they marched boldly into a hangar, took a starting handle from the locker of another plane there and were just starting up their chosen aircraft when a German sergeant stormed up and asked them what the hell they were doing.

"Well," said Morison casually in English, knowing the game was up, "we thought we'd borrow this, actually, and go home for the week-end." The sergeant looked faint, but soon recovered. The Germans wanted to try them for sabotage and kept them in jail for weeks, but finally purged them to Kolditz Strafelager.

Tough little black-haired Johnny Stower was nearly caught in the first half-hour of the escape. A guard questioned him a mile from the compound, but Stower had a forged pass from Walenn showing that he was a Spanish worker. He bluffed his way past and walked sixty miles to the Czech border, across fields and through woods, keeping away from the roads.

In a border town he made friends with a Czech innkeeper who gave him civilian clothes and money, and Stower went on by train to a spot near the Swiss border. He set out at night to walk across and actually walked into a narrow salient of Swiss territory, but not knowing just where he was he walked out the other side back into Germany and was caught by a frontier guard. After a few grim weeks in a Gestapo prison, he came back to us. It was tragic luck. Later, we realized how tragic.

Conk Canton had had bad luck too. He got into a train at Sagan Station, and as the train started a German officer got into the same compartment. Canton recognized him as a German doctor from the kommandantur and quickly hid his face behind a paper. He stayed that way for several minutes wondering how he could get to another compartment without being recognized when he felt an insistent tap on the knee. It was impossible to ignore it. He had to look over the top of the paper inquiringly, and there was the German doctor looking at him tolerantly.

"I'm sorry, Canton," he said. "You'll have to come back with me."

Around dusk, at lock-up time a few days after the delouser, three men in German uniforms and with rifles over their shoulders marched out through the compound gate, after perfunctorily showing their passes. There was nothing wrong with the passes. They all had the new mark on the back, and the three men vanished into the night.

Unfortunately two of them ran into Glemnitz on their way to Sagan Station, and the shocked and enraged Glemnitz recognized them as two prisoners and arrested them. The third man, Cochran, was picked up on a train a few hours later. It was bad luck, but at least Travis' dummy rifles hadn't been completely wasted.

CHAPTER 7

BY THE time the tunnels were about twenty feet long, Muller, Travis and McIntosh had the underground railways ready. Gone were the days when a man hacked away a basinful of sand at the working face and inched his way a hundred feet backward with it to the shaft to empty it, and then crawled up to the face again.

The trolleys had to stand up to a lot of work, so Travis used the beechwood bedboards to make the chassis. He had a trolley for each tunnel, and each one carried two detachable wooden boxes for the sand. Each wheel was three disks of beechwood screwed tightly together (the inside disks being larger to make the flange that held and guided the trolley on the rails). He screwed strips of metal from old food tins around the rims for tires and used metal rods off the stoves for axles. They turned in wooden bearings greased with margarine.

For the rails, Willy Williams went around the blocks tearing off the beading battens that lined the walls and the ceilings of every room. The carpenters split them lengthwise to make strips about an inch wide, half an inch thick, and a few feet long, and nailed them to the floors of the tunnels about a foot apart. The trolleys ran very smoothly on them, pulled each way by ropes made of plaited string tied to both ends.

Tunneling now was falling into a smooth routine. Each tunnel had about twelve permanent diggers on its staff, divided into shifts of four. Immediately after morning appell, Block X looked under the hut and in the ceiling to make sure no ferrets had hidden themselves away during appell, and when everything was clear the stooges kept guard while the trapfuehrer opened up and the shift of four went below. He shut the top, dismissed all except one of the stooges, and everything was safe on top till reopening time just before afternoon appell.

Down below, one of the shift squatted in front of the pump and started the rhythmic rowing action. Two men whipped off their clothes and changed into filthy long woolen underclothes. One of them lay on his belly on the trolley and wheeled himself up to the working face with a dog-paddle motion of his hands. The other hauled the trolley back by the rope and paddled himself up to the face. The fourth man back at the base of the shaft hauled the trolley back, clipped the sand boxes on, and the rear man in the tunnel hauled it back up to the face.

There was no room to turn around in the tunnel or lie side by side. Digger No. 1 lay full length and dug into the face, and as the sand piled up by his head, he pushed it down past his hips until Digger No. 2 (lying facing the other way—toward the shaft) could scrape it toward him and load it into the boxes on the trolley. When the boxes were full, he tugged the rope and the man in the base of the shaft hauled it back, whipped the boxes off, and emptied them into kit bags stacked in the dispersal chamber. He put the boxes back on the trolley, tugged the rope, and Digger No. 2 hauled it back to the face.

The man in the shaft spent most of his time finishing off the slots and tongues cut by the carpenters in the ends of the bedboards stored in the workshop chamber. When a new shoring frame or piece of air pipe or fresh fat lamp was needed, Digger No. 2 sent a note back on the trolley, and back came what he wanted.

They worked without a break below till evening appell. If

they wanted any lunch, they took it down with them. Mostly they didn't. Lunch was usually a slice of black bread and a couple of potatoes; at its best it still tasted like black bread and potatoes, and seasoned with sand it was even worse.

Now and then they switched jobs to ease the muscles and the tedium. Digging was the worst. You had a fat lamp by your head, you sniffed the fumes all day, and when you came back up again you did nothing but spit black. The pumps relieved this a lot. At the end of the air line there was a transferable nozzle which led up over the shoulder of the digger, gave him plenty of fresh air, and kept sand out of the air pipe itself. When another section of pipe was being fitted, the nozzle was taken off, the new pipe laid under the floor, and the nozzle put back.

Lightly-built diggers changed places by one lying flat and the other crawling over him, but with hefty characters like Tom Kirby-Green, they had to wheel themselves back to the shaft to change over. It was surprisingly warm below, and the diggers were in a constant sweat.

Sometimes a ferret wandered near the trap, and then the alarm tin in the shaft gave a soft rattle. Everyone froze where he was because sometimes muffled sounds of work below could be heard on top. They lay there without moving until the tin rattled again as the ferret moved away and they carried on.

The warning tin hung from the roof of the dispersal chamber. There were a couple of little pebbles in it and a string from it led up the shaft through the hut floor not far from the trap. It needed just a gentle tug from the stooge above whenever a ferret was approaching to rattle the pebbles.

About four-thirty the tunnelers changed into their ordinary clothes below and tried to comb the sand out of their hair. Above, the stooges drifted along to keep guard, and a German speaker stood by to lure away any ferret hanging about the trap areas. When they got the all clear the trapfuehrers opened up, the tunnelers came out, and the traps were shut. The tunnelers washed off any telltale sand in their huts and went on appell with everyone else.

After appell Block X's searched the huts again, the duty stooges kept watch, the traps were opened, and the second shift went below. They laid new rails, replaced any shoring frames that needed it, swept surplus sand out of the tunnels, and checked the fat lamps and the pump.

Travis had made two spirit levels, and every evening they carefully checked the levels of the tunnel floors to see that they really were on the level. It wouldn't have been so bad if they'd risen slightly (though not too much). They certainly didn't want them to go any deeper. The evening shift also checked for direction. Through the tame Germans the organization had two little prismatic compasses of the Wehrmacht infantry type. They only gave rough checks. The close checks were done by holding a fat lamp by the wall of the tunnel at the face and sighting along the same wall from the base of the shaft.

Then the tricky part started. If everything was clear, the traps were kept open and the kit bags of sand excavated during the day were hauled to the top by a rope sling. One by one the penguins stopped by, collected their sand, and wandered off. As soon as the last bag of sand had been emptied the underground men came up and the traps were shut for the night.

In the morning the third shift took over for the day's tunneling, and so they went in rotation, each shift working two days out of every three.

You needed stamina and steady nerves to be a digger. It was a heavy strain to lie for hours on one elbow carving away at the sand face with an outstretched arm, and you had to carve carefully if you didn't want a hundredweight of sand collapsing in your face. There were minor falls every day and sometimes bigger ones.

81

A mixed lot, the diggers. They came from nearly every British country, from America and France, Poland, Norway, the Argentine, and Czechoslovakia.

From Wales, there was Shag Rees, the little man with thick black hair and a nose that had been broken so often it was getting to be a habit. His friend, "Red" Noble, was a red-headed Canadian, built like a navvy with a slow, gentle drawl

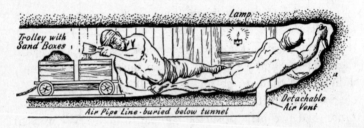

HOW THE TUNNELERS WORKED

and nearly always a half-grin on his face. He and Shag used to like baiting Rubberneck, and so they weren't always available because they spent a lot of time in the cooler.

Major Davy Jones was American, mostly known as "Tokyo" because he flew on the famous American raid in 1942, when General Doolittle led them off from a carrier and they bombed Tokyo and prayed they had enough fuel left to fly on to China. A few of them made it, and Davy finished up among the Chinese guerrillas. He got to the Middle East after that and was shot down on his first trip. A short but singularly violent operational career! He came from Oklahoma, a wild and lanky creature with jet-black hair, who looked like a hawk-eyed Indian.

Piglet Lamond was the little New Zealander who had dug his way out in the spectacular "mole" tunnel from East Camp. Danny Krol, a little Pole about five feet tall, used to be a

82

saber champion. He had a clean-cut face, straight hair brushed back, and the most perfect physique in miniature I ever saw.

Jean Regis, a Frenchman in the R.A.F., was dark and hairy and built like a gorilla. Regis was tireless. He used to sit pumping for four hours at a stretch and break into a tirade of French curses if you tried to give him a relief.

"Muckle" Muir, a tall, fair-haired Scot, had a huge handlebar mustache that he grew to keep the sand out of his nose.

Ed Tovrea's father was a big meat magnate in Arizona, and Tovrea, a good-looking youngster of about twenty-one, had been shot down on one of the first American Spitfire squadrons in England.

Buck Ingram was a big, tough Yank from Idaho with thick black hair and glinting eyes.

Johnny Staubo, the Norwegian, should have been in Hollywood. He was really a good-looking man, over six feet tall, with beautifully chiseled features and Nordic blond hair. He used to play Davis Cup tennis.

"Scruffy" Weir, another Canadian, had been flying without goggles the night he was shot down, and the plane caught fire. His helmet and oxygen mask saved most of his face but the fire caught him around the eyes, and the skin had healed thick and smooth like parchment, but was scarred purple and red.

The black-haired Birkland, also Canadian, was distinguished by a little fringe of beard around his jowls.

They all had their little peculiarities. Davy Jones had no nerves and a blind faith that a tunnel would never fall on him. Later he found out. Whenever Scruffy Weir dug, the tunnel used to take a diving turn to the left. Crump used to curse him every second day for going off course, but Scruffy kept making diving turns. Birkland used to veer to the right nearly every shift, so Crump always rostered him to dig after Scruffy to

83

even things out. For a long time, Birkland insisted on working stark naked below, and to see him, sweat-and-sand-stained, reversing down the tunnel was an unnerving sight. Floody noticed he was getting sand-scarred on the knees and elbows and made him wear the hated long underpants and vests. The sand scars looked too obvious.

When each tunnel was about thirty feet long, Floody changed the shoring system to conserve wood. Instead of solid framing all the way, they spaced the frames about a foot apart and laid boards over the tops.

Williams had already made three levies on bedboards throughout the camp, demanding a certain number from every room. Every bed now had about three boards missing, and the paillasses, which were never very comfortable, sagged in the gaps. You got used to it in time. Some of the rooms had double floors, and Williams sent his carpenters under the huts to rip off some of the lower floor boards. They sawed them into lengths of about eighteen inches and took them below to shore the tunnel roofs between the box frames.

With the new shoring the face had to be dug forward about two feet before they could put in a new box frame and line the roof, and the falls of sand immediately became worse. No matter how carefully you scraped the concave archway overhead, the stuff cracked and fell nearly every day. There was hardly ever enough warning to get clear; just the little cracking noise and down it came, usually burying the digger from head to hips and leaving a dome overhead.

Sometimes a couple of hundred pounds of sand fell and then number two worked fast, grabbed his half-entombed mate by the ankles and hauled him clear, sand in his eyes and ears and choking in his nose and mouth.

Nearly always the fat lamp and air line were smothered, and they were left in stifling blackness. Unable to write a note,

84

number two trolleyed himself back to the shaft and returned with another lamp, by which time number one would probably have coughed the sand out of his nose and mouth so he could breathe again. You'd know if he could breathe by the curses.

The last four feet of the tunnel would be blocked with sand. They dug out the nozzle of the air line, emptied the sand out, and refitted it. About a third of the sand that had fallen they sent back on the trolley, and then, with just enough room to work in, number one box-framed the area of the fall. He left a little gap in the roof through which he packed sand for half an hour till the dome above was filled in. Then he boarded over the gap and carried on tunneling. The exasperating thing about a fall was that, no matter how tightly you crammed it, you could only pack about two-thirds of the amount that fell back in the dome. The rest was so much extra sand to be dispersed.

One of Travis' men relieved the fat-lamp situation a little. He'd been an electrical engineer, and he went around every hut rearranging all the electric-light wiring. When he'd finished, he had about forty bits of cable from a foot to ten feet long. He spliced them all together, tapped the power lines behind the walls, and installed electric lights in all the shafts and for the first few feet of the tunnels. It wasn't any good during the day because the power wasn't on, but it was a great help to the evening dispersing shifts.

On a good day when there weren't too many ferret alarms or falls, each tunnel crawled forward about five feet. Often it was less, but by early June "Tom" was sixty feet long and the other two weren't far behind.

That wily man Glemnitz stopped Conk in the compound one day. "Ah, Mr. Canton," he said affably, "how many tunnels are you digging now?"

"Just above fifty at the moment," Conk said facetiously, and passed on.

A few minutes later Glemnitz encountered Floody and asked the same thing.

"Why should I tell you?" Floody said. "You wouldn't believe me."

At an "X" committee meeting a couple of days later it came out that Glemnitz had been asking dozens of people the same question. He had gone to every room in one block asking it.

"The cunning sod," Roger said. "I'll bet he's checking all the different answers and reactions to try and get some idea if there's a tunnel going."

He sent word around the compound that if Glemnitz spoke to anyone he was to ignore him completely.

THE Russian prisoners came back about June 10. About a hundred of them surrounded by German tommy-gunners deployed into the wood outside the south fence and started chopping the trees down. Convoys of trucks came and carted the trunks and foilage away, and in four days the edge of the wood had slid back fifty yards.

Massey found an excuse to see the Kommandant, and Von Lindeiner told him they were building a new compound.

"It is for the Americans," he said. "We are going to segregate you."

"Surely that's not necessary," Massey objected. "We speak the same language. They're our allies, and we get along very well together."

"I think," Von Lindeiner said dryly, "that is what the High Command had in mind. It is their order."

Massey sent for Roger, Goodrich, Clark, and Wings Day and told them.

"It's no good my working on the Kommandant," he said. "If it's an Oberkommando order, that's all there is to it. He turned to Goodrich. "You see what it means," he said. "If they finish the compound before we finish a tunnel, your chaps are going to miss out."

Goodrich asked if any date was fixed for the move to the new compound.

87

"Von Lindeiner either didn't know or wouldn't say," Massey said. "I myself think it should be about two months." He looked inquiringly at Roger. "What about it, Bushell?"

"The obvious thing, Sir, is to concentrate on one tunnel for the time being. 'Tom' is the most advanced. We'll go flat out on it."

"What are the chances?" asked Goodrich.

Roger said confidently, "We can do it if we're lucky. We might need a bit of luck because we might have to cut a few corners."

He told the committee the new program without hesitation. In view of the dispersal bottleneck there was no point in going ahead with "Dick" or "Harry" at the same time. Selected diggers could do up to twelve feet a day. Fanshawe guaranteed the penguins could handle that much. More would mean risks.

That night, Minskewitz scraped out the soap that sealed the edges of "Dick's" trap and put in cement. Crump cemented "Harry's" trap solidly all around so that it was again part of the floor.

Roger and Floody picked the fifteen best diggers and split them into three shifts to work "Tom." They included Lamond, Cornish, and Rees because they were short and wiry, tailor-made for underground work. They left off some of the big fellows like Kirby-Green. There was nothing wrong with Kirby-Green's work but he had such massive shoulders he occasionally knocked a box frame out of plumb and caused falls. Roger put all the American diggers on the team.

"Whether we break 'Tom' or not," Goodrich said, "I want to take as many experienced men to the new compound as possible. Some of the boys might get homesick."

There were Americans on every factory, and they didn't need much teaching. The ones with Travis could do anything with their hands.

Crump, Marshall, and Johnny Bull took over as the three shift bosses on "Tom," and Floody was overseer (and digger as well—all the shift bosses dug). Though he was tall and hefty, Roger himself insisted on going on one of the digging teams. He was tired of using only his voice.

They pressed forward ten feet the next day, and Fanshawe got rid of it all without trouble. The following day Floody was half buried in another bad fall that left a dome four feet high over the tunnel roof. His number two pulled him out by the ankles, and they were an hour and a half reframing and packing it. That day they made only eight feet.

There seemed to be a hoodoo on Floody for falls. His ear was so sharply cocked for the crack of falling sand that he could reverse down a tunnel nearly as fast as he could run. Tokyo Jones still had the blithe confidence that he'd never be buried. Floody sent him up to the face next day, and Jones had made about two feet forward and was just putting in the top board of the frame to shore the roof when about two hundred pounds of sand crashed down, and he just had his feet sticking out. Floody was able to pull him out and, when he'd got his breath back and finished cursing, the American got grimly and silently to work clearing the sand.

"I never knew anything would keep you so quiet so long," said Floody, amused, and Jones looked back over his shoulder, the whites of his eyes standing out in the lamplight in his dirty, sweaty face.

"The meek shall inherit the earth," he said. "Boy, I certainly inherited some that time."

Floody was buried again the following day, and this time the sand tipped the hot fat lamp against his leg and held it there. His number two pulled him out nearly screaming, a great patch of red and blistered flesh on his thigh. They had run into such a soft patch that they started box-framing all the way again.

By the end of the week, "Tom" was 105 feet long, and Floody, Crump, and Marshall built the halfway house. Floody wanted halfway houses every hundred feet. Beyond that distance the rope hauling the railways tended to scrape against the shoring and there was too much danger of knocking frames out.

They made the halfway houses about ten feet long and about six inches wider and higher than the main tunnel using longer boards for the shoring. It was a staging post, and no rails were laid in it. Two extra men lay there, with just enough room to turn around. As the trolley came back from the face, one man lifted the sand boxes off and passed them to the next man who put them on a second trolley and sent them back to the shaft. Travis had the second trolley ready as soon as the halfway house was finished.

Measuring below by string and above by trigonometry, Floody estimated that the halfway house was just about under the wire. About thirty yards on was the edge of the wood, and Roger agreed with him that about seven yards inside the wood was a safe enough spot to break out.

"We ought to be there safely in a fortnight," Floody announced to the committee, "then we're going to have a very tricky job to dig straight up about twenty-five feet."

"Why can't we slope gradually up from where we are now?" asked Marshall. "We'd only have a few feet to go vertically then, and it'd save a hell of a lot of time."

"I've been thinking of that," Floody said, "but I don't think it'd work. Too risky. If a trolley full of sand gets away on a downhill slope, it'll smash everything."

"I don't see why a trolley should get away," said Marshall. "We're out to save time, aren't we?" Marshall was the obstinate one. When he got an idea he hung on to it like a leech.

"If a rope breaks," said Floody, "you can kiss your tunnel good-by. The trolley'll tear half a dozen frames down, and you'll get twenty feet of sand collapsing. Over that distance it'll probably fall for a hell of a height, and you'll have twenty tons blocking the works. The trolley might run on and bring down a bloody sight more than that."

"Put double ropes on," said Marshall. "The time's the important thing. If we don't get it finished, the Yanks are going to miss out and be pretty sore, and I don't blame 'em."

Pulling on his mustache, George Harsh said seriously in his Georgia accent: "What about the guys down below if a trolley gets away and brings everything down?"

"I tell you there's no need for a trolley to get away," Marshall said.

"A man's only got to lose his grip on the rope," said Floody. "You can take all precautions, but it can happen. There'll be a couple of blokes trapped, and they won't have a chance."

"I'll take a chance on that," Marshall said.

"So will everyone," said Roger gently, "but that isn't the point. If we have to take a chance, we can. The thing is, do we have to?" He turned to Floody.

"No," said Floody. "I'm bloody sure we can make it in time my way."

"Then that's it," Roger said. It wasn't often he came into the technical arguments, and when he did it was always at the end with a decisiveness that settled it. Marshall fought tooth and nail for his ideas, but when the decision went against him he accepted it, muttering for a few minutes sometimes, but then resigning himself to it. He was an old regular, had been in the Air Force for donkey's years, and was always bubbling with high-strung enthusiasm. Outside tunnel work his only relaxation in the camp was playing the oboe, and his roommates wouldn't let him do much of that.

In Block 106 Jerry Sage and Davy Jones had been sitting up all night for two nights running. Their vigil was by the light of a fat lamp around the kitchen stove where a great covered pot was bubbling. Out of the lid of the pot stuck a long thin tube made out of bits of jam tin rolled around a pencil. There were yards of the tube; it angled down from the pot into a tin of water where it curled around and around and then stuck out through a fat-sealed hole in the bottom. Every few seconds a globule of colorless liquid dripped and fell with a glistening splash into a jar on the floor. The Fourth of July was approaching, and through one of Al Hake's stills the Americans were preparing for it.

The camp was drier than Prohibition ever made the U. S. Once a year the Germans produced a few barrels of a liquid which mocked the traditions of German beer and was compared detrimentally with the natural product of the horses that pulled the honey wagon.

For state occasions the substitute was raisin wine and its by-products. About a dozen men saved all the raisins and sugar from their Red Cross parcels for several weeks and tipped them into half a barrel of water with a fermented raisin as a starter. For three weeks it bubbled like a witch's cauldron, and when all the raisins had fully fermented the pulp residue was strained through a towel. The sludge that came out was courteously called raisin wine. It had phenomenal alcoholic ferocity and would lubricate one good party, leaving a feeling of impending doom in the morning.

The fastidious ones double-distilled it into raw spirit, and one of the Poles, who had been a chemistry lecturer at Kraków University, used to make from it an imitation rye whisky in return for a share in the party. He poured in some viscous stuff that looked like honey and added a little white powder. He would never say what they were, which was probably just as well. The spirit turned a pale amber, and if you couldn't remember very clearly what rye whisky tasted like, it wasn't a bad substitute. When July fourth dawned, a dozen American syndicates had gallons of the stuff prepared.

They started toasting the day as the sun edged up behind the pine trees, and half an hour later hell broke out in the British blocks as Paul Revere came riding through, followed by forty whooping Indians. Paul Revere was Jerry Sage, in a paper tricorne hat and long woolen underpants for knee breeches. He threw Bushell out of bed, and Roger, grinding his teeth slightly, took it quietly, largely because Sage and Harsh were sitting on him. He was rostered for the tunnel that day and went below after appell with a wistful glance at a bottle of hellbrew that Sage was brandishing.

The party went on all day until about three o'clock a senior officer suggested they should ease off in case some exuberant soul wandered over the warning wire. Half a dozen senior British and American officers threw him into the firepool, clothes and all. Goodrich, with bland apologies, leaned down and offered to help him out and the man in the pool dragged Goodrich in too. Goodrich climbed out and threw Wings Day in, and within five minutes everyone had been thrown in the pool.

After they had climbed out, someone noticed a body drifting sluggishly on the bottom of the pool. They hauled it out, laid it flat, and started squeezing the water out with artificial respiration until you could almost hear the ribs cracking. The body stirred after a while and eventually sat up with a wan smile. "The water wouldn't hold me up," he said foolishly.

George Harsh wagged a solemn finger at him. "It's the faith you lack," he boomed, and vanished in the direction of his hut.

He was back again in a minute with a blanket draped around him in biblical style. Standing on the edge of the pool, he raised an arm for silence and intoned: "Thou shalt have faith

93

and walk upon the waters." He took a firm pace forward, and the water closed ruthlessly over him.

They pulled him out, and he stood in dripping dignity, wrapping his cloak around him.

"I got two steps," he lied shamelessly, "but my faith gave out."

"T OM" had gone fifty feet past the halfway house when one of the penguins slipped up. He was a little careless, pulling the pin out of his trouser bags on the fringe of a crowd around a volley-ball game instead of in among them. It only needed a little slip. Glemnitz was prowling about and saw the yellow sand before it was covered up. He didn't say anything at the time. Glemnitz never signaled his punches.

Every ferret was in the compound next morning, and they turned over all the gardens. In several of them they found more yellow sand than should have been there. Roger and Valenta watched them and saw Glemnitz and Rubberneck walk out, grim and thoughtful.

Roger sent for the committee.

"Glemnitz knows there's a tunnel," he announced. "Now there won't be any peace till he finds it. It's going to be a race, and we're on the dirty end of it. They'll be searching every hut, and that means they'll be concentrating on all the concrete floors. There's nothing more we can do about 'Tom's' trap. Maybe it'll hold, maybe it won't. Dispersing is going to be the toughest part. Glemnitz'll be watching the compound like a hawk."

"If he knows there's a tunnel, why worry so much trying to hide the sand?" someone asked. "We're not giving anything away they don't already know."

"You bloody stupid clot," Roger turned on him. "They'll identify the penguin traffic and trace it back to 123. Use your brains, for God's sake."

"Have you seen the guys in the goon-boxes?" said Harsh. "Every son of a bitch has got his field glasses up watching all the time."

Probably marking the numbers that go in and out of every block," Roger said. "I want an immediate restriction on traffic in and out of 123."

"You can't stop it all," someone said.

"I don't want to stop it all," Roger said cuttingly. "That'd be just as fishy. I just want the camp to know they're not to go to 123 during dispersal hours. There ought to be about enough penguin traffic to make it look natural. There's one thing we've got to keep in mind. Glemnitz doesn't know how many tunnels there are or how advanced they are, and he won't have the faintest idea everything is so organized. He mustn't get to thinking it's anything more than a little effort of a few blokes. If he does, he'll turn the whole bloody camp inside out. He mustn't find anything more."

"Well, what about the dispersal areas?" Floody asked. "It's going to be bloody risky putting it in the compound."

"We can put some in the gardens they found the first lot in," Roger said. "I know the Goons. They won't think of looking there again. For the rest, we'll just have to have bigger and better diversions."

Sage said he'd get the whole goddam camp out.

Glemnitz, Rubberneck, and a dozen ferrets searched block 106 the next morning and nearly took it to pieces in the process. It was one of the three blocks along the western wire. The others were 107 and 123.

About 11 A.M. three heavy wagons drove in and careered around the compound, mostly along the sides of the huts, trying to collapse any tunnels by weight. They wrecked half the camp gardens, but tunnels thirty feet deep were safe from that sort of thing.

Next morning they searched 107 for five hours. The Keen Type had had an attack of cold feet and wouldn't tell Axel Zillessen what huts were next on the list, but Blind Peter could have made a pretty good guess. There were no shifts down "Tom" that day. With the ferrets busy on 107, Minskewitz spent the morning carefully cementing the edges around "Tom's" trap. Very thin cement, so it would dry quickly.

We came off appell next morning and found the screen of tommygunners around 123, the ferrets inside. Roger, Floody, and Crump couldn't bear to watch and walked silently around the circuit all morning. At two o'clock the ferrets came out carrying a few nails and some wire—all they'd found in the way of illicit property.

They searched another block the next day, and that morning the stooges on the routine searches found ferrets hiding in the roofs of two blocks. They'd climbed up there while we were on appell and had their ears glued to the ceilings. There was no point staying up there after being spotted, and the embarrassed ferrets dropped out of the manholes and walked off.

Outside the south wire the first huts of the new compound were nearly finished. They were prefabricated and went up quickly. With all the ferret activity there had been no tunneling for three days. Time was getting short.

Roger went and talked it over with Massey, Goodrich, and Wings Day. The senior men, less experienced in tunneling, never tried to throw their rank about and interfere, but they shouldered responsibility where they could help on policy matters. They advised Bushell to take the calculated risk.

Roger sent a special security warning around the camp that night. In the morning Minskewitz chipped the new cement away from the edges of "Tom's" trap and Floody took a shift down. They dug ten feet during the day, but the penguins, working very cautiously, could get rid of only three-quarters of it.

Birkland was walking round the circuit that evening and saw a ferret moving in the wood outside the compound. As he watched, curious, he saw the ferret slip down behind a pile of branches on the edge of the wood. Birkland stood there for a quarter of an hour but the ferret didn't come out again. He went to Roger's room.

"I think we've got a peeping Tom," he said, and Roger collected Clark and Harsh and went to look. From an angle by the recreation ground they could just make out a vague shape behind the branches. They wandered around the circuit and spotted two more piles of branches on the edge of the woods. One of them was right at the spot where "Harry" was eventually intended to surface. For half an hour they watched quietly from a hut window and saw a ferret crawl away from behind one of them into the woods. He was carrying a case that looked like field glasses.

At two o'clock in the morning Pieber and half a dozen guards came into the compound. The people sleeping in 101, nearest the gate, were the first to find out. There were hoarse shouts of "Raus! Raus!" and the trampling of jackboots in the corridor. Doors were flung open, and everyone was hauled out of his bunk and paraded outside the rooms. Pieber counted them, and the guards searched the rooms.

Pieber did the same in every block, and to several hundred blinking, tousled men he was a very unpopular man. A dour and muttering Crump told him irritably that he didn't have a hope of finding anything, and Pieber made an unfortunate essay into English.

"You think I know damn nothing," he said indignantly. "Actually I know damn all."

He didn't find anything. "X" had not worked at night since

98

a snap 2 A.M. appell at Barth the previous year had found men working on a tunnel.

In the morning, Glemnitz found more freshly dispersed sand in the gardens by 119 and walked straight out of the compound. At eleven o'clock a long column of about a hundred fully armed troops marched in and went straight to the western side of the compound. They turned everyone out of 106, 107, and 123 and posted tommygunners to cut off that area of the camp. The Kommandant drove in in a staff car with Broili and a little civilian with a bony face. The civilian seemed to be on equal terms with the Kommandant and Broili was being very respectful.

A wagon drove up, and the soldiers unloaded picks and shovels. Glemnitz marked out a narrow strip between 123 and the barbed wire, and about forty men set to work digging. By three o'clock they had a long trench four feet deep. Rubberneck and ferrets Herman and Adolf took some thin steel rods about five feet long out of the wagon and began sinking them into the floor of the trench. They hammered them down almost to the hilt hoping to hit against the roof boards of a tunnel. Von Lindeiner and the civilian stood watching them. So, from a distance, did we. Floody was making insulting remarks under his breath. The ferrets would have needed probes five times as long to get anywhere near "Tom." Roger was standing with his arms folded, watching, not saying anything.

When the ferrets had sunk a probe as far as it would go and struck nothing but yielding sand, they pulled it up and tried a foot further on. Once they hit something about four feet down and there was a rustle of excitement among the Germans. Half a dozen shovelers got to work, slinging the sand over their shoulders out of the trench, the sweat pouring off them. As they reached the obstruction, the Kommandant leaned over the trench. It was a rock. Floody nearly had hysterics.

99

Just before appell, the Germans gave it up. The guards filled in the trenches and made a dignified withdrawal. It was another day lost on the tunneling, and that night Roger learned from a kitchen Goon that the bony-faced civilian was second in command of Breslau *Kriminalpolizei*. Sagan was in the Breslau Gestapo and Kriminalpolizei area.

"We're up in the big stuff now," Roger told the little gathering in his room. "They must be pretty sure we've got something big on to call the coppers. From now on anything can happen."

"Well, it's just a bloody race then," someone said. "We'll have to cut a few corners."

"That's exactly what we can't do. It's too late for that," Roger said. "Don't you see the implication? If they get any more evidence they'll go crazy and bring in a few hundred troops or something. You'll find yourselves sleeping out in the dirt while they tear up all the hut floors. We can't afford another slip."

Colonel Clark suggested that everything might be closed up for a few weeks till the fuss died down. He added quietly, "As far as the Americans are concerned, it's more important that the tunnel be saved rather than risk it now in the hope that we can use it before we move."

"Hell no," said Floody. "You've put in a hell of a lot of work. Don't miss out."

"We'll have our own tunnels going in the new compound soon," Clark said.

"Too late to close up now anyway," Roger, as usual, put his finger on the vital point. "The Goons'll go on hunting till they find something, and the longer they go on the more chance they'll have of finding 'Dick' and 'Harry' as well."

"Let 'em find 'Dick' or 'Harry,'" said someone, "and they'll probably stop looking."

"We're not giving anything away," Roger snapped. "We're

going on with the original plan. The only thing is we've got to do it without leaving any more traces or we'll have the damn Gestapo in. Glemnitz mustn't find any more sand."

And then Fanshawe achieved fame.

"Why not," he said, "put it down 'Dick'?"

It was so simple.

One of the northern blocks was searched in the morning and a shift was down "Tom" again. In the evening the penguins carted all the sand to the washroom of 122 where Mike Casey passed it below in jugs. Crump and two helpers dumped it at the far end of "Dick," taking out the box frames and trolley rails as they filled it in. They took the frames and rails across to use in "Tom."

They made twenty feet in two days without much trouble from the ferrets. Glemnitz seemed to be ignoring 123 and was concentrating on the other huts. They were searching a new hut every day, and the ferrets were diving under the blocks looking for sand. Willis-Richards saw Glemnitz himself disappear under 119 and took a cup of tea and a piece of black bread and laid them by the trap door in the base of the wall.

Leaning down, he called cordially into the darkness, "Oberfeldwebel, do come and have some tea. It must be very hot and dirty under there."

A wall trap door on the other side of the hut opened and Glemnitz crawled out and walked away, his hard-bitten face flushed a delicate pink.

That evening, the duty pilot reported that Rubberneck had come into the compound soon after appell and had not been checked out. The stooges crawled under the floors and up under the roofs of every block, but there was no sign of him. And then someone reported they'd seen him go into the kitchen block. The lageroffizier used a little office there, and a stooge found it was locked. We went around the block and closed all the blackout shutters (they couldn't be opened from the inside). At dusk, Rubberneck emerged glowering from the door and stalked out of the compound with a dirty look at the duty pilot sitting on the steps of 112 as he passed.

A tame ferret reported the next day that Rubberneck had gone straight to Glemnitz and asked him to throw all the duty pilots into the cooler. Glemnitz refused because, he said, a new team of duty pilots would only watch the gate from various windows and he'd rather have them out in the open where he could see them.

Glemnitz never did quite know what to do about the duty pilots, and as there was actually nothing effective he *could* do he tolerated them philosophically as an innocuous irritant. He even went so far as to be light-hearted about them. Coming in the gate one afternoon a couple of days after the Rubberneck incident, he walked straight up to the D.P. and grinned benevolently.

"Put me down," he said. "I'm in."

The D.P. courteously entered his name.

"Who else is in?" asked Glemnitz affably.

"No one," said the D.P., and Glemnitz's smile died.

"Show me that list," he said. The D.P. hedged for a while, but there was no way out and he handed it over. Glemnitz read it grimly and handed it back.

"You can mark me out again," he said; "I have some business," and he walked back out of the gate and over to the kommandantur where he found Rubberneck, the ferret Adolf, and another new ferret in their barrack blocks. Would they please explain, asked Glemnitz, why, if they were listed for duty till 5 P.M., they had been marked out of north compound at four o'clock.

Four days' cooler for Adolf, four for the new ferret, and two weeks' extra duty and confinement to barracks for Rubberneck. (Oh frabjous day in north compound!)

CHAPTER 10

PARTLY because he couldn't do anything about the duty pilots, Glemnitz sent in a team of men with axes and saws and they started felling all the pine trees that had been left around the huts. The trees were almost all down in about three days, and the compound looked naked without them.

From outside a watcher could obviously see any movements around the huts. Clark and Harsh spread the word that all factory and tunnel stooges were to watch from inside the huts if possible. If they had to be outside the huts they were to try to change position every day. Clark sent a standing patrol around the circuit watching the little piles of branches that the ferrets had stacked by the edge of the woods. The ferrets were still spying from them, and he broadcast a warning to all stooges that they were to consider themselves under observation all the time.

"Tom" was going ahead nicely, from eight to ten feet a day, and Floody estimated that in two days they would be under the edge of the wood. He and Roger met after appell to discuss a way of digging straight up without the sand falling in on them when Clark stuck his head through the window.

"Come and look at this," he said, and took them over to the western fence by 123. Men were swarming along the edge of the wood with axes and saws, and a tree was falling every five minutes. They were working like beavers, and in three days the edge of the wood had moved back about thirty yards. There the woodchoppers left it for the time being.

The tunnelers and other people in the know surveyed it with frustration and fury. "Tom" was just over two hundred feet—and still now a hundred feet short of the shelter of the trees. Pieber told Valenta they were going to build a new compound on the spot.

"Bloody funny coincidence," Roger commented acidly. The only thing to do was dig on. That was unanimous. Breaking out where they were in the open was a permissible risk for one or two, but not for a big show involving a hundred.

The dispersal problem was raising an ugly head again. Sand had been pouring out of "Tom," and "Dick" was full now to the base of the shaft. Roger refused to let them fill the shaft because he wanted it for an equipment store and underground workshop. He wouldn't let them touch "Harry" either. If "Tom" was found, he wanted "Harry" as it was.

The ferrets were rooting around the gardens and the dust of the compound every day, and it was too risky to dump more than small amounts of sand there. It was Roger's idea to store it.

"Everyone keeps Red Cross boxes full of junk under their bunks," he said. "Why not put sand in the boxes and stow them under beds all over the camp?"

"We won't get away with that for long," Conk said.

"Put 'em in a couple of the unlikely blocks they've just searched," Roger said. "They'll be safe there for a couple of weeks. That ought to give us time."

Floody backed him up, and Block X's went around collecting Red Cross boxes. That evening the penguins picked up sand from "Tom" in boxes and stowed them under bunks in 101 and 103 which had both just been searched.

They got away with it for five days, and "Tom" shot ahead

nearly fifty feet. The atmosphere in the compound was rather electric. Floody had scrapped the idea of a second halfway house as a refinement he couldn't afford, and they went hell for leather all the way. Then Glemnitz sprang a surprise search on 103 and a ferret found the boxes of sand. Glemnitz stormed out of the compound, and the wagons were in half an hour later trundling around each side of 103, wrecking the gardens again.

One of the ferrets (we learned this later) remembered seeing a couple of prisoners coming out of 123 with Red Cross boxes. He told Glemnitz, and the wagons rumbled over and wrecked the gardens around 123 too. Glemnitz wandered thoughtfully through the block, but apparently decided that the two searches it had already had were enough and wandered away again. Red Cross boxes, after all, were a common sight in the camp.

Von Lindeiner issued an order in the afternoon that no more of the boxes were to be taken into north compound. The rest of the day passed quietly and tensely, but in the evening Roger sent Minskewitz across to seal down "Tom's" trap with cement again. He had decided "Tom" had gone far enough. It was 260 feet long and still 40 feet short of the wood, but it was about 140 feet outside the wire and clear of the pools of light around the goon-boxes.

Roger—and most of the committee agreed—thought it was reasonably safe in the circumstances to break out at that point and crawl to the edge of the wood. It was too dangerous, and in any case there was no time, to try to go any further. Across the south fence the last hut of the new American compound was up, and the roofers and painters were at work. The barbed wire was strung around the fence, and the goon-boxes were in position. As far as the contacts could learn, the Americans would move within two weeks.

Floody thought it would take about four days to dig up to the surface. Fanshawe was worried about dispersing the sand, but said he'd fix it somehow, even if he had to eat the stuff.

"You don't have to worry for a couple of days anyway," Roger said. "I want to shut things down for three days and try to divert Glemnitz somewhere else. There's a faint chance we can get him to think the whole thing might conceivably be a hoax. There won't be any convincing him, but it might relieve the pressure a bit." He turned to Jerry Sage. "I want a big gang of stooges," he said, and explained his idea.

Sage went down to his block, 105, stamped into the corridors, and bellowed, "I want fifty volunteers right away." He knocked on all the doors and repeated it. After a while two or three men appeared.

"Where the hell is everyone else?" Sage demanded.

It appeared that everyone else was either peeling spuds, playing cards, reading, sleeping, or just not in a volunteering mood. Sage barged into the first room, and there were knocking and trampling sounds. A couple of bodies came hurtling through the window, followed by a couple more. A fifth man escaped through the door. Sage went from room to room, his progress marked by thuds, noises of running, and more bodies tumbling out of windows. "When I call for volunteers," he bawled, "move!"

When he'd infiltrated about fifty people into 103, he handed each man a Red Cross box, and at short intervals he sent them walking in twos and threes across the compound to 119. Rubberneck noticed them within ten minutes and stood off at a distance watching. He had a word with Adolf, and Adolf went out of the gate at a fast walk.

Glemnitz was striding into the compound in a quarter of an hour followed by a dozen guards and half a dozen ferrets. Poker-faced, he marched them straight to 119; they hustled everyone out of the block and searched it for four hours.

One of Valenta's contact men, a reliable-looking soul who placidly smoked a pipe, took Glemnitz aside that evening and told him he was being ribbed. He hinted vaguely that there was actually no tunnel, and that the whole thing was a camp stunt to pull the German legs and tie up their men for weeks searching fruitlessly for something that wasn't there. For the next two days a couple of contacts trailed Glemnitz and Rubberneck, and now and then flashed sardonic grins at them. One of them made the mistake of laughing openly at Rubberneck, and the sensitive Rubberneck lost his temper and had him sent to the cooler.

The bluff campaign partly fooled Glemnitz. Only partly. He was sure there was a tunnel—he took that for granted—but he thought the Red Cross boxes being taken out of 123 might have been a blind, like the Red Cross box trail out of 103. He had a night conference with the ferrets. Herman, flushed with victory, told his contact about it later.

Glemnitz thought there was probably a tunnel in one of the huts along the north fence. It was a less obvious spot than 123, and he had great respect for P.O.W. cunning. He ordered searches of 104 and 105, and then at the last moment he changed his mind and ordered one last search of 123. Floody was sending a shift down that morning to start digging up for the surface, but when we came off appell the cordon of guards was around 123.

Floody walked grimly over to 110, collected Bushell and George Harsh, and they took up position in a room of 122, standing silently by the window, watching, getting occasional glimpses of the ferrets as they moved about inside 123. For two hours they stood there, frozen-faced, and hardly exchanged a word. Bushell said briefly once, "If we get away with it this time, we'll make it. They're bound to concentrate on the other huts." There was something about the tension in that room like the heavy stillness before an electrical storm, and it spread to other people in the camp. Nearly everyone now had a fairly accurate idea of what was going on. Many months' work by many people, many hopes, were hanging on this, and for two hours, time seemed to be motionless, as though it, too, were waiting.

About eleven o'clock Herman was jabbing his probe around the concrete floor by the chimney listening for hollow sounds when the spike suddenly stuck in the concrete. Herman, startled, wiggled it and pulled it out with a jerk. A little chip of concrete came away with it. Herman was short-sighted, and it was only when he got down on his hands and knees that he made out the faint outline of the trap and let out a shout of wild triumph.

Glemnitz was beaming with a loathsome joy. Even Rubberneck looked happy. They stood in the doorway of 123 waiting for Von Lindeiner and Broili. Behind them the trap was still unopened—because they didn't know how to—but they had scraped the edges clear, and a ferret had gone for a sledge hammer. A group of us stood about twenty yards off eyeing them stonily and then gave it up and wandered away rather than give them any more satisfaction.

When Von Lindeiner came, they smashed the trap in, and Rubberneck went down the shaft and looked up the tunnel. He wouldn't go into the tunnel. Only one ferret ever had the nerve to do that, a grinning little gray-headed fellow with a flat face called Charlie Pfelz. Charlie was everyone's friend, including the prisoners'. He was always stationed at east camp.

Glemnitz sent for him, and Charlie came over and vanished into the tunnel with his torch. It took him half an hour to go right to the end and crawl back again, and Glemnitz's grin slipped a little when Pfelz bobbed up again, still grinning, and told them how close the tunnel had been to success.

Bushell was in a vile mood all day but snapped out of it

toward evening, and he, Wings Day, and the committee had a three-hour session to plan the next move. It was a dispirited gathering. Roger said he wanted to keep the other two tunnels sealed until all the fuss had died down.

"No risks at all from now on," he said. "I know if we don't get on to them soon it'll be winter. That's O.K. by me. I'd rather keep them safe through winter than risk losing them."

Depression comes easily in prison camp. Some of the older prisoners had been working on tunnels for three and four years, and they were still stuck behind the wire, becoming obsessed, a few of them, with the hopelessness of it all.

"It makes you wonder," Tovrea said to Crump, "whether we'll ever break one of these things out." Tovrea would be one of the experienced tunnelers going to the new American compound.

"Don't let it bother you," Crump said. " 'Tom's' only the ninety-eighth one they've found." Crump had been keeping score since 1941.

There was a mass meeting in the camp theater the next afternoon.

"As most of you know," Bushell announced, "we started this project with three separate schemes, knowing we might lose one or two—and prepared to lose them—to make pretty sure of succeeding with at least one. We've still got two up our sleeves, and the Germans probably think we've shot our bolt. We're going to lay off the other two for a while to make sure they think this. Then we're going ahead. I don't think they can stop us this time."

Wings Day hit the best note. "The Kommandant," he said, "wants to retire as a general. It's our job to see he's retired— but not as a general."

After the first flush of joy, the ferrets didn't quite know what to do about "Tom." Usually they flushed out tunnels with a hose, but "Tom" was too long and too strongly shored.

Finally Von Lindeiner rang the Army engineers, and they sent along a tiny little man with a happy but cretinous face. He pottered about "Tom" for two days and laid gelignite in it. Everyone cleared out of 123 and waited expectantly while the little man pushed the exploder. He wasn't a very good engineer. The charge roared out of the tunnel up the shaft. A great mass of 123 roof flew into the air, the concrete floor disintegrated, and the chimney ponderously tilted on one side. The little man went away in disgrace, and workmen came in to repair 123. Even in death, "Tom" had done his part for the war effort.

Glemnitz made the mistake of talking too loudly in the compound to a ferret, and one of Valenta's German-speakers overheard him saying that he didn't think there would be any more trouble in north compound because the prisoners must have used every scrap of available wood to shore the tunnel. If they ever tried another big one in the future, he would notice bedboards gradually disappearing.

Roger heard about it within an hour and sent Willy Williams around every room organizing the biggest bedboard levy yet. Within two days he had collected nearly two thousand and stored them down "Dick" and behind false walls. Roger reasoned that if Glemnitz considered he'd broken the major effort he wouldn't be watching bedboards for a while. When he *did* start checking them again, he'd be reassured by the fact that none were disappearing. Meanwhile the tunnels could be shored from the hidden stocks.

Roger set an example by giving up every one of his bedboards and persuaded Bob Tuck, who shared his little room with him, to do the same. He got Travis to make them both a string bed—a net of plaited string slung between the side frames of the double-decker bunk. For once Travis' handiwork failed. Roger climbed into his top bunk the first night, the string gave way, and he crashed through onto Tuck below. The weight smashed Tuck's strings, and they both went through onto the floor. It took them all the next day to mend them both so they would hold.

A week later the Americans were marched out to their new compound, laying bets they would break a tunnel out before us. Jerry Sage and Junior Clark, and a lot of other good men went with them. Though he came from Atlanta, George Harsh stayed with us because he'd been in the R.A.F. Apart from the fact that he was such a fanatical watchdog, it was good to have him around because he was such a character, pulling at his great gray mustache, glaring furiously at the Germans, and mumbling ingenious American curses.

He used to sit on the edge of his bunk, massaging his mustache, dreaming about food, and after a few minutes he'd explode, "Goddam, I'm a hungry sonofabitch. Why did I ever pull that rip cord!"

"How were you shot down, George?" a new boy asked him, and George eyed him gloomily.

"I was sitting on a barn door over Berlin," he said, "and some bastard shot the hinges off."

Glemnitz also went with the Americans. Von Lindeiner had detailed him to look after security in their new compound, and we hardly ever saw him in north camp after that. We grieved not.

Actually it didn't help. Rubberneck was as smart and more unbending. He also wanted to be a feldwebel instead of an unteroffizier and started riding the ferrets hard. He threatened the Keen Type with the *Ostfront* for loafing in Zillessen's room, and the Keen Type wasn't much good with information after that. Instead of slackening off after the break, the ferrets were more of a nuisance than ever.

Smarting after his four days in the cooler, Adolf found a

111

new conscientiousness and began haunting the forgery factory wherever they went. He was a somber little man with a thin face, a blue chin (what there was of it), and a black toothbrush mustache that gave him a faint, caricature resemblance to that other, more notorious, Adolf—hence the nickname. Roger had toyed with the idea of opening the tunnels again after a few weeks, but with the ferrets so keen and one tunnel already gone, he decided to hold off indefinitely. All the other factories worked steadily on.

◼ CHAPTER 11 ◼

WITH a nice feeling for gentle and ironic humor, Tim Walenn gave his factory the code name of "Dean and Dawson," after the British travel agency. Getting around the Third Reich was largely a matter of having a fistful of permits and passes, and one couldn't go far, particularly by train, without having to submit them to the cold eyes of the Gestapo or *Sicherheitspolizei*.

Walenn had that methodical and precise nature which, if you didn't know it before, is essential for good forging. He had a smooth, unruffled face—and hid most of it behind a spreading, Jerry Colonna–type mustache which revolted every artistic feeling in the compound. Artists liked to work with him because he was so unfailingly courteous.

His first efforts in east compound were faking gate passes and simple travel permits in the form of typewritten sheets. A tame Goon had produced the originals from the kommandantur and Walenn hand-lettered copies with such incredible care and accuracy it was impossible to tell them from the originals without looking very closely. Gordon Brettell was one of his first assistants, and no one ever figured out how Brettell came to be a good draftsman. He was a dark, tough customer with a thickset jaw and had been a racing driver before the war.

He had tested one of the passes just before the move into north camp. Wangling his way into a working party, he had drifted into one of the half-built huts and hidden in some paillasses. Pieber searched the camp for him, even fussed about the spot where he was hiding, but didn't find him, and at night Gordon sneaked away from the empty compound. He was only picked up through bad luck. At Chemnitz he asked for a ticket to Nuremberg, not knowing that Nuremberg was verboten territory because of a recent bombing. And the Gestapo collared him. He had one of the passes saying he was a French worker. The Gestapo accepted it, but Gordon's French wasn't good enough to confirm it and he did three weeks' solitary before coming back to us.

The Gestapo never woke up to the fact that the pass was hand-made. Walenn had gone to such pains over it that he'd even hand-lettered strikeovers, as though some of the letters had been mistakes and been typed over with the right one. Others he did as though the shift key hadn't completely returned, showing part of the capital of one letter slightly above the line and the top of the lower-case letter slightly below.

The factory grew, and more artists joined the gang. One of them was a curly-haired little man who smoked a pipe nearly as big as his head—Dicky Milne, D.F.C. and Bar, who'd been fighter wing commander at Biggin Hill before he was shot down. Henri Picard, the Belgian youngster with the Croix de guerre, was the man who had got the German rifle measurements with home-made calipers for the delousing break. The most distinctive, in appearance anyway, was Alex Cassie. No one could look like Cassie without working hard at it. He had a great thatch of long ginger hair that fell over his eyes like a Skye terrier and little tufts of ginger beard sticking out of isolated spots around his jaw.

One of the forgers was an American, Donald Stine, a very quiet, slim, dark lad with a crew cut. He was a beautiful artist who also made many drawings and paintings of camp scenes and personalities. Ley Kenyon, tall, fair Englishman, was another magnificent artist who became a forger.

They started working in north camp in an empty room in 120 until Adolf, suspicious of the stooges outside the block, started hanging around and walking up and down looking in the windows. One of Dean and Dawson's occupational hazards was that they had to sit by a window so they could get enough light for the finicking work. Adolf nearly caught them a couple of times, but they were just able to cover the work before he reached the window.

Adolf was getting too dangerous, so Walenn moved the factory to a room in the kitchen block next to the room where the camp orchestra practiced. They worked there with peculiar noises in their ears. It wasn't a very good orchestra. They took the duty stooge into the room with them. He sat on a high stool looking over their heads out of the window at a little chair standing beside 122. If a ferret approached, a man sun-baking by 122 moved the chair; the stooge muttered a sharp "pack up," and the work was covered in a moment. The only time Walenn ever lost his gentle courtesy was if he saw the stooge take his eyes for a second off the chair by 112. When the orchestra finished practice, the forgers packed up too, and the stooge walked out with the musicians, carrying a violin case. He took it over to 104 when Pengelly opened it, took out the forged papers, and stowed them behind a secret wall panel.

Bit by bit, mostly through Valenta's tame Goons, Walenn built up his stock of originals. He had an *Ausweis* for being on Reich property, gate passes, two types of *Urlaubschein* for crossing frontiers, about three different forms of travel permit, and a French worker's identity card.

Once when Pieber was away on leave, a new hauptmann came in as lageroffizier. He didn't understand P.O.W. morality very well and was induced to take his tunic off and sit down

115

in a room for a brew one day. It wasn't till he got outside the compound that he found his personal identity card missing. He was in an awkward spot. He couldn't very well report that the prisoners had stolen it because the Kommandant would have given him, figuratively speaking, a disciplinary kick in the seat of his well-cut breeches.

He chose the lesser of two evils, and in some embarrassment and as politely as he could in the circumstances, he asked the squadron leader who had been his host if he would be good enough to arrange the return of his card. He couldn't very well be rude about it because the squadron leader would have blandly denied all knowledge of it, and there would be nothing the hauptmann could do about it without getting in hot water himself. The squadron leader said he would do what he could, and two days later handed the card back. Walenn didn't want it any more. He had a very accurate copy of it.

The *Soldbuch* of the ordinary soldaten was easy to get hold of. The soldbuch was a combination pay-book and identification card, and the very young obergefreiter who had signed the receipt for the chocolate used to hand his soldbuch to his contact when he came into the compound.

"But you *must* let me have it back when I go out," he pleaded.

One of the complications about the soldbuchs and a couple of the other passes was that they carried a photograph of the bearer. The meticulous Tim told Roger that they must get genuine photographs of the people who were to use them.

"We'll have to get a camera, that's all," said Roger, and passed it on to Valenta. Valenta told the contact, and the contact put it up to the young obergefreiter who nearly passed out with fright on the spot and pleaded to be excused this time. Valenta, a little conscience-stricken, went to Roger.

"We can't ask the poor little Goon to do this," he said. "He's liable to be shot if he does."

116

"Tell him," said Roger grimly, "he's liable to be shot if he doesn't."

The little Goon brought in a tiny camera. Later he brought some developing and printing materials and Chaz Hall, the compound meteorological expert, set up a little studio in his room. Tommy Guest supplied imitation German uniforms and civilian clothes for the sitters.

Forging was a slow business. Some of the documents were covered with line upon line of close print; others had a background of fine, whorled lines almost like a banknote, and it all had to be reproduced with fanatical care and accuracy with pen and ink or brush and paint. Tim scrapped any forgery that he didn't consider to be nearly perfect. One careless line would wreck a little document that a forger might have been working on for days.

One of the urlaubscheins used to take a skilled forger, working five hours a day every day, a whole month to make. Altogether, Dean and Dawson eventually turned out about four hundred documents. It was a little hard to believe. They had fifty forgers and stooges on the job three to five hours a day for a year. All the phony documents were endorsed by official Nazi stamps, bearing the eagle and swastika and the titles and signatures of various police branches. Tim used to paint the designs on rubber boot heels, and Al Hake, the compass maker, carved them out with bits of razor blade.

As well as passes, Tim used to fake letters for escapees to carry. If a man got out, say, as a French worker, Tim would give him a little bundle of letters in French bearing loving bits of gossip from his "wife" back in Cherbourg or somewhere. They were rather convincing. One of his favorite stunts was the letter of authorization. These, hand-"typed" on a business firm's letterhead, authorized their employee, Herr So-and-So, to travel to Stettin or Danzig or some such strategic place. Stettin or Danzig were both favorite spots because neutral

Swedish boats docked there, and if you could stow away on one of them your troubles were nearly over.

From tame Germans Tim got a couple of actual letterhead sheets to copy. If he wanted something different, he designed it himself. He produced an imposing embossed letterhead purporting to come from a near-by Focke Wulf factory. Gordon Brettell did the embossing by pressing a toothbrush handle on the back of the hand-painted "print" against a pad of paper. It looked quite genuine.

One of the documents was a travel permit in the form of a typed foolscap sheet. They did a few laboriously by hand, but each one took ages. Valenta got Thompson working on the little German juggler in the kitchen, and he agreed to help. Tim gave him one of the sheets, and the little German took it out of the compound in his boot. He sent it to Hamburg, where his wife had a typewriter, and she typed stencils of the form and sent them back to her husband, who delivered them to Tim.

Travis made a tiny printing press with a roller made of a carved piece of wood covered with a strip of blanket. Brettell and Cassie made printing ink from fat-lamp black mixed with neat's-foot oil, and they ran off dozens of the forms.

Getting the right quality, thickness, and color of paper for some of the passes was a constant problem. They used to tint paper with water-color backgrounds, and for some of the better-quality paper Tim ripped out the flyleaves of a few Bibles. The soldbuchs and a couple of the other identification ausweises had stiff linen-faced covers. The forgers glued tracing linen over thin cardboard, tinted it the right color, and painted the lettering over it. You couldn't pick them from the originals.

On some of the originals, the eagle and swastika stamps were embossed, particularly over the identification photographs. Jens Muller cut out a mold of the stamp in soap and cast a replica in lead from melted silver paper. Travis made a stamping machine with a centering device, and that difficulty was overcome.

Rubberneck began to hang around the kitchen block so Tim put muslin over the windows of the forgery room, ostensibly to keep out flies. They went on working there till Adolf whipped around the corner one day and, before they could cover the work, he was peering in at them through the muslin. Apparently he couldn't see very clearly because he wandered away again, but Tim thought it was getting too hot and moved the factory across to the church room in 122. The padre raised eyebrows and voice in protest, but Roger claimed it was all God's work in a good cause, and as there didn't seem to be any specific ruling on this point in church dogma, the forgers kept going to church every day to indulge in a little Christian counterfeiting.

It wasn't long before the wretched Adolf was hanging around again. He must have noticed the stooges because he kept wandering around 122 looking in the windows, and a couple of times every day the forgers had to cover up in a hurry and sit around innocently while Cassie gave an imitation of a lecture in psychology until Adolf went away. Tim thought it was getting too hot again and moved across to the library in 110. Travis, who'd had his engineers there, moved down to the bottom of "Dick's" shaft. There wasn't much room there, but it was quiet and safe for such noisy pursuits as tin-bashing and filing.

The other departments didn't seem to be troubled so much by security. Des Plunkett, a nuggetty little man with a fierce mustache, had a staff of map tracers dispersed in various rooms throughout the camp. Through the contacts he had collected all sorts of information about the surrounding country, and his local maps showed all the quietest paths away from the area. His general maps illustrated the escape routes down through

Czechoslovakia to Switzerland and France and through the Baltic to Sweden.

Tracing was too slow to do all the maps he wanted, so he got a contact to scrounge some invalid jellies through a German in the hospital block in the kommandantur. He cut them up, soaked them in hot water, and wrung them through a handkerchief, tasting the fruity solution that streamed out until it was no longer sweet. Having extracted the sugar from the mess in the handkerchief, he had the straight gelatine, which he melted, poured into flat trays made from old food tins, and there, when it set, was his mimeograph.

He drew his maps for reproduction with ink made from the crushed lead of indelible pencils (strictly verboten, but the tame Germans supplied them). After pressing the maps on the mimeograph, he ran off hundreds of copies. Tim Walenn used his mimeograph sometimes for his forged papers.

Tommy Guest also dispersed his tailors in rooms throughout the compound. Cloth was his main trouble. Mostly he took old uniforms to pieces and recut them along civilian lines. He got bits of cloth smuggled in from outside and sometimes used the heavy linings from old greatcoats. The only jackets and trousers ever issued in the compound came through the Red Cross, and they were either rough old Polish uniforms or the unlovely stuff they issued (and still do) to R.A.F. "other ranks"—made of heavy serge. Guest had a couple of people shaving the serge nap off with razor blades to fine the cloth down, and then he dyed it—with beet-root juice, or a boot-polish solution, and once or twice in dyes made from the covers of books soaked in water.

He made himself a stock of paper patterns of various sizes by cutting them out of sheets of German newspaper. It greatly simplified the business of reshaping clothes. If he didn't have time or cloth to make you a suit himself, he would—if he was in a very good mood—lend you his paper patterns. He usually did the cutting for the difficult suits himself.

One man who wanted to try to hack his way through the wire at night had the idea of traveling outside as a German railwayman and asked Guest if he could make him a porter's uniform. Guest ran a ruler over him.

"Come back at one o'clock for a fitting," he said.

The man reported back at one, had his fitting and collected the finished uniform, complete with cap, at 5 P.M. He would probably have got a long way in it if the searchlights hadn't picked him up on the wire as he was trying to cut through.

Al Hake had his compass production line in a room in 103. He made the compass casings out of broken gramophone records, heating the bits till they were soft as dough and then pressing them in a mold. Artists painted the points of the compass accurately on little circles of paper, and they fitted neatly into the base of the casings. He sank a gramophone needle in the center of the base for the needle pivot. The direction needle itself was a bit of sewing needle which he rubbed against a magnet.

With great delicacy he soldered a tiny pivot socket to the center of the magnetized needles. (The solder came from the melted joints of bully-beef tins, and he dug resin for the soldering out of the pine trees, and after the trees were cut down, out of the resinous wood of the huts.) Valenta even got him some luminous paint for the needles so they could be used at night without the danger of striking matches.

Glass for the compass tops he took from bits of broken window. If there weren't any broken windows handy, he broke one himself and then cut the pieces into circular disks under water so the glass wouldn't crack or chip. He made a little blow lamp out of a fat lamp and some thin tubing rolled out of old food tins. Through the tube he blew a gentle jet of air against the

121

flame, playing it around the rim of the compass case, and when it was melting soft he pressed in the glass and there it set, tight and waterproof.

He was finishing one a day, and they were so beautifully done you'd have thought they were bought in a shop. I think the neatest thing about them came from the inscription he had carved in the bottom of the mold for the casings. When you turned the finished compass over, there on the base was professionally engraved, "Made in Stalag Luft III."

As they turned their stuff out—maps, compasses, clothes, and forged papers—Roger dispersed them behind the false walls and down in "Dick." It occurred to him that though the Germans searched the huts with Teutonic, but not particularly imaginative, thoroughness, they never thought to search the huts of the outside earth latrines, so he hid a lot of the bulky clothing up in the roof of one of them.

They kept two or three of Tommy Guest's creations, including a German uniform, behind a wall panel in the room which Chaz Hall and Cornish used as a passport photograph studio. It was safer to have them right on the spot. Hall produced a striking shot of "Unteroffizier" Roger Bushell of the Luftwaffe, looking out of the picture with that sinister drooping eye. Later Roger had one taken as a businessman, and that was the one he eventually used on his passes.

Von Lindeiner flatly refused to allow any communication with the Americans in their new compound, so Massey put a semaphore signaler in an end room of 120, standing well back from the window so that he was outside the field of view from the goon-boxes. The Americans spotted him in about two minutes, and put their own signaler in a window. They chattered away every day for half an hour exchanging compound gossip. He used to send the B.B.C. news over for a while, but the Yanks didn't take long to get their own radio going.

Ellan, our radio man, was collecting more stuff through the

contacts with an eye to making a transmitter if the need should ever arise. One had to be a shade prudent about that. If Rubberneck came across a transmitter or the signs thereof, the other seven in his room could look forward with confidence to a bullet in the back of the head, preceded by a little gathering in a sound-proof Gestapo room to discover what had been going on.

Johnny Travis made them a bolt hole by putting a tall locker against the thin wooden wall in Ellan's room and another locker in the same spot in the next room. He put detachable panels in the backs of the lockers and another detachable panel in the wall so that stuff could be passed through in emergency.

The summer lingered on, and the weather stayed good for escaping. That was probably why Rubberneck kept the ferrets up to the mark. He got the idea (only too justified) that a foolish little ferret known as "Young 'un" had been wooed from the path of duty. I don't think Rubberneck ever proved that "Young 'un" brought in contraband, but he had him sent to the Russian Front, and even the Keen Type smartened up after that. The Ostfront was the bogieman.

The woodchoppers came back and cleared the rest of the wood outside the west fence, and a new compound started to go up there. That ruled out "Dick" for good, except as workshop and store, leaving only "Harry." Roger kept it sealed down. He wouldn't risk his last tunnel while Rubberneck was so active. Autumn was suddenly on us, and Roger faced the fact that there was no chance of breaking out "Harry" safely before winter and that they would have to wait till the spring.

"Don't get the idea we're sitting back till then," he said. "We want 'Harry' finished by the time the weather's right again."

He was moody and irritable in the next few weeks, and it was worse when a man came in on a new purge whom Roger had known before he was shot down. The new man had been an engine mechanic on his squadron. Now he was a squadron leader. Bushell never did take kindly to rusticating in a backwater while the rest of the world went ahead.

He found some relief for his frustration in the camp theater, taking parts in nearly every play—and playing them brilliantly. One couldn't have a personality and ego as powerful as Bushell's without being a good actor. Sometimes he was difficult to live with, but he was mostly forgiven that except by a few who experienced his wrath. Bushell's way with the lazy or the foolish was blunt and lacerating, and yet he had enormous charm. He was two people, really—one ruthless and autocratic, and the other the generous playboy.

"He's got killer's eyes," Travis said, "but he's a helluva nice chap." They weren't killer's eyes. That was only the effect of the ski gash. They were brooding. There had been a hint of it when he was first shot down.

He wrote to his old adjutant in England, "That devil, the human mind, makes one go crazy at times. The hardest part here is being out of things."

And to his mother in South Africa, "The most tiring job is doing nothing."

At the time he was learning Czech, Danish, and Russian, as well as acting, teaching German, and playing rugger. Massey and Wings Day encouraged his activities because it helped to lull German suspicions. They never ceased regarding Roger as a marked man, though. Valenta had had his contacts very delicately spreading the word that Roger was a reformed character, had given up tunneling as hopeless, and was content to wait for the end of the war. Rubberneck came to believe it almost completely, and Roger certainly gave the impression of a man living a blameless life. He recovered his spirits after a while and was the playboy again. That was about the time he and Canton raided Travis' room and emptied their sugar bowl.

They filled it with sand and put a thin layer of sugar over the top. There was a roar of dismay from Travis' room at brew time that night. They suspected Bushell immediately and tackled him. Roger turned on his best declamatory barrister's manner.

"The bloody Goons," he roared in outraged sympathy. "They must have pinched it during appell. I'll tear a strip off Pieber for that."

"I'm not so sure it was the Goons," said Travis, suspiciously.

"Must have been," said Roger indignantly. "Who else but the Goons would think of putting sand in its place?"

"You're a hell of a barrister," Travis said, eyeing him flintily. "No one's mentioned sand yet," and Roger bowed his head in shame.

"It was for raisin hooch," he said disarmingly. "I was going to invite you."

ROGER still found time for escape work. With "Harry" still sealed down, he organized "wire jobs." Anyone who wanted to try it applied to the committee and had to convince Roger he had a sound travel plan and had made up a good enough story about himself to pass casual police checks on trains and roads. The committee gave him a little money, ausweis, compass, maps, clothes if he needed them, and a pair of wire-clippers.

The man waited for a stormy night or an air raid when the boundary lights were turned off, then crawled out of his hut, prayed he wouldn't strike the hundfuehrer, made for the boundary wire, and tried to cut his way through.

A couple of dozen people tried it before winter set in, but there were too many guards and searchlights. One or two got clear, but only for a night or two. The usual form for wire jobs was out of the hut, up to the wire, and down to the guard-room with hands up and pistol in the back, then into the cooler.

Jacky Rae, a New Zealand Spitfire pilot, decided that the reason most wire jobs failed was because on a dark night the guards were always on their toes around the wire by the huts. He thought there was a better chance of making it if one could get to the wire on the far side of the appell ground where the guards wouldn't be expecting anyone.

The area was swept by searchlights, but there was a slight dip in the ground across the appell ground where the Germans had been thinking of making a road. Rae and a Canadian called Probert got out of their hut one night and crawled on their bellies along the dip, the searchlights flashing just above them. They were so careful it took them seven hours to crawl 250 yards, but they finally made the wire and then only had about two strands to go when a guard picked them up.

The Kommandant was so angry at their audacity he gave them a month each in the cooler. Probert had claustrophobia and couldn't stand it. He got out of his cell to go to the toilet one day and made a dash for the cooler door, but a bullet got him in the shoulder before he made it. It was months before he recovered enough to return to the compound.

Travis made the wire-clippers for these jobs out of tie bars which he ripped off the huts. He riveted them together like scissors and filed cutting notches in them. It was very soft steel, so he hardened the metal himself. In a home-made forge he heated the clippers till they were red hot, poured a few grains of sugar on the metal around the cutting notches, and heated it up again so the carbon in the sugar was baked into the metal. Then he plunged it into cold water, and the steel came out hard enough to cut wire. It was the same technique he used for making his cold chisels.

As the weather got colder, even the most incurable optimists faced the fact that it was too late now for any Second Front in 1943, and people, with varying degrees of patience, resigned themselves to another year of prison. Some who had been behind the wire for three and four years were developing little eccentricities—"wire-happy" was the polite name for it. One man became convinced he was General Smuts and insisted the people in his room call him "Sir." The German doctors took him away for treatment.

There was another one who cut his wrists on two occasions

with a razor blade to finish it all, but there is no privacy in prison camp and he was seen bleeding and it was stopped. The Germans took him away to sick quarters, but he got out of his bed one night and climbed up on the roof where a guard spotted him, challenged him and, as he ran across the roof, caught him with a burst of machine-gun fire.

Another one was to be taken away by train for treatment, but at Sagan Station, as the train came in, he wrenched himself away from the guards and jumped onto the tracks right in front of the engine which had no time to pull up. Over in the east compound, a man could suddenly stand it no longer, jumped over the warning wire, and ran for the fence. He was tearing his hands to pieces on the barbed wire when the machine guns put him out of his anguish forever.

It was about this time in east compound that Eric Williams and two of his friends escaped through the most brilliant and ingenious tunnel yet devised.

They made a vaulting horse with covered-in sides and parked it every day by the warning wire in exactly the same place. While a team of men had vaulting drill over it, Williams and his colleagues, who had been carried to the spot inside the horse, were tunneling underneath. Being able to start by the warning wire instead of under a hut gave them a couple of hundred feet less to dig to freedom. After weeks and weeks of dogged and courageous work, they broke through outside the wire one night and all three of them got back to England by way of Sweden. That effort (described in Eric Williams' brilliant book, The Wooden Horse) is already acknowledged as one of the classic escapes of history.

By the middle of 1943, Germany was finding it hard to cope with the millions of prisoners and slave laborers within her borders. Himmler was pressing Hitler to give him full control of all prisoners of war. In October, Keitel, Chief of the High

Command, issued the "Igel Order," which laid it down that all prisoners in transit henceforth should be chained.

About two months after Italy fell, Von Lindeiner sent some workmen in to fix a loud-speaker in the compound so we could be dosed with German radio. They were stringing up several hundred yards of wire to connect it to the master set in the vorlager and while they worked dumped a couple of reels of wire behind them. Roger got the news in the theater where he was rehearsing and sent Canton off with a gang of diversionists to collar some of the wire. They hid behind a near-by hut, planning a disturbance to divert the workmen while one of them sneaked up and grabbed some of the wire.

At that moment the compound gate opened and Red Noble wandered in, carrying his blanket over his shoulder, just out after his latest spell in the cooler for trying to sneak into a hut that was being searched. He wandered up the dusty path, and a quiet gleam came into his eyes as he spotted the wire about fifty yards in front. Changing course just a fraction, he scooped up a coil of wire, tucked it under his blanket, and walked on. The workmen, ten feet away, didn't notice a thing. A minute later, two of Canton's men started fighting, and the workmen downed tools to watch. The fight didn't last long. Neither did the other reel of wire.

That night it was all smuggled down "Dick." There was over eight hundred feet in the two coils—more than enough to light "Harry" when work started again.

The committee's joy was tempered with doubt and worry.

"There'll be a hell of a row," Floody said. "Rubberneck will know bloody well why we've taken it, and we might be starting a new bunch of searches just when we're getting them to relax a bit."

Roger, strangely enough, wanted to take a chance.

"I don't think he'll necessarily assume we've got anything

129

going underground," he said. "He knows we'd pinch the stuff on principle anyway, and in any case I think 'Harry' is pretty safely stuck down. It's worth taking a risk. It'll be pretty handy if we get away with it."

As usual, Roger got his way and, as it happened, the foolish workmen were too frightened to report that they'd lost the wire. Later they were sorry they didn't.

A German general came in to look us over that week, a great plump character with red slashes down the side of the riding breeches, a large bottom, and white lapels on his greatcoat. He drove into the compound with Von Lindeiner in a big shiny Mercedes and about a hundred scruffy prisoners clustered around to gape at that strange sight from another world, a motorcar. Von Lindeiner, knowing his prisoners, told them to keep their distance, but that jolly and benevolent extrovert, the general, wouldn't hear of it.

"Ach no," he said. "Let them see how Germany can make motorcars. My chauffeur will keep watch." And away they marched on their inspection, Von Lindeiner still looking doubtful.

The chauffeur didn't know much about prisoners either. He did his best, but as soon as he hauled a man out of one door there were half a dozen more scrambling in the other doors, looking in the tool kit and crawling underneath. A couple of the German speakers started firing questions at him about the car, offered him cigarettes, and others milled around him, smiling, innocent and admiring.

They drifted away after a while, with admiring comments, the general's gloves, his torch and map case, all the portable tools in the tool kit, and a German Army handbook they found in the glove box.

I do not know what happened later between the general and the chauffeur, but I expect it was a fairly testy and one-sided conversation. The chauffeur probably caught the next train to the Ostfront, but there were no reprisals in the compound. The general, it seems, was too embarrassed to make any official fuss because the book that vanished from his glove box was a secret military handbook—and generals are not supposed to lose such things, particularly to enemy officers.

Von Lindeiner came into the compound the next day and had a private talk to Wings Day (Massey was in hospital having his foot treated).

"We know you have all these things," Von Lindeiner said. "Let us not argue about that. If you will return to us the book, we will say nothing about the other things and no further action will be taken. But we must have the book. You understand the situation."

"I am most surprised to hear about this," Wings said politely (and not very truthfully). "I will have some inquiries made, and if one of my officers has forgotten his principles in his zeal, I will see what can be done."

Von Lindeiner withdrew, a little prickly.

There wasn't any point in hanging on to the book. The German speakers had been through it thoroughly, and it was only one of those fatuous military tomes that lay it down oracularly and pompously that if you have your right arm shot off above the elbow you may salute with your left arm.

It was Roger's idea to have a special boot-heel stamp cut for the book and, after this had been applied, Wings handed it back to Von Lindeiner. I'd love to have seen the general's face when he got it back. The boot-heel stamp was right across the cover—"Passed by the British Board of Censors."

Snow fell heavily, early in December. It was too cold to be outside, so some of the stooges looking after the factories stood out like sore thumbs as they loitered around the same spots in the snow day after day, and it didn't take long for Adolf's watery eyes to fasten on Dean and Dawson's stooges at each end of 110.

"Adolf, it would be bloody Adolf," muttered Tim, ruffled for once. He was getting an obsession about Adolf, who was tramping around the block every day, a quaint little figure with earmuffs and a blue nose, looking impassively through the windows. His expression never changed. Neither did his tactics. As soon as he saw the stooges, he was circumnavigating the block. The forgers were getting warnings four or five times an afternoon, and there was a mad rush to cover the work and look innocent while one of them stood up and held forth as though he were giving a lecture. It didn't matter what he said. Adolf didn't speak English.

He took to walking into a couple of the rooms, and that meant they had to shoot the stuff into the wall panel, damaging some of the work before the ink was dry and wasting time while they sorted it out again afterward.

So far, the stolid Adolf had been immune to any approaches from the contacts, but Tim got a contact to beguile him into a Christmas raisin wine party. They poured a couple of potent slugs into him, and he began to thaw and talk, his nose turning from blue to a luminous pink.

"You have some tricks going on in Barrack 110," he said solemnly after a while. "I know. I have seen your postens outside. They are always there, and they give warnings when I approach."

That gave Walenn an idea.

"Take the stooges away," he said. "Adolf will think work has stopped there and won't worry us."

"Oh . . . risky," said Cassie doubtfully.

"No more than it is now," Tim said. "We're giving ourselves away and losing a hell of a lot of time."

132

We decided to give it a try and told the stooges to take a holiday. Adolf's attentions stopped immediately. It was miraculous. The forgers were happy; the stooges were happy (stooging in the snow in leaky boots and on poor food is not funny), and presumably Adolf was happy too.

For a week they went forging ahead with no interruptions from Adolf or anyone else. They got twice as much work done, and it was easier on the nerves. Then one afternoon Henri Picard looked up and saw Adolf's bony face peering through the window.

"Oh hell," he said. "Look!"

There was a paralyzed silence, and then Tim quietly said, "Go on working as though nothing is happening."

Adolf continued to peer through the window, but the cold outside and the warmth of the room inside had condensed moisture on the window and it was running down the glass, blurring it so that Adolf couldn't quite make out what was going on. He must have thought they were writing letters or studying, because after a minute his face vanished. There was a mad rush in the room, and in a few seconds all the documents were shoved behind the wall panel and the forgers had dispersed, but Adolf never came in to investigate.

"The stooges have got to go back, obviously," Tim said.

"Correction," said Cassie. "The stooges have got to go back —but *not* obviously."

The problem was how to hide them so they could cover all approaches to the library room and still be able to give the pack-up in time. Hiding stooges from the ferrets also usually meant, to a certain extent, hiding the ferrets from the stooges. The ferrets, if they suspected a hut, had a habit of approaching it under cover of another, then darting around the corner and up and down, peering through the windows.

We worried over this one for a couple of days because Dean

133

and Dawson were so exposed there couldn't be any slips. Eventually we worked out a real cloak-and-dagger system which sounded very complicated.

The library room was midway along the western side of 110 with a door to the corridor and two windows facing west to be

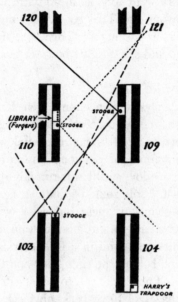

HOW THE STOOGES PROTECTED
THE FORGERS

covered. One stooge stood by a window in an end room of 103, facing the northern end of 110, so he could see down both sides and around the near end. Another stood by an east window of 109, facing the library room so he could see past both ends of 110. The third stooge stood in the window next to the library (he couldn't go in the actual library itself because the forgers were all around the windows). This third man could see anyone approaching from the west, and the outlooks of all stooges overlapped for double security.

134

When the stooge in 103 saw a ferret approaching, he opened his window. The man in 109 immediately saw this and put a folded paper against the window. The stooge next to the library caught the signal, knocked on the wall, and the stuff was out of sight in a few seconds.

With no stooges in sight, Adolf stopped hanging around 110 again. Occasionally he and other ferrets had a routine peek through the block but there was no deliberate concentration on it, and the stooges always warned in time.

Roger wrote home, "It can't last much longer. This is definitely our last Christmas in the bag." Grimly true for him.

On the last day of the year, the "X" chiefs threw a raisin wine party in 110, and by evening appell the world was sweetness and light. Canton and Bob Tuck charitably got on each side of a prominent tunneler and carried him on appell, his legs making walking movements about six inches above the snow. They held him up, swaying, in the ranks but when Pieber came past counting, the tunneler swayed out of their grip and staggered to one side.

"Please stop moving," said Pieber severely. "I cannot count you properly."

"Tisn' me moving," said the tunneler, focusing desperately. "T'syou."

There weren't any more raisin wine brews after that. For two reasons.

A young squadron leader went to a hooch party in another block, and early in the morning, hours after lock-up, he felt so good he decided to slip out of the window and crawl back to his own block. He hadn't gone far when the hundfuehrer's dog caught him and was mauling his arm when the hundfuehrer himself walked up and emptied his pistol magazine at him. He was a rotten shot. Only one of the five bullets hit the man, low down in the stomach, and he lived, but hooch was banned after that.

The ban was hardly necessary. Freezing weather had brought sharper hunger and people wouldn't spare a single raisin for a brew. The only vegetable from the Germans was sauerkraut. For weeks everything was sauerkraut, and the charm and novelty of sauerkraut are as fleeting as an English summer. A certain American summed it up when, for the tenth time in ten days, they handed him his sauerkraut ration.

"Jesus Christ," he muttered disgustedly. "The same yesterday, the same today, and the same forever more."

The compound dust was frozen hard under a foot of snow, and most of us tried to keep warm by going to bed during the day. It was no time for escaping and Rubberneck knew it. The rest of the ferrets were very glad to be invited into rooms for a brew, out of the cold.

CHAPTER 13

THAT, reasoned Roger, was the time to open up "Harry" again. It was about January 7, when he called the committee together.

"The idea is a blitz campaign," he said. "If we can finish 'Harry' in a couple of months while the Goons aren't expecting it, we can seal it again and break as soon as the weather's right."

"What about dispersal, for Pete's sake?" Floody asked. "We can't get rid of the stuff while the snow's about."

"That's what the Goons'll be thinking," Roger said. "We've got to find some way of doing it now. Anyone got any ideas?"

They talked about it for an hour and got nowhere. There didn't seem to be any way of doing it. If they packed it under the huts, it would be found. If they stored it up in the roofs, it would probably be found there too. Likewise if they hid it, as before, in the rooms, once the ferrets found sand, the hunt would be on again till they located a tunnel. And "Harry" was the last hope. They wouldn't risk it.

Canton suggested digging a small tunnel as a blind and letting the ferrets find it but that only meant more sand dispersal. Also, as Roger pointed out, they might find "Harry" instead. Now that the new compound was up outside the west fence, the north side was the only practicable tunnel route. That would mean tougher searches of the northern blocks, including

104. He closed the meeting and told them to go away and think of something.

Crump and Fanshawe stood talking for a while outside 110, and Fanshawe suddenly said, "What about the theater?"

"Under it!" said Crump. "God, I was just thinking of that."

"Is there any room?"

"Bound to be. It's a sloping floor."

They ran back inside and told Bushell, who was peeling potatoes. He put them down with a dawning glint in his eye and said slowly, "I really think you've hit it. That floor's a couple of feet high."

"It ought to be safe," Crump said. "I don't think the sods have ever bothered to search it properly."

"They can't." Roger was grinning. "Not underneath anyway. We didn't put any trap doors in the walls."

The theater people weren't happy about the idea. They thought if the Germans found sand under their floor they might shut the theater down and put a stop to camp entertainments.

"Escape is more important," Wings Day said, and issued a tactful but uncompromising order that the theater was to be used for dispersal.

Travis fixed a seat in the back row of the auditorium so that it tipped back on hinges, and under it he cut a trap door in the floor. Fanshawe slipped below with a fat lamp and found there was enough space to disperse more sand than "Harry" would ever yield.

Immediately after appell on January 10, Floody, Pat Langford ("Harry's" trapfuehrer), and Crump started chipping the cement away around "Harry's" trap. They thought they could get it done in about twenty minutes, but Crump had made such a good job of it that it took them two hours. They lifted the stove off the tiled square, the trap swung up easily, and they clambered below carrying a fat lamp each, wondering nervously what they would find. "Harry" had been shut for three months, and tunnels need constant maintenance to stay in good order.

Crump had made a good job of "Harry." The air was still fresh down there because he had left the by-pass valve open on the pump. He crawled up the tunnel, finding a little sand had seeped through here and there, but only four shoring frames had twisted out of plumb and he chalked them to be replaced later. Floody found the kit bag bellows on the pump had rotted, and that afternoon Travis went down with a couple of carpenters and fitted new bags. The pump seemed to be working stiffly, and Crump reported from the face that not much air was coming through.

"I guess there's a blockage in the air line somewhere," Floody said gloomily. There was nothing to do but unearth the line till they found the damage—the stickiest job possible because it meant reefing up floor boards with the risk of the frames above sinking and starting dangerous falls. Luckily they found the worst trouble in the first few feet, near the tunnel mouth. Some of the tins of the airline had buckled and sand had leaked in. They replaced them and the pump worked normally again, but Crump found jets of air hissing up through several floor boards and they had to take out more boards, dig down, and seal the leaking tins with fresh tarred paper. It was a long and exasperating job and took several days.

On January 14, Floody was able to take the first full shift down for digging. He trolleyed up to the face and ran his finger gently down the sand. It was fine and felt fairly firm so he knew he could space his frames about a foot apart and board them on top. He dug ten feet that day, and the sand flooded back to the shaft where Crump packed it in kit bags.

After appell, the evening shift laid fresh rails, and about 8 P.M. Langford opened the trap for the first dispersing. It had never been so easy to get rid of the sand, because as it was the off season for escape, Massey had persuaded Von Lindeiner to let the prisoners walk about between the blocks till ten o'clock. Covered by darkness, there was no need to use the trouser bags.

As each penguin reported to the trap, Langford hauled up a kit bag of sand on a sling, and the penguin swung it over his shoulder. George Harsh signaled the all clear from the corridor, and the penguin nipped swiftly out of the hut and across the path into the door of 109 opposite. He reported to a controller's room there, and if ferrets were about he slung the bag under a bunk and waited. If it was all clear he moved out of the far door of 109 with his sand and walked around 120 through the snow straight into the theater. Fanshawe, by the trap, passed the kit bag below.

A faint glow was coming out of the trap where, down below, a dozen dirt-stained men in long underpants were crawling on their bellies by the light of a couple of fat lamps. In turn each one took a bag and wriggled to the side of the floor and emptied it, packing it down as hard as he could. The penguin took an empty kit bag back with him, folded under his coat.

Over in an end room of 112, the duty pilot kept a team of runners, and if any German—ferret or otherwise—came into the camp, he sent one man to tell George Harsh who it was and where he was heading, and two more to tail the German. One of them kept him in sight all the time and periodically sent the other to tell George his latest movements. George sat most of the time in the room across the corridor from "Harry's" trap, knowing at any time where every German in the compound was. If a ferret headed for 104, George slipped across and warned Langford.

Langford had a drill for closing the trap and could do the whole operation in just over twenty seconds. Closing the trap itself was easy enough, but there was more to it than that. First, a quick warning to the people below to keep quiet, then he slipped the grill in position and used blankets to muffle the hollow sound. The trap came down, and he slipped the extension flue off the stove, moved the stove back on the trap, and slipped on the usual short flue. Langford always had the stove burning red-hot so any ferret prowling about the room would be discouraged from moving it to investigate the tiled base.

"Harry" was electrically lit all through at night, the stolen cable being taken right up to the face, tacked to a corner of the tunnel roof. It made work much easier, though the day shift still had to use the fat lamps because the power wasn't on. They were getting rid of so much sand that Floody sent down a couple of extra workers on the night shift to keep on digging. Fanshawe dispersed it all, and in a week "Harry" had gone forward fifty feet, and Crump and Floody built a halfway house. It was on the same lines as in "Tom," about seven feet long and two feet six inches square. They called it Piccadilly, and it was just about under the cooler.

Sound travels through loose sand, and Shag Rees swore he could hear the jackboots rasping on the concrete floor of the cooler.

"I ought to know," he said. "I know the bloody sound well enough."

Roger insisted on going down and working a couple of shifts. He was in grim good spirits again, obsessed with the prospects of escape.

"There'll have to be at least one more halfway house," Floody told him. "I think we can probably leave it at that. We've done just over 100 feet now, and I'd say there's another 250 to go." That was across the rest of the vorlager to the far fence, under the road and the grass verge to the shelter of the woods.

George Harsh was getting grayer every day. There was a little ginger-haired ferret called Rudy, and his contact lived in 104. It had never mattered a great deal before but now Rudy went on the late ferret shift and came in after appell every evening. He made a beeline for his contact's room and sat down to talk, smoke his contact's cigarettes, and get his brew. He sat there for hours behind the closed door, while the trap was open down the corridor and penguins went traipsing by, lugging their sand. For a time George considered making the contact move to another block, but dropped that idea because he knew Rudy might still haunt 104 to scrounge cigarettes from his other friends in the contact's room.

"We'll have to let Rudy stay," he gloomed to Floody, pulling agitatedly on his mustache. "I guess we can take enough precautions."

Rudy was always given the chair farthest from the door, and his contact and at least two others always sat between Rudy and the door. Outside, George had a stooge standing hour after hour with a cooking pot, and if Rudy ever got up in a hurry to go, there would have been a loud scraping of feet in the room, and as Rudy opened the door, he'd have been been bowled over by the stooge bringing in the pot. George also always had one of Valenta's German speakers loafing in the door of the kitchen, and if Rudy or any other ferret wandered in at short notice, he would hold him up with half a minute's conversation while Langford went through his trap drill.

"Harry" was nearly two hundred feet long when the full moon came. The sky stayed clear, and for a week the moonglow off the snow filled the compound with a soft radiance.

"It's too risky," Fanshawe told Roger. "It looks like day outside. The penguins'll be spotted in no time. They could see them from the goon-boxes."

Roger, impatient and irritable, gave the pack-up order, and there was no tunnel work for a week. Every day he went along to Chaz Hall and asked what the weather would be that night, and every day Hall gave him the same answer, "Bloody moon. No cloud."

Crump used the time to make new ropes for the trolleys, as the old ones were rotting. Williams had been saving up string from the parcel store, and Crump took on the exasperating job of making three hundred feet of four-ply plait, the long ends constantly tangling so that he had two men standing behind him clearing it.

The moon faded and digging started again. Floody made a new record of twelve and a half feet in one day. Then they ran into a soft patch and Floody was buried again, badly. A couple of hundred pounds of sand slipped from the roof, and Floody was nearly unconscious from the force and weight of it. Crump had a little trouble dragging him clear, yelled back, and Canton came crawling up from the halfway house. Together they dragged Floody out, and he recovered quickly and insisted on staying to clear the mess.

There were other falls, too, just as dangerous. A bedboard slipped out of a pile at the top of the shaft, fell nearly thirty feet, and got Cooky Long on the head as he was coming out of the tunnel. They brought him up concussed, green and sick, and he was two days in his bunk.

A day or so later a metal jug fell from the trap and hit Floody on the head—luckily not a direct hit from the rim but a glancing blow on the side, otherwise it would have split his head open. As it was, he had a wicked contusion, and his head was in bandages for days. He told Pieber he'd tripped and cannoned into a door, and Pieber was very sympathetic.

Langford dropped a bedboard and nearly brained Crump, who cursed him for a couple of minutes.

"I suppose you think I bloody well did it on purpose." Langford called down, and then apologized. Langford lived in the

143

trap room and ruled it with a rod of iron. The trap was his baby. Nerves were getting very frayed. The volatile Johnny Marshall had a couple of outbursts; in fact everyone did, even the limping, good-natured Johnny Bull.

By February 10, they had finished the second halfway house. It was nearly under the outer wire and Crump named it Leicester Square. There were about 130 feet to go for the woods, and Johnny Marshall again wanted them to start digging gradually up so they would finish near the surface. Floody opposed him, and there was a heated debate in the committee. Roger settled it by saying they would dig straight on. On a long uphill haul, he still wouldn't trust the trolley ropes.

Wings Day was doing an occasional digging shift on "Harry." Floody wouldn't let him dig too often because Wings, like Roger, had a notorious record as far as the Germans were concerned and was supposed to keep in the background as a sort of over-all controller, lending his advice whenever it was needed.

Pop Green was another one of the old brigade who wouldn't be out of it. Pop had won an M.C. in the 1914–1918 war and got into this war as a tail gunner by lying about his age. He was about fifty and had been one of Fanshawe's penguins since the days of "Tom." He still insisted on being a penguin and used to collect his kit bag of sand weighing about fifty pounds from Langford and stagger down the corridor with it. Fanshawe tried to make him take an easier job, and Pop refused in terms that hadn't been used to Fanshawe since his midshipman days.

Pop shared a little room with the Dodger at the end of 104 —next to the room which sheltered "Harry's" trap. Bushell thought it would be a good idea to help divert any suspicion if they boldly had Pieber in to tea, nonchalantly rubbing shoulders, so to speak, with the trap. It was a fair assumption that if the Germans were invited in they would tend to believe that nothing sinister could be going on in that area. So Pieber was invited; and about the time he was due to arrive, the Dodger, that amiable and nerveless Anglo-American, sighted the Kommandant striding majestically in the compound; so he invited the Kommandant too, and the four of them spent a pleasant half hour in innocuous chit-chat with the trapdoor only 10 feet away behind a wooden partition. The duty shift of tunnelers was down below and George Harsh was standing by to see that nothing went wrong, glowering, tugging on his gray mustache and muttering curses.

At the end of February, Himmler had another victory in his campaign for more ruthless treatment of prisoners. Keitel issued the order known as "Stufe Roemisch III." It said that every escaped officer prisoner, other than British and Americans, was to be handed over on recapture to the Gestapo. Recaptured British and American officers were to be kept in military or police prisons, and the High Command would decide in each case whether they were to be handed over to the Gestapo. The recapture of the officers must be kept secret, and they were to be officially reported as "Escaped and not recaptured."

We came off appell one morning and found the tommy-gunners around 104, Rubberneck and the ferrets inside. Floody, Crump, Harsh, and Roger walked around and around the circuit telling each other airily that Rubberneck didn't have a hope, and all of them feeling butterflies in their stomachs. Rubberneck came out three hours later, looking his usual lugubrious self.

Adolf was making himself a nuisance again. He came in on the late shift and wandered restlessly all over the camp and in all the blocks, causing a near-panic in 104. The German-speaker delayed him in the corridor and Langford got the trap closed, but dispersing was held up and George Harsh had bitten his fingernails right down and went around muttering horrible threats. Adolf was still the friendless one. No contact was able to inveigle him into his room for a brew. Adolf might exchange a few words with them, and then he shut his stolid mouth and gloomed off.

It seemed like an Act of God when, for no accountable reason, he suddenly developed a friendship for a tall red-bearded Scot called Jim Tyrie who spoke fluent German. Tyrie took him into his room in 103 for a brew, and Adolf settled down there comfortably for a couple of hours. He went back the next night and made it a habit.

Valenta had cultivated Walter, the bookfuehrer, a thin obergefreiter with glasses who came in the compound nearly every day and often helped Pieber count the appell. He was harmless, rather a gentle type, and he told Valenta that Rubberneck was getting the idea there was a tunnel somewhere in the compound.

"What, in winter?" Valenta said innocently, fishing for more. "Where the hell does he think we can hide the sand?"

Walter shrugged and spread his hands expressively.

"I would not know," he said. "It is nothing to do with me. I think you can expect more searches."

"Where?" asked Valenta, and Walter nodded toward 110.

Roger cleaned out his wall panel that night. There wasn't much bulky stuff in it, but there were some lists of names. He hid most of them behind a panel in another block, but, a little carelessly (unusual for Roger) he carried the rest in his pockets.

There was no search next morning but halfway through appell Rubberneck walked on to the appell square with half a dozen guards. They split up and approached various squads, one of them being the inhabitants of 110. Roger, conscious of the papers in his pockets, had a sudden instinct of what was

146

going to happen and his heart was bumping a little. He shoved his hands in his pockets and muttered out of the corner of his mouth, "Conk, stick around."

Canton, Piglet Lamond, and McIntosh moved up close to him, and as they did so, Rubberneck and Eichacher, an English-speaking German, reached the squad. Eichacher had a word with Bob Tuck, who was at the front, and then turned and called, "Squadron Leader Bushell, please. Come out and follow me."

As he shouldered forward in the crowd, Roger pressed the papers into the hands of those around him, and they passed them on to others down the line. Rubberneck didn't notice a thing.

In 104 squad, another ferret had called out Floody and George Harsh, and they marched, a forlorn little group, across the square. Rubberneck stopped by Wings Day.

"Komm!" he said.

Half a dozen armed guards fell in around them, and they were marched off to their huts, Rubberneck stripped them all naked and searched them, finding nothing. Poker-faced, he let them go and marched out of the compound.

Walter had been right. Rubberneck searched 110 the next morning and, probing above a window in a room on the east side he sprang a secret wall panel. It was empty. No. Not quite. Rubberneck pounced on a little piece of paper lying in it. There was some writing on it. He passed it to Eichacher.

"What does it say?" he asked.

"It says," Eichacher translated a little nervously, " 'Sorry. Too late!' "

It wasn't a very wise thing for the roomfuehrer to do. Rubberneck was a bad man to goad, and judging by his next move, he was ready to do anything to unearth the tunnel he was beginning to suspect.

Floody called Bushell out of his room.

147

"For God's sake, come and look at the circus."

In the vorlager just outside the fence a little procession was walking along the wire. Rubberneck was there, Broili in his shiny black boots, one or two other German officers, and a few ferrets. Leading them was an old man in a cloth cap and a ragged corduroy jacket. He held a rod in front of him and was looking at the ground over his drooping mustache.

"What the hell. . . !" Roger said.

"A bloody diviner." Floody was hugely amused. "Ever heard of a tunnel diviner?"

"I never thought I'd live to see the day," Roger said, shaking his head.

The old diviner had started opposite 101, and now he was opposite 103. A couple of times he stopped and cocked an eye pensively at the sky while the rod gently waved in his hands. Once he turned back a few paces, Rubberneck and Broili stepping devoutly aside, watching, it seemed, a little self-consciously because Rubberneck was swiveling an occasional eye sideway at the compound. A few prisoners stopped on the circuit and gaped at them open-mouthed.

"No, I never heard of a tunnel diviner," Roger said after a short silence, "but I think we ought to be in this. The old boy might imagine he's found something and start a panic." He moved down to the wire, Floody after him, and they muttered to the spectators by the warning wire. A few seconds later, groans and catcalls started to rise, followed by wild, shrill laughter. People came running up to see what all the excitement was, and the chorus of derision swelled. Rubberneck wouldn't look across any more, but his face was scarlet. The old diviner looked up in offended dignity, then Broili spoke to him and he dropped his eyes again.

But he was a rattled man. He doddered on, passing over "Harry" opposite 104 without a tremor, dithered for a while round 105 (where there was nothing), and continued on to the end of the compound, followed behind him by the Germans and along the warning wire by a hundred derisive prisoners. He tried again on the return journey but the ectoplasm didn't seem to be working. It was the first time the ferrets had ever tried diviners.

And the last.

"It's not really funny," Roger told the grinning committee later. "It means we're going to have that sod Rubberneck on our tails. Everyone's got to be doubly careful from now on."

Harsh sent out a special security warning and threatened he would personally bash to a pulp any stooge who slipped up or anyone talking about escape where they might be overheard. Langford noticed the white-washed cement facing on the wall behind "Harry's" trap was a little scarred where the open trap had leaned against it. He carefully "whitewashed" it again with a solution of foot powder, smearing it on with a shaving brush.

As a further blind for himself, Roger took on another part with the camp theater. In addition to his escape work and his language classes, he started rehearsing every night the part of Professor Higgins in *Pygmalion*. The fact that Rubberneck had still suspected him enough to search him personally was making him very cautious.

149

ROGER expected Rubberneck might put on a couple of snap appells during the day. That had happened once at Barth when the Germans suddenly ran into the compound and a couple of people down a tunnel didn't have time to get up again. The count showed they were missing, and the tunnel was found because of it. He sent an order around that in the event of a snap appell, everyone was to dawdle as much as possible, and Floody fixed an emergency procedure for the men underground.

The timing was uncanny. A score of guards marched in for a snap appell in the early afternoon a couple of days later. If the fools had done it properly they might have trapped the day shift underground, but with boneheaded Teutonic thoroughness they had to go through the usual bullshine routine of falling in by the gate, numbering off from left to right, and then dismissing to clear the prisoners out of the huts. Harsh saw them from 104, and Langford went through the new drill. He had the trap up in a moment and called down the shaft the one word, "Ferrets!"

At the bottom, the shaft man flashed a torch up the tunnel and the diggers dropped what they were doing and trolleyed back hell for leather, Langford just had the trap in position again as the jackboots sounded in the corridor and the voice was bellowing, "*Raus! Raus! Alle rausgehen!*"

Early in March, S.S. General Mueller, Berlin Gestapo chief, issued the "Kugel Order." It was an extension of the "Stufe Roemisch" order. Kugel means bullet, and the new order said that recaptured escapee officers, other than British and Americans, were to be taken in chains to Mauthausen Concentration Camp.

Mauthausen was instructed that prisoners transferred to them under the "Kugel Order" were not to be entered on the camp books but taken to the underground cells and either gassed or shot, whichever was convenient.

About that time security police visited Sagan and had a conference with Von Lindeiner about counter-escape measures. They hinted to Von Lindeiner that prisoners who escaped in future might suffer very harsh penalties. One of them suggested that reprisals might even consist of shooting people in the camp. (To one of his officers, Von Lindeiner later remarked that if he was ordered to shoot prisoners, he would take his own life.)

Von Lindeiner sent for the senior officers, doctors, and chaplains in all the compounds and asked them to put a stop to all escape activity.

"It is not worth it, gentlemen," he said. "The public temper outside is running very high, particularly against the Allied Air Forces, and escapers may suffer harsh consequences. The war may be over in a year or two . . . it is not worth taking unnecessary risks now."

It was a pity he could not have been more explicit. A captive officer cannot give up the idea of escape just because the enemy asks him not to.

Walter, the bookfuehrer, told Valenta that Rubberneck was going on fourteen days' leave on March 1. That was in three days. The committee could hardly believe their luck.

"We can finish it before he's back," Floody said exultantly. "I'm bloody sure we can if we really get down to it. Then we can seal up and wait for the weather."

He reckoned there was just over a hundred feet to go and then they could dig straight up under the trees.

Floody's joy was premature. Rubberneck struck the day before he was to go on leave. We were on morning appell when thirty extra guards marched on to the square. Broili and Rubberneck were with them, and Broili went from squad to squad calling out names. One by one the men he called walked suspiciously out of the ranks, and the guards closed around them. Floody was one of them. So was George Harsh (still in pajamas). Fanshawe was another. There were nineteen of them, including Bob Tuck, a couple of diggers, and Jim Tyrie, the man with the beard who had kept Adolf out of the way for the past vital fortnight.

Broili marched them down to 104, giving Floody, Harsh, and Fanshawe some nasty moments wondering if they had located "Harry." They hadn't, but they spent two hours searching them, and then, without giving any of them a chance to go to their rooms to get their few belongings, they marched them out of the gate to a compound at Belaria five miles away.

It was a stunning parting pick from Rubberneck. Three key men lost without warning at the critical moment! No one knew how they'd chosen the nineteen. Some of them were completely harmless types who had nothing to do with "X," and about a third of them were fairly important workers. It was a wonder they didn't take Bushell, but apparently his outside activities had really convinced Rubberneck that he was a reformed character. (Walter later revealed that the ferrets had gone through all the identification photographs and picked out those they suspected might be on escape work. Why they suspected them we never did find out.)

Floody, Harsh, and Fanshawe were seething when they were

taken away. They'd been slogging on the tunnel for nearly a year; they would all have been certainties to get out, and now this . . . right on the point of success.

Later they felt rather differently!

Crump took over the next day as chief tunnel engineer, and with Rubberneck away they dug like furies. There were eight men down the tunnel on every shift now; two at the face, two in Leicester Square, two in Piccadilly and the frame cutter and pumper in the shaft. The sharp-eared Shag Rees got a shock when there was a sudden rumble right overhead, and he cringed back expecting the whole roof to come crashing down. The rumble passed and he realized it was a heavy cart above. They were under the road.

There were almost no falls over the last stretch. With Rubberneck away everything seemed to go smoothly, and there was still plenty of room for dispersal under the theater. In nine days they dug nearly a hundred feet. Rubberneck was due back in five days. On the tenth day they built the whole of the last halfway house, ten feet long. Crump trolleyed backward and forward trailing a long piece of string, checking the measurements. "Harry," from shaft to face, stretched for 348 feet.

The surveyors had said it was 335 feet to the edge of the wood. Crump crawled out of the trap that night feeling that the whole thing was unreal. It didn't seem possible that they were really inside the trees as they had planned nearly a year ago.

"The ground falls away outside the fence," he said to Roger. "If the mathematical marks are right, we've only got about twenty-two feet to go up. Barring the unforeseen, I'll guarantee it before Rubberneck gets back."

He already had the framing for the outlet shaft stored below. Travis had been working on the sections for a week. It was to be solid box-framing around four bedposts.

Digging up was tricky and dangerous. The sand kept clump-

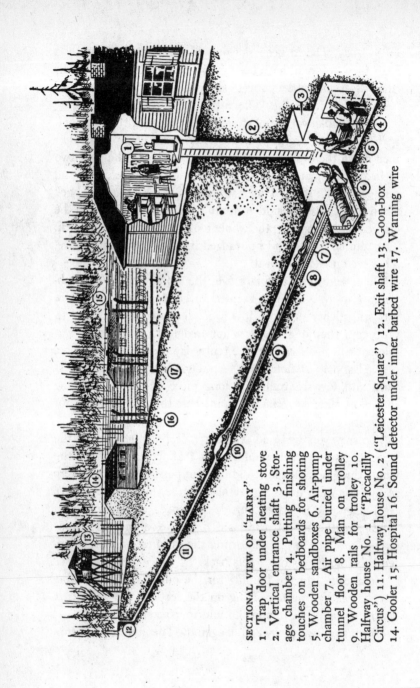

SECTIONAL VIEW OF "HARRY"
1. Trap door under heating stove
2. Vertical entrance shaft 3. Stor-
age chamber 4. Putting finishing
touches on bedboards for shoring
5. Wooden sandboxes 6. Air-pump
chamber 7. Air pipe buried under
tunnel floor 8. Man on trolley
9. Wooden rails for trolley 10.
Halfway house No. 1 ("Piccadilly
Circus") 11. Halfway house No. 2 ("Leicester Square") 12. Exit shaft 13. Coon-box
14. Cooler 15. Hospital 16. Sound detector under inner barbed wire 17. Warning wire

ing down, and as Crump fitted the sections of the framing he roofed over half the top to minimize the falls and scraped the sand down on the open side. Then he changed the roof to the other side. They fixed the ladder in sections as they burrowed up and stood on it to dig. It was backbreaking work.

Just before appell on the fourteenth, Crump came to pine roots and gathered he had only three feet to go. His idea was to stop about two feet from the surface and roof it firmly. With two feet of earth it wouldn't sound hollow if anyone walked on it above. To break out they could remove the roof and hack the two feet of soil away in a couple of minutes. It could drop to the bottom of the shaft, and they could leave it there.

He came up for appell and told Johnny Bull, who was doing the evening shift:

"Test it to see how far you can go. I think you ought to be able to put in two more frames and leave it at that."

Bull vanished up the tunnel after appell. He was back twenty minutes later shaking with excitement.

"There's only six inches of dirt there," he said. "By Christ it's lucky I tested it first. I'd have broken right through."

He'd stuck a metal rod up into the sand, and after six inches' penetration there was no more resistance. He went back and roofed it strongly, packing the sand above the roof as tightly as possible so it would be solid above if anyone trod on it.

At a quarter to ten they were all crawling out of the trap; still with that feeling of unreality, unable to believe it was the last shift and "Harry" was finished. They brought up all the unused bedboards and pipe-line tins, the dispersal bags, the tools, and spare shovels, even the sand boxes off the trolleys, and either burned them or stored them down "Dick." They weren't going to need them any more. It was hard to believe that too. Langford stuffed the muffle blankets very carefully under the trap and lowered it.

"Well that's it, you old bastard," he said, sounding deeply satisfied. "Next time you come up you'll be useful." He added soberly to Crump, "It's none too soon, you know," and pressed a foot gently on one corner. It made a little knocking noise as it rocked.

"Warped as bloody Hitler," Langford said. "It won't matter so much now." He spent the next half hour cementing it down around the edges, completely sealing it as he had done twice before. Then before he went to bed he scrubbed the floor. (He scrubbed the floor every day after that, sloshing water all over it. It wasn't fanatical cleanliness. The water made the boards swell, and they filled in the last vestige of crack around the edges of the trap.)

Crump went over to tell Roger it was all done. Roger was staying away from the trap area as much as possible now, not because he wanted to, but because of the time Rubberneck had searched him. He knew he was probably still suspect, and Massey and Wings were insisting he didn't take any chances. He'd been rehearsing as Professor Higgins that night. He and Crump sat quietly for a few minutes, not talking much but conscious of a feeling of elation, and Crump drifted off to sleep still trying to convince himself it was fact, not fiction.

Rubberneck was back in the compound in the morning. He didn't waste much time. Just after lunch a squad of ferrets and guards ran in the gate and headed at a fast trot for 104. Rubberneck loped down the corridor throwing the doors open so he could see anything that might be going on before they had a chance to cover up. He cleared everyone out, and the ferrets went through it for four hours. It was the worst four hours we had known and oh, the blessed relief when Rubberneck walked out again as solemn as ever.

"There's nothing to be smug about," Roger warned that evening in the library room. "Rubberneck's obviously got it into his head there's something in 104, and we probably won't get away with it next time. I don't see that we can risk a next time."

"Well, we can't break it now," someone said. "Not in this snow."

"We damnwell can if we have to"—Bushell was speaking roughly at that meeting.

"Doesn't give the hardarsers much chance," said Marshall.

"Johnny, they haven't got much chance any way," Roger said. "You know as well as I do they'll nearly all be caught. We can't lose 'Harry' just because conditions are tough. It isn't only to get people home, it's to muck the Goons about too and get them to divert troops to look for us."

Roger had thought of just about everything. There were, he said, four factors he wanted for the night of the break: (1) no moon, (2) a wind to cover up noises, (3) reasonable weather, and (4) no Rudy in 104. He had three days in mind —the twenty-third, twenty-fourth, and twenty-fifth of March. They were the three most moonless nights for the next five weeks. Almost immediately he ruled the twenty-fifth out.

"It's a Saturday night," he said, "and that means Sunday timetables for most of the train traveling."

They talked it over for two hours and didn't reach any hard and fast decision. Crump and Langford sided with Roger in breaking out as soon as possible. They didn't think the trap would stand up to another search.

"We'll work toward the twenty-third or twenty-fourth," Roger said, "and see how the weather turns out."

He had worked it out that at the most about 220 people might be able to get through the tunnel on the night of the break. That meant "no joy" for most of the "X" workers. There were about 600 of us who had taken part in the project in the various departments.

Roger and the committee picked 70 names from among those who had put in most work and those, particularly the

German speakers, who had most chance of getting home. They put the rest of the names in a hat and drew out another 130, and then Roger approved another 20 names of deserving people who hadn't drawn a place. They were all to go in the order they were drawn.

The lucky ones were told to get ready, and the committee appointed marshals to help them. Each marshal was allotted ten men, and it was his job to see they had everything they needed. For a start they concentrated on seeing that each man had a fake name and a fake personal background so he could answer questions if he was picked up and interrogated. The marshals carried out mock interrogations on them, firing questions about their home life, where they were going and why, and then doubling back on questions to see if they gave the same answers. They found out what each man wanted in the way of ausweises, money, civilian clothes, compasses, food, and maps.

The marshals held mannequin parades of all the men in their charge, the would-be escapers dressed in their escape kit parading up and down while the marshals ran their critical eyes over them to correct anything that looked unnatural. A ferret passing a window nearly stumbled across one of these parades—and would have if the strutting models hadn't dived under bunks and into corners to get out of his field of vision. Roger was furious when he heard about it and threatened unseemly forms of mutilation against any marshal or stooge who gave the game away.

The whole organization was buzzing with activity. They had several thousand marks in the kitty by this time, enough for about forty people to travel by train. The rest of them would have to "hardarse" across country by foot. Most of them planned to strike down to Czechoslovakia, where they would have a chance of contacting friendly people. The border was only sixty miles to the south, though there was a mountain range in between. Johnny Vesley, a Czech in the R.A.F. who knew the area, lectured the hardarsers in batches on how to go about it, and Johnny Stower, who had got to the Swiss border after the delousing break, lectured them on his experiences.

Roger himself checked all the train travelers' stories and gave them all the information Valenta's men had been able to collect on timetables and routes. He gave general lectures to everyone on German customs. Marshall and Crump spoke to them on how to get through the tunnel without coming to grief.

Travis' engineers had switched to the production of metal waterbottles. They cut old food tins into sheets according to patterns, and a team of solderers, drawing heavily on stocks of bully-beef-tin solder and resin got to work with home-made blow lamps and turned out little flat flasks by the score.

Plunkett had his mimeograph going and rolled off something like four thousand maps, from local maps to strip maps of routes.

Stooges all over the camp were working overtime, and by the grace of God, no slips were made that week. Rubberneck was still prowling about as alert as ever, but nearly all the huts had been cleaned out and the stuff was down "Dick."

Al Hake shut down his compass production line. He had about 250 of them stored down "Dick."

Guest's tailors kept on working to the last day, and by that time they had hand-sewn nearly fifty complete suits; and most of them would have been a credit to some of the tailors I have met. They were mostly for the train travelers who had to look the part. A lot of the hardarsers were converting old uniforms. It didn't matter so much if they looked as though they were wearing hand-me-downs. However smart they were when they left, they were going to look pretty scruffy after a few days' trekking. Guest showed them how to shave the nap off the cloth and dye it, lent them his paper patterns and gave them civilian-type buttons.

For some months past "X" had been making a levy on the

Red Cross food parcels, and in a room of 112 half a dozen cooks were mixing "fudge," the concentrated escape food. It was the recipe of David Lubbock, a naval type, and was a compound of sugar, cocoa, Bemax, condensed milk, raisins, oats, glucose, margarine, chocolate, and ground biscuits. The beaten mixture looked like old glue, and it was taken across to the kitchen block where Herrick baked it into cakes, or rather bricks, and packed it into flat cocoa tins. Lubbock had worked it out that one four-ounce tin held enough calories to last a man two days. The difficulty was to get it down past the ribs, where it tended to stick tenaciously. The train travelers were each allowed four tins, and the hardarsers could take up to six.

Massey gave a final warning to those who had drawn a place for the tunnel and told them he had been informed that the German population was becoming increasingly hostile, particularly toward the Allied Air Forces.

"If you are caught, some of you may not be treated very well," he said. "I do not think the Germans would dare to take extreme measures, as you are protected by the Geneva Convention, but do please avoid any provocation."

Roger spoke to a few of us who hadn't drawn a place.

"I can promise you plenty of entertainment later," he said. "Once they find there's been a mass break under their noses, it'll be a case of 'après nous, le déluge.'"

In between his lectures and rehearsals, Roger drew up the scheme to get the 220 people into 104 on the night of the break without exciting the ferrets. It was two and a half times more than the block was supposed to hold, and they had to be hidden when the Germans came around to lock up. Everyone in 104 who wasn't escaping was allotted a bunk in some other hut on the night of the break.

Rudy's contact moved out immediately to another hut and told Rudy he'd had a row with his roommates because they didn't like the idea of associating with a German. Rudy cut them dead after that.

Roger knew well enough the ferrets had periodical checks on people moving between the blocks to see if any unusual activity was going on. He put traffic checkers around 104, and for two days they logged the numbers of people who normally moved in and out. From their figures Roger worked out a timetable and routes to control people moving to 104 on the night of the break.

Dean and Dawson had the hardest job of all because everyone's papers had to fit his stories. The forgers were working full pressure filling in fake names and particulars, sticking on the photographs that Hall and Cornish had taken in their studio, and stamping them. All told they had about four hundred forged papers of various kinds. Everybody was to have at least one, and many were taking two. Men with elaborate identities like Bushell and some of the German speakers had up to half a dozen, including letters of credit and incidental forged personal letters just for effect. Tim had a folder for each man.

Meticulous as ever, he wouldn't risk leaving them in the wall cupboards, but insisted on hiding them down "Dick." It was damp down there now, so Travis made four large metal cans with sliding lids which were quite waterproof when smeared with margarine. The forgers were working on the papers morning and afternoon, and Tim wouldn't even leave them out during lunch. They had to go back down "Dick."

The stooges reported to "Dick" every morning after appell. Mike Casey lifted the iron grating in the middle of the washroom floor, baled out the well, scraped the soap off the edges of the slab, lifted the slab out. Tim went down, got the cans, and while he was carrying them to the workroom under a box of potatoes, Casey replaced the slab, sealed it again with soap, ran the water into the well, and put the grating back. At midday the forgers broke off for a spell because they found they couldn't keep going all day without botching the work. Tim took the cans back to "Dick," and Casey went through the complicated procedure of opening up and closing again. An hour later, after lunch, he did the same again while Tim collected the cans, and again about four-thirty, just before appell.

The forgers worked till their heads were splitting and the points of their nibs and brushes and the letters they were forming seemed to jump and wriggle and blur under their eyes.

Most of the escapees were going as foreign workers coming from nearly every country in Europe. Tim was going as a Lithuanian.

"And what happens, please," asked Marcinkus, who really was a Lithuanian (in the R.A.F.) "if the Gestapo get hold of you. How much Lithuanian do you know?"

"None," said Tim, "but then I don't suppose the Gestapo bloke would know any either."

The snow still lay six inches deep on March 23, but there was a hint of mildness in the air and the white carpet was wet on top and a little squashy underfoot. The bush telegraph had sent a whisper around the compound that the break might be in a couple of days, but most people didn't believe it. It was too tough for the hardarsers.

There was a committee meeting in the morning at which Chaz Hall said he thought the weather would hold fine.

"Looks like the thaw's starting just in time," Roger said. "We'll wait and see how it is tomorrow. If the weather keeps like this, I'm all for getting cracking, but we won't decide until we have to."

"I'll have to know as soon as possible," Tim cut in. "We've got to cut a date stamp and stamp all the papers."

"I've got to know too," Crump said. "I must know by lunch-

162

time on the day of the break. I've a lot to do to get 'Harry' ready."

Marshall was concerned again about the cross-country men.

"Some of the poor devils'll freeze," he said.

"I'm sorry, Johnny, but it just can't be helped," Roger said. "I wish to God we could do something about it, but if we wait till next no-moon period, we're about certain to lose everything."

"What about putting out a few of the train travelers and then closing up again?" Marshall asked.

"No," said Roger. "We'd lose the tunnel, and a few people getting out won't upset the Goons as much as a mass job."

He thought about it all day, and after afternoon appell he went to Wings Day and they walked round the circuit in the gathering dusk.

"We've got to go tomorrow," said Roger, "but I hate having to make the decision. Bloody few of the hardarsers'll have any chance."

"They wouldn't have much chance even if there wasn't any snow," Wings said. "You know yourself what their chances are . . . a hundred to one. If things get too tough out there they don't have to freeze to death. Once they know they can't make it, they'll have to give themselves up."

"You think I'm right then?"

"Look," Wings said, "it's an operational war. Don't forget that. It isn't just a question of getting a few people home. It's just as important to mess the Goons about. Most of the boys will be caught anyway, but if we get a good team out there'll be a flap all over Germany, and we'll have done something useful . . . more useful than getting a few back home."

"All right," said Roger. "Thanks."

After dinner he went across to the theater for the dress rehearsal. *Pygmalion* was to open in two days for a four-day season. Roger stood and watched them. McIntosh was playing Professor Higgins. He'd understudied Roger for the past three weeks just in case.

The twenty-fourth dawned fair, and by appell the sun was well over the pine trees, unchallenged in a clear sky. The surface of the snow was glistening, and it was quite mild.

They met at eleven-thirty in Roger's room. It was one of the shortest meetings on record, certainly the tensest. There were only a few words spoken. After the last man came in there was a dragging silence. People were looking up at the ceiling or sitting with their arms folded on the bunk, staring at the floor. Roger looked at Langford.

"How do you feel about it?"

"I won't guarantee the trap another month. I can't . . . not with that wobble."

"Crump?"

"I think I can speak for all the tunnel men," Crump said, "including those who are hardarsing. I don't think we could take it if we lost everything now. Morale'd go for a burton."

"Right. Tonight's the night," Roger jumped energetically to his feet. "Get cracking."

THE entire camp must have known about it within five minutes. You could feel the tension. It was absolutely electric.

Langford and Crump made a beeline for "Harry." Langford chipped the cement away, and Crump and one other tunneler went below and trolleyed up to the far end with a load of blankets. Crump nailed one blanket as a curtain across the end of the last halfway house at the foot of the exit shaft, and nailed another about three feet back in the halfway house. They were to act as light traps and silencers when the shaft was broken through. They nailed blankets to the floors of all the halfway houses so that people could crawl over them without getting their escape clothes dirty.

Crump tore more blankets into strips about six inches wide, doubled them over, and nailed them on the railway lines over the first and last fifty feet of the tunnel so the trolleys would run silently. Travis came down with the board platforms he'd made for the trolleys and nailed them on so the escapers could lie comfortably on them with all their kit.

Up in the compound, there was a sort of ordered chaos as the 220 made their final preparations. So many things had to wait till the last day in case the ferrets stumbled across them. "Little X" in every hut called together the men in his block who were going out and handed them their water bottles, fudge, compasses, maps, and money. He also told each one the exact minute he was to leave his room and where he was to report to the controller. They went back to their own rooms and started sewing all their special kit into extra pockets inside their clothes. A lot of them had made little fat-lamp heaters for brewing cocoa on the trek across the snow-clad country. They kept inside the huts as much as they could so the Germans wouldn't notice too much rushing about.

The stooges were on duty that day in scores. Tommy Guest raided his secret clothing stores and passed the suits out to the lucky ones.

Dean and Dawson, as usual, had the most hectic time. Tim had asked Al Hake the previous night to start cutting the date-stamp out of a rubber heel, and it was ready by the time the decision was made. The forgers went to work stamping all the papers and then they sorted them all and distributed them.

Crump had to come up from below for five o'clock appell.

"Still got a hell of a lot to do," he told Roger.

"Can you make it by eight-thirty?" Roger asked.

"I think we might just," said Crump. "Have a bloody good try anyway."

He and Langford were back in 104 as soon as appell was over. The stooges searched the block as usual in case any ferrets had hidden there and gave the signal. Langford swung the trap up.

"The last all clear," Crump said and scuttled below. He seemed a little sad about it. Crump and Canton were barred from the escape this time because Massey wanted a nucleus of experienced tunnelers left in the camp for the future.

Carrying a little box of electric-light globes (filched from the huts), Crump made his way slowly along the tunnel, tapping the cable in the roof about every forty feet and fitting extra globes. He trolleyed back to the base, praying that they'd all work, and clicked on the switch. The tunnel lit up like

Blackpool illuminations. It was rather a thrill to see the blaze of light stretching into the distance.

He trolleyed slowly back along the tunnel looking for damaged frames, found four side boards twisted out of line, and carefully started replacing them. Darkness had settled over the compound, and people were sitting restlessly in every room trying to talk of innocent things and thinking only of the tunnel.

At six o'clock there was an early dinner party in Travis' room. Half a dozen people present were hoping it would be their last meal in prison camp—Bushell, Lamond, Van Der Stok, Armstrong, McIntosh, and Osborne. Travis had made an enormous pile of bully-beef fritters mixed with flour he'd milled by grinding barley under a bottle and seasoned with garlic. To follow he had a great bowl of "barley glop"—barley boiled like rice with milk powder, sugar, and raisins. He pushed a massive plate of fritters over to Roger.

"If you can get outside that," he said, "it'll keep you going for a week."

There wasn't much conversation. Roger ate methodically, trying to relax. He'd been working like a machine all day on last-minute details. Someone broke the silence and asked him how he felt about it.

"O.K.," he said laconically. "I'll make it this time." He must have felt the silence and known what they were thinking because he pushed the plate away and grinned easily.

"You don't have to worry," he said. "They won't be getting me this time. I think I know the score pretty well now."

At five to seven a man in a rough black suit got up from his bunk in a room in 107 and pulled on a greatcoat that seemed to bulge in a few directions. Richards was one of the hardarsers, and with a grin that was a shade too tight and on one side to be natural he shook hands around the room.

"Good-by, you bastards," he said. "Sorry I can't stay. See you in London after the war."

"See you looking out of the bloody cooler window in a couple of days, you mean," said the roomfuehrer. "Good luck, old boy. Don't get your feet wet."

Richards picked up a folded and tied blanket, and at seven o'clock sharp he walked out of the south end of the block and down the path into the end of 109 away from 104. He went into room 17. A stooge was standing at the window, and Wings Norman was sitting at a table with a list.

"On time," said Norman. "You're first. You can go right away."

Richards turned and walked down to the north end of the block. Another stooge was standing there and ten yards away across the path was the door of 104.

"O.K.," said the stooge. "All clear. On your way."

Richards walked straight out across the path and into 104.

Torrens, block commander for the night, was standing in the doorway of the hut kitchen with a list in his hand.

"Richards?" He ticked the name off with a pencil and pointed to a door. "Room six. Get into a bunk and stay there. Keep fairly quiet and talk about the weather . . . if you have to talk."

Richards went in and lay down. He tried to relax but couldn't. He was fairly tingling with wakefulness.

At thirty-second intervals all over the compound, farewells were being said, doors were opening, and men in bulky greatcoats walked out and went by a dozen circuitous routes to 109 where they reported to Norman. In ones and twos he sent them at intervals across to 104 where Torrens ticked them off on his list and sent them to the rooms allotted to them.

Stooges were bringing Norman reports every couple of minutes as to the position of every German in the camp. Luckily it was a quiet night, and after a time only Rudy was in, firmly ensconced in his contact's new room in 112. He was enjoying himself. Everyone in the new room seemed terribly friendly, and that very decent fellow, his contact, had given him half a bar of chocolate. They sat there a long time, smoking cigarettes and talking.

Outside in the corridor three men were loafing by the stove, a German speaker and two stooges. If Rudy had come out, the German speaker would have started a conversation. One of the stooges would have gone to warn Norman, and the other would have tailed Rudy.

So far it was going like clockwork and 104 was filling fast. There were ten stooges standing beside the windows, watching into the darkness and edging back out of sight as the fingers of the searchlights came probing past. The stooge at the north window could see the goon-box over the roof of the cooler. "Harry" would break somewhere among the dark trees almost directly behind. Outside the fence he watched two greatcoated sentries pacing their beats. One patrolled slowly from the goon-box down to the guardroom by the gate and back again, and the other paced in the other direction from the goon-box to the west fence. They would be more of a danger than the man up in the goon-box swinging his searchlight with his back to the exit.

About a quarter to eight, Torrens had his bad moment. The door of 104 opened and he saw a German unteroffizier walk in and stride down toward him, jackboots clumping heavily on the boards.

There were three escapers in their civilian clothes in the corridor, and they scuttled in panic into the nearest room. Torrens, petrified for a moment, recovered and headed down the corridor toward him to try to stop him, head him off, do anything to get him out of the block. He had a shattering, sick feeling that everything was lost, and then he saw it was Tobolski, the Pole.

A controller had forgotten to warn him that Tobolski was going as a German, in one of Tommy Guest's home-made uniforms. The uniform was a terrifyingly good imitation, with all the right swastikas and eagles and badges on it. If you compared it with a German uniform by daylight, you could see that the color was a shade bluer than the German gray.

Tobolski apologized, and Torrens, weak with relief, waved him into his allotted room. The people in that room nearly died when Tobolski opened the door and walked in. Tobolski was traveling with Wings Day, who had converted a Fleet Air Arm tunic into a double-breasted civilian coat and had a pair of gray trousers and a cloth cap. They planned to make for Stettin and stow away on a Swedish ship.

In Room 23, Roger, Marshall, and Johnny Bull were standing with Langford by the trap waiting for Crump to finish up below. Langford had pulled a couple of lockers out from the wall, blanking off the trap area from the window, and he had the blackout shutters closed.

Massey limped in to wish them au revoir and Godspeed. He didn't say much. The atmosphere was too tense. A week earlier a board of doctors had told him he was going to be repatriated soon because of his injured foot.

"I can't tell you how proud I am of you," he said quietly. "I'm hoping you will get to London before me, and you know how much I'll be looking forward to meeting you there."

He shook hands. "Now I'll get out of your way and give you a clear run," and he limped off down the corridor and into the snow.

At eight-thirty Crump was still somewhere in the tunnel. Marshall and Langford were fidgeting restlessly, but Bushell, vivacious and bright-eyed, was talking gaily. A little too gaily. He looked very smart in the gray lounge suit that he'd saved from Prague, a black overcoat (an R.A.F. coat dyed with boot polish), and a dark felt hat he had somehow scrounged through a contact. His papers described him as a French businessman, and, carrying a little attaché case filled with his kit, he really looked the part. His traveling companion was the Frenchman, Scheidhauer, a lieutenant in L'Armée de l'Air attached to the R.A.F. Scheidhauer knew people in Alsace and Paris, and they planned to link up with an escape chain in France.

Up by the trap the minutes dragged like hours, and even Roger was getting restive. They were behind schedule already. Langford climbed down the shaft and met Crump as he trolleyed back to the base.

"For God's sake, how much longer?" he asked.

"All O.K. except the new rope on the end trolleys," Crump said. "Bull and Marshall can fix them on when they go up. Save time."

Langford went back up and reported, and at eight-forty-five Bull and Marshall clambered down the ladder. Crump handed Bull the new trolley ropes and quietly shook his hand.

"Good luck," he said. "Wish to God I was going with you."

Bull lay flat on his belly on the trolley and paddled himself up to Piccadilly. He tugged on the rope, and Marshall hauled the trolley back, climbed on himself, and Bull hauled him up the tunnel. Bull went ahead to Leicester Square to fix the trolley rope.

Roger was next down the shaft, shaking hands with Crump. He hauled the trolley back, climbed on, holding his case out in front of him, tugged the rope, and Marshall hauled him along.

One by one, in strict order, men were clambering down the shaft and shooting up the tunnel on the shuttle service. There is a terrific sensation of speed rumbling up a tunnel on a trolley with your nose about three inches from the floor.

Eventually seventeen men were in position underground

and everything was ready to open up. In the end halfway house lay Johnny Bull and Marshall, side by side. Just behind, overlapping their feet, lay Bushell and Scheidhauer, then Valenta and Stevens, who were to follow them out, and Dowse who was to haul the next bodies up. In the tiny space they were packed like sardines. In Leicester Square a man was lying on the trolley, another man waiting to go next and a hauler. In Piccadilly, the same. At the base of the shaft there was a man on the trolley, Langford waiting to go next, the pumper, and Crump, in charge of operations.

It was about half-past nine when Roger set the ball rolling, speaking quietly as though it were an everyday occurrence, "I think you can have a shot at it now, Johnny. Everyone ought to be in position."

Bull grunted and crawled carefully through the blackout blankets. A couple of seconds later they heard him clambering up the shaft in the darkness. After he had opened up, Bull was to lie outside the hole in the trees to control the first people out. They were to climb up the ladder and stop just below the top so he could feel their heads in the darkness. When it was all clear, he would give them a gentle tap on the head, and out they would go. He had landed that job partly because he was traveling third class by train as a workman, and it didn't matter if he got his clothes dirty opening up and lying in the snow.

Down below the remaining six lay quietly, breathing slowly and deliberately because the air was thick and heavy. In the heat and the crush they were all running with sweat. They could hear Bull scraping at the roof boards at the top of the shaft with the special trowel that Crump had left there earlier in the day. Travis had carved it out of wood because it would be quieter than the metal ones.

He seemed to be scraping away up there for hours and the minutes dragged endlessly. They could hear him grunting a

172

little now and then. Johnny Marshall crawled through the blankets and called softly up the shaft:

"How long?"

"Can't loosen the damn top boards," Bull whispered down. "They're wet and they've jammed. Must be swollen with water."

He worked on in the darkness, standing precariously on the ladder and trying to lever out the unseen, tightly packed boards that roofed the shaft, the sweat running off him.

Time dragged, and down through the tunnel and up in the hut nerves were stretching tight. Everyone was thinking that something must be wrong but had no idea what it could be, and imaginations were running away with some of them. Crump was looking vainly up the tunnel trying to see what the matter was. He noticed the air by the tunnel roof getting thick and hazy and told the pumper to give it all he had.

People kept on calling down from the trap asking what the hell was wrong. They should have opened up at nine o'clock. It was now ten o'clock.

Marshall, up at the end, looked at his watch and saw that Bull had been up there half an hour.

"For God's sake go and see how he's getting on," Roger said, his voice a little strained.

Marshall went through the blankets again and, as he did so, he heard Bull coming down the ladder, and a moment later he stood beside Marshall at the bottom, breathing heavily.

"You have a go," he gasped. "I'm done in."

With hardly an inch of space to move it, Marshall laboriously stripped off his smart suit and climbed up the ladder in his long woolen underpants. He couldn't risk getting into a first-class train compartment with his clothes streaked with dirt. At the top he hooked an arm around the ladder and tugged at the roof boards. He kept at it for ten minutes before

173

he felt one shift just a fraction, and then he worked at it madly and felt it loosen bit by bit. In another five minutes it came away and then the others came easily.

Marshall eased himself sweatily down the ladder again, wiped his face on his shirt-tail, and started to dress while Bull went aloft and gently scraped away the last few inches of soil covering the top. Cramped in the halfway house the others heard the music of the sand as it pattered down to the floor of the shaft.

Bull felt his little shovel suddenly move unresistingly and knew he was through, and then the cool air was caressing his upturned, sweating face. He scraped a widening hole and in a minute he could see stars above—a glorious sight and an epic moment—and he hoisted himself up the last two rungs and stuck his head up into the open.

He got the shock of his life. The surveyors had blundered. "Harry" was too short! Instead of being a few yards inside the wood, he saw that he was out in the open, ten feet short of the dim line of trees. He looked back at the compound, and the full tragedy of the situation hit him. The goon-box was only fifteen yards away, a stilt-legged monster outlined against the glow of the searchlight. He could see the German guard's shoulders and his ugly square helmet as he peered over the rail into the compound, swiveling the beam of light.

Bull felt naked out there. He ducked his head and softly felt his way back down the shaft. Crawling behind the blankets, he broke the news. There was a stunned silence.

"God, we can't be short. We can't be," Marshall said. "Right out in the open?"

"Go and look," Bull said tiredly. "You'll see."

All of them felt the sick dismay. It looked as though every-thing was a flop . . . six hundred men working every day for a year . . . the escape fever of those who had been behind the

174

wire for up to five years. They couldn't quite grasp the reality of it.

Bushell recovered first.

"Could you be seen from the goon-box?" he asked.

"Couldn't be certain," Bull said, "but I think you would sooner or later. It's dark all right but a man couldn't lie on the snow for long. He'd show out against it so bloody plainly."

"Well, we can do two things," Roger said. "Either go ahead now and get as many out as we can before we're caught or put a couple out and let 'em close up the outside. Then we can dig on a few more feet, put up another shaft and break next no-moon period . . . if we get away with it that long."

They talked it over in whispers for a few minutes, shying away from the idea of postponing everything. Worse than the anticlimax was the probability that Rubberneck would find the tunnel. They all knew about the wobbly trap.

It was Roger who thought of the vital factor.

"We can't put it off now," he said. "All the papers are date-stamped. They won't be any good next month, and we won't get far without them. We've got to go tonight." He paused and then went on slowly, thinking as he talked.

"We've got to have a new way of getting people out without a man lying by the hole in the snow. Someone's got to control it from outside somehow."

And funnily enough it was the ferrets who gave the answer.

"Just a minute," said Johnny Bull, with dawning inspiration. "About ten feet from the hole right by the edge of the wood, I saw one of those spy nests the ferrets put up while we were digging 'Tom.' Put the controller behind that."

"Pretty remote control," Roger commented.

"Tie a rope to the ladder," Bull said, his voice rising in excitement. "The controller holds the other end. When it's all clear, he gives a couple of tugs and the bloke crawls out."

It was so obviously the solution that Roger agreed on the spot.

Cramped against the side of the halfway house, he fumbled through the buttons of his greatcoat to a pocket and brought out a pencil. Inching over onto his back, he began to write the new procedure in scrawling print in the wall:

"Pause at the top of shaft. Hold signal rope tied to top rung. On receiving two tugs, crawl out. Follow rope to shelter."

He spoke to Dowse.

"Warn everyone coming through of the new procedure. Make sure they understand. Tell your relief hauler to do the same when he comes through and make sure he tells the man who relieves him." He spoke generally, "Everything clear?" and there were quiet grunts of satisfaction.

"Well, here we go," said Bull, and crawled out through the blankets and up the shaft, carrying a long coil of plaited rope. He tied one end to the top rung and cautiously stuck his head out of the hole to get the lay of the land. It seemed to be clear, and he gently eased himself onto the snow and crawled noiselessly till he was behind the shelter of the ferret fence, paying out the rope as he went. The snow fell wet and the crust broke through easily.

The sentry in the goon-box was still looking into the compound. He did not seem to be worrying about the woods behind. Probably he never thought to look there. His searchlights roamed over the vorlager, up and down the fences, and then joined the beams from the other goon-boxes playing over the huts and the churned-up snow in the compound.

Bull heard a man approaching from the west and then saw him dimly, a German soldier walking along the wire, the barrel of his slung rifle sticking up behind his shoulder. He walked to the sentry tower, stamped his feet once or twice and walked back. A few moments later the other sentry came into sight in the other direction, reached the goon-box, and turned back.

Neither of them seemed to be glancing toward either the woods or the compound, but just tramping in frigid unhappiness up and down, up and down.

Over the top of the sheltering brushwood, Bull could see the black outline of the hole in the snow. When he lowered his head it narrowed, and he thought that from the eye level of the sentries it would not be very obvious. He waited a while to see what would happen, and shortly the two sentries appeared again, one shortly after the other, and then turned and tramped away.

As soon as they were out of sight, he tugged sharply twice on the rope and a moment later Marshall snaked over the edge of the hole, keeping low, and crawled on his belly, keeping one hand on the rope till he was beside Bull. Marshall stayed with him a while, his eyes getting accustomed to the dark. He put his lips close to Bull's ears and whispered, "Doesn't seem too bad."

"No," Bull answered. "I think we might get away with it."

The wire patrollers came into sight again.

"I have to wait till they're both out of sight before I can get anyone out," Bull said. "It's going to make it a bit slow."

"No help for it," Marshall whispered. He waited till the sentries were out of sight again. "Well, see you in London." He felt for Bull's hand. "Good luck, Johnny." Then, picking up the rest of the coil of rope, he crawled off into the darkness of the wood, paying out the rope behind. About sixty yards inside the trees, he came to the end of the rope and tied it to the trunk of a tree, pulling in the slack. He gave it a couple of tugs to let Bull know he was in position and waited.

Back at the ferret fence, Bull tugged on the shaft line, and Valenta crawled out and joined him behind the brushwood.

"Marshall's up there," Bull said, and Valenta crawled off, keeping the rope running loosely throught one hand so he could receive signals if Germans came close. If he felt a tug he was to freeze on his belly in the snow, and wait till he got two tugs, the all clear.

He joined Marshall at the end. A couple of minutes later, Bushell arrived.

"Doesn't look too bad," Roger whispered. "I think it'll be all right. Off you go. See you back home. Good luck."

Marshall and Valenta crawled another hundred yards deeper into the woods before they stood upright and walked swiftly away. Marshall had his compass cupped in his hand, and they followed the luminous needle, heading north. Less than half a mile through the woods lay Sagan Station. They were catching a train down through Hirschberg to Czechoslovakia, where Valenta had friends.

Bushell was joined by Scheidhauer and they waited, sheltering behind two trees by the end of the rope, till Stevens, the South African, reached them. Then they headed north after Marshall and Valenta while Stevens waited for his partner.

So it went on.

and makeshift suitcases, smoking and trying to look natural—and looking, in fact, like refugees from the underworld.

At quarter-past ten Crump felt cold air on his cheek. He turned and peered up the tunnel, and there was no mistaking the cool draft sweeping past his face. A great exhilaration swept over him, and he lifted his head and whispered up the shaft, "They're through. They've broken through. Tell Torrens."

Torrens came and leaned over the trap.

"You're sure?"

"Yes," Crump called throatily. "You ought to feel the draft down here. They should start moving soon. Warn the next man, but don't send him down till I tell you."

They waited nearly a quarter of an hour, and it wasn't till half-past ten that the man on the trolley at the base felt the rope tug as the hauler in Piccadilly signaled. He tugged back and went rolling softly up to the halfway house over the blanket-deadened rails.

Crump called up, "Next please," and a few seconds later a bulky shape was moving down the ladder.

The trolley was back in a minute, and another man lay his belly on it and waited.

Gradually the movement got under way.

Torrens had two runners by his desk to carry instructions. As one escaper crawled down the shaft Torrens sent a runner to warn the next man on the list to be ready in five minutes. The man struggled into his kit, whispered farewells around the room, and was ready to go when the runner came back for him.

He went to the door by the trap and waited till Crump called for him. Davison, at the trap with another list, checked his name and gave him the patter: "All right, now sit down here on the edge of the trap. Feel that ledge a foot below with your feet. Stand with your right foot in the far corner. Feel the

BACK in 104 the tension had been nearly [...]
able. The first men had been up at the far end for over [...]
and there wasn't a sign of anything happening. Peo[...]
calling down the shaft to Crump, asking what was wr[...]
Crump, harried and fearing the worst, called back in a [...]
whisper, "For Christ's sake wait, will you. How the [...]
know what's happening?"

Shortly after ten o'clock the lock-up guard went ar[...]
camp as usual, shutting and barring all the hut doors. [...]
bothered to look into the huts as a rule. He walked u[...]
and the stooges held their breath while he slammed t[...]
shut, slipped the bar in position, and walked off. It h[...]
lieve the tension a little.

Torrens set up a table outside the trap room and [...]
himself there for the night. Now that the huts were lo[...]
only the hundfuehrer would be left in the compo[...]
overflow of bodies in the rooms moved into the corri[...]
of all Torrens ordered a dozen of them to lay blanket[...]
the corridor floor to muffle the sound of anyone movir[...]
Everyone took his boots off.

The corridor was an amazing sight; bodies lying all [...]
floor, Tobolski in his unteroffizier's uniform stepping [...]
in his socks over people in rough suits, and plus f[...]
types in berets and cloth caps, sitting up beside blar[...]

top rung of the ladder with your left foot. Got it? All right now, let it take your weight. It's quite strong. Turn your body and down you go."

At the bottom Crump showed them how to lie on the trolley and hold their kit. When they reached Piccadilly the hauler there had the trolley from Leicester Square, and the escaper crawled on, rolled along on the next stage, and changed trolleys again for the last lap.

The haulers were all experienced tunnelers like Noble and Rees and Birkland, so that everything underground would go smoothly. As each hauler pulled ten people past him, the eleventh, twelfth, and thirteenth men successively relieved them, and the old haulers continued on down the tunnel and out. The controller outside the hole behind the ferret fence got twenty men out, and then the twenty-first relieved him, and so on.

It wasn't long before Crump realized that they were falling badly behind schedule. Barring hitches, Bushell had aimed at getting a man out every three or four minutes, but the first hour soon settled those hopes. Only six people were called in that hour. The suitcases were the trouble, and it looked as though they were going to be the trouble for some time.

The first thirty-seven were all going by train, and they nearly all had suitcases, made mostly out of cardboard or plywood and rubbed with boot polish. Nearly all of them found trouble in handling the cases on the trolleys. Some of them dropped them and some got the corners dangerously wedged against shoring frames. Trying to hold them out in front, several men overbalanced on the trolley platform, lifted the wheels and derailed them. The derailing was the worst.

The tunnel was so cramped that the men on the trolleys couldn't do anything about getting the wheels back on again. The hauler would feel the rope tighten and then jib altogether, and usually he knew what the trouble was. He had to crawl down the tunnel and get the man on the trolley to take his weight on his hands and toes while he fitted the wheels back on the rails. Then the hauler crawled backward to his halfway house, started hauling again, and like as not the trolley would be derailed again before it reached him.

Crump turned once to see who was next and was surprised to see not a man but a suitcase. In fact, not so much a suitcase as a trunk. Behind it grinned a strange face which he recognized after a second or two as Tim Walenn without his great mustache, which he had shaved off for the occasion.

"Where the hell d'you think you're going with this?" Crump demanded with a blend of wonder, exasperation, and amusement.

"Home, I hope," Tim said soothingly, "but I expect to the cooler, actually."

"You'll never bloody well get that thing through," Crump said.

"Don't worry. I'll cope."

"Not a hope," said Crump. "Can't be done," and they argued for a couple of minutes.

In the end Crump sent the case up on the trolley by itself, and Tim followed after.

Nerves were affecting a lot of them. Even some of the veteran diggers who had been riding on trolleys for months found themselves fumbling and getting stuck.

Rockland and Muller, the two Norwegians, went through very smoothly, Muller with a parting affectionate glance at the pump he had designed. They both looked very smart in plus fours. Neely, a Fleet Air Arm man, was another who went through smoothly.

A little after midnight the men in the hut heard the sirens and groaned. There had been no air raid alarms for a fortnight, and Roger had been praying that this would be a free night too. As the wail of the sirens died, the stooges at the windows heard faintly the rumble of the first bombs dropping on Berlin, sixty miles away, and almost in the same moment a German over in the kommandantur switched the power off, and all the lights went out.

Down in the tunnel it was Stygian, terrifying blackness, and everything stopped at once. Further progress was impossible. In the halfway houses, the confinement, the stuffiness, the fear of moving in case of a fall combining with the blackness gave rise to claustrophobia, and nerves were at snapping point again.

Wings Day, who had just been about to set off for Piccadilly, stayed and helped Crump light the fat lamps stored in the shaft and took them up on the trolley with him. His nerves seemed steady as a rock, and Crump watched with thankfulness as he receded into the tunnel, a moving, flickering pool of light.

Wings carried the lamps right through the tunnel, leaving one in each halfway house. When he got to the far end he found the hauler there had vanished. When the lights had gone and his relief did not arrive the hauler had apparently thought that something had gone wrong or that the Germans had entered the hut and found the tunnel, so he decided to leave. It was just lucky that Wings was experienced. He hauled through his partner and stayed to pull the next hauler up before he continued on his way. By the time men were moving slowly through again, a good thirty-five minutes had been lost, and, but for Day's coolness, the time lost would have been a lot more.

There was one cheerful side to it. The camp boundary lights and searchlights were off too, leaving everything in blackness, and the guards by the wire were watching closely all the time into the compound, looking for optimists trying wire jobs in the darkness. The exit controller took advantage of it to speed up the departure.

The stoppages had already dislocated the plans of most of the escapers. The train travelers all had certain trains to catch and apart from four or five of the early ones they had all missed them. Some were able to catch later trains, but the delay meant they wouldn't be as far away as they had hoped to be when the alarm was raised.

Up above it had been time for camp "lights out" at midnight and Torrens ordered "lights out" procedure. All the blackout shutters were opened (they had to be, because it was the usual practice), all fat lamps were doused, and everyone in the rooms had to stay in a bunk. No movement was allowed except in the dark corridor, and there was little enough movement there. The whole floor was covered with bodies huddled in blankets trying to snatch a few minutes' sleep before their turn came.

Not many were sleeping. They were too keyed up. Nearly all of them were hardarsers, and they knew they weren't going on any picnic. The trek across snow-clad country would beat most of them, and there were bound to be a few Gestapo beatings.

By the windows the stooges saw the hundfuehrer and his dog several times within a few yards of the window of Room 23. The stooge whispered a warning, and everyone froze out of sight but the German never came near enough to look in.

Crump had had his fingers crossed for hours praying there would be no falls but about one-thirty the luck gave out. Tom Kirby-Green was halfway between Piccadilly and Leicester Square when he moved position slightly on the trolley and the rear wheels rose and came off the rails. He tried to squeeze himself off the platform and back to fix it, and his burly shoulders caught on a damaged box frame and tore it out. The roof collapsed and down came the sand, bringing down about three more feet of roofing and more sand crashed down.

It was a bad fall. In two seconds Kirby-Green was buried from legs to shoulders and the tunnel was blocked. Wrapped in all his escape kit the big man couldn't move, but luckily his head was clear and he could breathe.

Up in Leicester Square, Birkland, who had been hauling him, felt the rope tighten and stop. Looking down the tunnel he could not see the dim light of the fat lamp in Piccadilly and knew that the tunnel was blocked. He crawled down to the accident and slowly pulled Kirby-Green clear, then made the big man crawl over him up to the halfway house. Birkland started patching up the tunnel, working like a sweating madman in almost total darkness, feeling where the boards had come away and then probing for them in the fallen sand.

It was a dangerous job in the darkness, with a constant risk of more sand coming away, burying him alone there and wrecking the tunnel. As far as he could judge there was already a dome about three feet high over the fallen roof. He got the side boards in place again and then some of the roof boards and started packing the fallen sand on top. It was a solid hour before he had finished, soaked in sweat and sand and breathing heavily with exhaustion.

Just as he was finishing the sirens wailed again, sounding the all clear and over in the kommandantür a German switched on the current and the tunnel was flooded with light. The cable, luckily, had survived the fall. Birkland found himself, as usual, left with a pile of sand that could not be packed back above the roof. He did the only thing possible and spread it out over the floor of the tunnel for several feet between the rails, then crawled backward to Leicester Square, and the shuttle service started again.

About a quarter to three the last of the suitcase carriers went through, and the rate speeded up a little as the blanket brigade started. They all carried a single blanket rolled and tied tightly and slung on a string around their necks. It left their hands free so they could hold themselves more steadily on the trolley.

There were still too many stoppages. Some of the men

185

hadn't tied their blanket rolls as they'd been shown, but had made them too long and the ends jammed between their shoulders and the walls of the tunnel. They had to keep freeing themselves every couple of feet and one man took seven minutes to go a hundred feet. Others had the string too loose about their necks so that the blankets dangled under the platform of the trolley, caught under the wheels, and the next thing they knew the trolley was derailed and they were nearly strangled.

Some of them had so much food and spare kit packed around them that they looked like swollen editions of Falstaff, and down at the base of the shaft Crump ruthlessly went through their corpulent forms emptying out their accessories till he thought they were lean enough. The Dodger was one of his victims. He was swaddled in so much stuff that he looked like a cocoon, but, courteous as ever and with only the most considerate of protests he submitted to Crump's reducing treatment and then went trundling smoothly through. Pop Green was another, but after Crump's merciless fingers had done their work he, too, went through with only minor trouble.

Men had been moving for over four hours now. There were less than three hours to first light and less than fifty had reached the far end. Now the hardarsers were going through, the procedure outside was altered slightly. At the end of the rope in the wood, men waited until a party of ten had assembled, one of whom had been specially briefed on leading them through the wood, around the west side of the camp, past a French and a Jewish compound, and on to a little dirt road leading south toward Czechoslovakia.

The numbers had just passed the half-century mark when Cookie Long stuck on the trolley within twenty feet of Piccadilly. Bob Nelson, who was hauling, tried to pull him gently through, but a box frame suddenly dragged away and the sand crashed down, burying Long. He was able to drag himself off

186

the trolley and crawl up to the halfway house and Nelson crawled down to the fall. It wasn't quite as bad as the first one, but working flat out it took him half an hour to clear it.

Two more prisoners were stuck soon after that but eased themselves through without further falls. As the fifty-seventh man was being hauled in the middle section a trolley rope broke, and there was another hold-up while it was mended.

Crump climbed up to the top and saw Torrens.

"Not much more than two hours to go," he said. "We won't make the hundred at this rate. We'll have to do something drastic. Blanket rolls are causing most of the trouble so from now on blankets are out. They'll just have to take their great-coats and nothing more."

"It's a bit desperate," Torrens said.

"It's got to be desperate," said Crump.

The hardarsers took it with good grace. The wakeful ones padded up to the desk and asked what their chances were of getting out. By this time Crump knew they wouldn't be able to beat the century and told most of them to go back, forget about it, and get some sleep.

He dived back down the shaft, and without the blanket rolls, the rate immediately speeded up. Then there was another fall in the second section, and Cookie Long, who had relieved Nelson hauling in Piccadilly, crawled up to the scene. It wasn't a bad one, and working in the usual mad sweat he fixed it in about twenty minutes. There wasn't any more serious trouble after that, and men began to go through comparatively swiftly, as swiftly, that is, as the exit man at the far end could dare to signal them out.

About four o'clock, Roy Langlois, Number 60, went through and relieved the exit man behind the ferret fence. Lang had signaled two men out of the exit, when guards started to tramp along the road only about seven or eight yards from the hole. They were going past in ones and twos and didn't seem to have anything in particular on their minds. Lang puzzled about it for a while and then realized that it was guard-changing.

It meant another hold-up. For the next twenty minutes guards were strolling back along the road after being relieved, and Lang only got about two people out in that time. Then the last sentry tramped past, and the exodus from the hole quickened once more.

At half-past four, Lang jerked his head up in fright as he heard the sentry suddenly start shouting in the goon-box. He wasn't looking into the compound now but leaning over the side, and for a terrifying moment Lang thought he had been spotted.

He saw the guard wasn't talking to him but calling to one of the sentries patrolling the wire who was approaching. The patroller climbed up into the goon-box, and the searchlight sentry clumped down the steps, and to Lang's horror turned straight across the road toward the hole.

Langlois' heart was choking him in his throat. The German kept coming straight toward him in the gloom. He was right on top of the hole, and then he casually turned away as though he wasn't worried about it. A bare four feet from the black opening in the snow he squatted down, busying himself with one of the less dignified functions of man. The exit was just to his side and he took absolutely no notice of it. Lang, a bare ten feet away, burrowed face down in the snow wishing to God his heart wouldn't thunder so loudly, couldn't believe it was real.

The German must have been blind—what actually happened, of course, was that he'd been looking through a searchlight beam for hours and couldn't see a thing in the darkness after the dazzle. A broad black trail of slush led away from the hole showing where the prisoners—the ex-prisoners—had crawled away, and out of the hole itself Lang could see, against the glare of the searchlight, a thick column of steam rising, a peculiarity of all newly opened tunnels.

For five minutes the guard crouched there communing with Mother Nature, and then he hitched up his pants, strolled casually back to the goon-box, and clumped up the steps. The patroller who had taken his place clumped down and resumed his monotonous walk, and Lang breathed again for the first time in five minutes.

Back in 104, Torrens had ticked off Number 83 down the shaft. They were going through fairly smoothly now, and there were few hitches. Crump looked at his watch and climbed up the shaft to check on the light outside. It was still dark, but he knew it couldn't last much longer and he lingered by the window, trying to keep his eyes away from the searchlights and fix them on the wood to see if the trees were becoming clearer.

About five minutes to five he thought there was a shade more light coming off the snow and imagined he could see the trees across the wire in a little more detail. He called Davison over.

"I think it *is* getting a bit clearer," Davison said.

"Right. About time to pack up," Crump said. "Get the next three down and that's the lot. If we can get 'em all out of the way without being seen, the Huns won't know a thing till appell, and the boys'll have an extra four hours before the hunt's on."

Davison hurried the next three down—Michael Ormond, a tough New Zealander who used to play glamorous girl parts in the camp theater, Muckle Muir, and Tim Newman. Newman was just vanishing up the tunnel on the trolley when a rifle shot cracked across the snow. It came from outside the wire in the direction of the tunnel.

☐ CHAPTER 17 ☐

J UST before ten to five, a big burley air gunner called Reavell Carter climbed out of the hole, went crawling past Lang, and followed the rope into the wood to the rendezvous tree. He was to lead the next party of ten through the trees to the road running south from the camp.

A couple of minutes later Oggy Ogilvy, a Canadian, emerged and snaked past Lang toward the tree. Next was Mick Shand, New Zealand Spitfire pilot. Len Trent (Squadron Leader Trent, V.C., D.F.C.), who followed him, had just crawled clear of the hole when the sentry who'd been patrolling the east beat along the wire came into sight again. For some unknown reason, he was walking on the near side of the road, along the edge of the wood. No sentry had done that yet. If he kept on going he must walk across the hole.

Lang could make out the buttons and cross belts over his greatcoat and went even colder than his long vigil in the snow had made him. He tugged sharply twice on each rope and Shand, halfway to the tree behind him, and Trent, just outside the hole, froze where they lay. The German kept steadily on. He was ten yards away, and Lang felt his eyes were sticking out like organ stops. The German was seven . . . six . . . five yards away, and still he came on and still he hadn't seen anything. He seemed to be looking dead ahead and not at the ground at all.

His boots were crushing methodically through the snow,

190

left, right, left, and then he put a boot down within a foot of the edge of the hole *and still didn't see it*, and his next foot missed by a couple of inches treading on Trent, lying doggo and quaking by the hole. *Still the guard didn't see him.* It was unbelievable.

He took another pace—and then he came out of his coma. He must have noticed the slushy track the bodies had made through the snow. A little muttering came out of him as he swung toward it, and in the same movement he shrugged the rifle off his shoulder and into his hands. Then he must have seen Shand lying on the track. He lifted his rifle and was about to fire when Reavell Carter, who could dimly see the drama from the tree, jumped into sight waving his arms.

"*Nicht schiessen, Posten!*" he yelled. "*Nicht schiessen!*" ("Don't shoot, sentry! Don't shoot!")

His sudden appearance gave the German the shock of his life, and his rifle jerked upward as he fired. The bullet went wild. So did the quiet woodland scene. Shand bounced up from where he lay on the track and made a crouching dash for freedom, dodging in and out of the pine trees. Ogilvy jumped up from behind the far tree where he had been burrowing into the snow and did the same thing, tossing away excess kit as he ran.

As they vanished among the dark trees, Reavell Carter came forward—there was nothing else he could do—and then, right beside the paralyzed guard and still unseen, Trent slowly rose to his feet. The guard saw him, jumped about a foot in the air, and stood rooted again, staggered with shock. He was a simple peasant type and quite speechless.

A second later, Lang—with no option—also stood up behind the ferret fence about ten feet away. The guard, seeing him, could only shake his head unbelievingly, and then he saw the hole in the ground right at his feet, and his mouth opened and shut like a fish.

For about three comical seconds he stayed paralyzed, and then he recovered, whipped out a torch and shone it down the hole. Just below the surface, hanging on to the ladder, was Bob McBride, who was to have been next man out, the eightieth.

The sentry fished up his whistle and blew it shrilly, then found enough presence of mind to point his rifle at McBride and beckon him out. McBride crawled sheepishly out, and the sentry covered the four of them with his rifle. He was making hoarse speaking sounds, but no one knew what he was saying, least of all, probably, the sentry.

Lang heard the guard up in the goon-box frenziedly telephoning the German guardroom, and along the road from the guardroom by the gate a couple of hundred yards away a horde of German soldiers came running. The man in the goon-box yelled to them, and they fanned out into the woods. The sentry prodded his rifle at the four and nodded meaningfully down the road. They turned, hands in the air, and trudged off.

Back in 104 a hush had followed the shot. Around the trap the silence lasted perhaps three seconds as the people in the room, frozen into the attitudes they had been in, looked at each other. Crump said quietly, with magnificent understatement, "That appears to be a shot."

"That was indeed a bloody shot," someone else said, his voice sharpening as he spoke.

"Christ!" Crump was the first to move. "Someone's got it. Davison, get the blokes back from down the tunnel." And as Davison slipped down the ladder Crump spoke to Torrens in the doorway.

"Get everyone in the hut to start destroying their papers and all their incriminating kit."

He darted over to the window but could see nothing. The cooler was in the way of the tunnel exit. He crossed back to the trap, knowing that most people in the tunnel wouldn't have heard the shot and would still be traveling through. As he was vanishing into it a stooge from the front room called out that a mob of Germans had come out of the guardroom and were running along the wire toward the exit of the tunnel.

As it happened, the people in the end halfway house *had* heard the shot. Denys Maw, Number 81, had been just about to crawl into the exit shaft when right above his head, and echoing down the shaft came the shattering crack of the rifle. One awful thought flashed through his mind. "The bastards! They've known all along and they're plugging each bloke as he crawls out."

He realized immediately that couldn't be or they'd have heard it before. The guards must have just found the hole. Maw turned back into the halfway house where two other people, the hauler and the next man out, had reached the same conclusion.

"Let's get to hell out of here," he said, and the other two needed no persuading. One man lay on the trolley and propelled himself back to Leicester Square, and then the trolley was hauled back and the next man paddled himself down. Maw hauled the trolley back and set off on the return journey himself.

So the shuttle service was reversed as the men started to scurry like moles back toward the compound. For a few minutes, however, the people in the first section of the tunnel still didn't know the flap was on, and they did not find out till people started to scuttle back from the far end. Meanwhile Crump and Davison, at the base of the shaft, were trying to inform them.

Peering up the tunnel, Crump could just see the trolley up by Piccadilly with Newman's bulky shape lying on it. He howled; "Come back! We've been spotted. Pass the word along."

His voice was muffled in the long, narrow space, and the man on the trolley could just hear a faint voice but didn't know what it was saying. A vague, muffled shout came back to Crump in reply.

"Come back! Come back!" Crump howled again. "It's all up. The tunnel's been found."

Again the muffled answer. It developed into a shouting match, and neither man could make out what the other was saying. Crump grabbed the trolley rope and tried to haul it back with Newman still on it, but Newman would have none of it. He was on his way out, and he wasn't coming back for anyone. He grabbed hold of the rails and held the trolley firmly. Crump shouted again and hauled back more strongly. He heaved and heaved, and then the rope snapped.

Crump realized there was no point crawling up the tunnel after him. People at the far end would soon find out the game was up and come pouring back, and he would only block the exodus if he crawled up. Newman sensed that the rope had broken and began to realize something was seriously wrong. He was just able to twist his head over his shoulder to look back and saw Crump beckoning frantically in the mouth of the tunnel. Crump, with enormous relief, saw him begin to paddle the trolley backward, and in a few seconds Newman emerged feet first into the shaft.

"What the hell . . ." he started, red-faced and sweating.

"Tunnel's spotted," Crump snapped. "Someone's been shot out there. Duck up to the block."

As Newman went up the ladder Crump tossed the trolley into the dispersal chamber. With the rope gone, it was better out of the way. He looked up the tunnel again and saw a body crawling down. Soon a face stuck out into the shaft and the man scrambled out, perspiration pouring off him. He'd come all the way from the end halfway house.

"We're spotted," he said superfluously. "I think the ferrets are coming down. There's someone just behind me."

There were more sounds in the tunnel, and Crump saw another body crawling down. In a few seconds Muckle Muir's head stuck out.

"It's all up," he gasped. "They've found the hole, and I think ferrets are coming down. There's someone just behind me."

More sounds in the tunnel. Mike Ormond appeared and breathlessly hauled himself out. "They've found us," he said. "Ferrets are coming along."

One by one they came crawling down the tunnel, panting and sweating, and as each one emerged he burst out excitedly, "Look out! There's a ferret just behind me."

Each time it was only another prisoner, but Crump felt his scalp prickling. The last three back were Red Noble, Denys Maw, and Shag Rees. Shag had been hauling in Leicester Square and had had a nasty moment. When he heard Maw returning from the far end, Shag didn't know whether it was a prisoner or a ferret. He took the light bulb out of its socket in the halfway house and squeezed himself against the wall in the darkness to get out of the way of any bullet that came whistling down. Unable to stand the tension any longer, he called, "Who's that?"

Maw answered reassuringly and said he was the last man. Back they scuttled toward 104, Shag expecting a bullet at any moment. When they emerged at the top Crump closed the trap door and moved the heavy stove back over it. He and Davison picked all the blankets off the floor and tossed them on the bunks, then slid the lockers that had shielded the trap back against the wall.

Crump went out into the corridor and thought for one frightened moment the block was on fire. There were a dozen fires in the corridor and more in the rooms as people burned their papers and maps, and the hut was full of smoke and lit palely by little flames. They crushed some of their compasses and tried to hide others and their German money in paillasses. They tore civilian buttons off their converted clothes and either hid or burned them.

A few leapt out of windows—strictly against orders—into the lightening compound and dashed back to their huts. The guard in the goon-box by the cooler sent a couple of bullets whistling after one of them, and the practice stopped.

Everyone was suddenly still, looking at the door of the hut. They heard the bar withdrawn, and the door opened and in walked the hundfuehrer and his dog. The dog looked unconcerned but the hundfuehrer stood there a moment uncertainly, eyeing everyone warily. He was a simple soul and didn't quite know what to do. Rather halfheartedly he told a few people to go into the rooms, and they largely ignored him. Wandering up and down the corridor, he collected greatcoats off the hooks and piled them in a heap by the hut door. The Alsatian knew what to do. He lay on the coats and went to sleep.

The hundfuehrer could think of nothing more. He sat down near the coats and contemplated his toes.

Now that the show was over the tension had relaxed and about 140 prisoners sat around in the rooms, talking, laughing, and letting off steam. They knew they would be searched soon and probably sent to the cells on bread and water, and after a while the main occupation was eating escape rations. The stuff was too concentrated to get much down and before long no one could swallow another mouthful. In Room 23 Crump heard a faint scratching and scuffling under the trap door. The ferrets had arrived. As they had found their own way there, Crump decided to let them find their own way out again.

In the guardroom by the gate, Von Lindeiner was standing in front of the four men caught at the tunnel mouth. He was red-faced, shouting at them, and little flecks were flying off his lips. They stood up straight at attention and kept quiet, unable to make out much of what he was saying. He was nearly incoherent. Lang caught one part.

"So, you do not want to stay in this camp"—Von Lindeiner's voice was high and shaky. "You wish to be out so the Gestapo will get you. They will shoot you—get rid of the lot of you."

He went on in that strain. No Kommandant, to a prisoner, is a good man, but I think Von Lindeiner was. At least as good as a Kommandant could be in Hitler's Germany. It was not his fault if he could not give us enough food, or if someone went wire-happy and was shot by a trigger-happy guard. And he knew the tunnel was going to break him and that his own arrest could not be far off.

About six o'clock the first helmeted German column came tramping through the trees from the kommandantur into the compound, roughly seventy of them, in full riot squad kit. This time they were carrying mounted machine guns as well as tommyguns. They fanned out through the compound, closing the shutters around every window, and then formed a silent ring around 104. Four squads set up machine guns on tripods covering the hut doors.

Von Lindeiner walked into the compound, very upright and moving fast, staring straight ahead, still red in the face. Broili was just behind him, pale in contrast and almost running to keep up. And then the Kommandant's adjutant, Major Simoleit, and Pieber, who was looking owlishly solemn. Rubber-neck came running up, and behind him marched another squad. As Von Lindeiner stalked up to the hut, the guards all stiffened to attention. There was a succession of salutes, a rattle of boot-clicking, and all the ferrets drew their revolvers.

Several guards threw the doors open and clumped inside yelling the old familiar "Raus! Raus!"

One by one the prisoners started to emerge, half expecting the chatter guns to open up on them. Snow was just starting to fall, and about a dozen ferrets were waiting for them. As each man came out a ferret grabbed him and made him strip naked in the snow, even to his boots. The ferrets closely examined every garment, and anything that looked as though it had been modified to look like civilian wear or could remotely be an aid to escape they tossed on a pile to one side. A lot of the boys lost their pants and were left standing up in their woolen long johns. It began to have a faintly funny side but not so that you'd burst out laughing.

Simoleit came running agitatedly out of 104, streaked past the prisoners in the snow, and headed toward 101. He was a dapper little man shaped like an undernourished gorilla, and his back view, running in breeches and boots, looked absurdly bandy-legged. He burst into Bill Jennen's room and breathlessly announced that Unteroffizier Pfelz had gone down the far end of the tunnel an hour before and they couldn't find the entrance trap to let him out. He would suffocate—die. Herr Major Jennens was to come at once and get him out.

Big rough Jennens was still in his bunk. Slowly, stretching and yawning, he roused himself and demanded what the hell Pfelz was doing down the tunnel. (It was amazing what Jennens got away with by shouting and banging his fist. He was always doing it, and the Germans always respected him.)

Simoleit explained that Unteroffizier Pfelz had gone down to see if any more prisoners were left there. Would Herr Jen-

198

nens be good enough to hurry. The Unteroffizier would be suffocating. Simoleit was hopping up and down in his distress.

Jennens leisurely dressed and leisurely followed Simoleit down to 104, where he found that Red Noble had taken pity on his old friend Charlie Pfelz and was lifting the trap door. Down at the bottom of the shaft a relieved Charlie blinked up at them and scrambled up the ladder. He went out, saluted smartly and told the Kommandant what he had seen. Then he grinned at Rubberneck. A big moment for Charlie. He loathed Rubberneck.

Von Lindeiner had his pistol in his hand now and so did the other officers as well as the ferrets. Broili's hand was shaking so much he probably couldn't have hit a barn door, but Rubberneck's hand looked remarkably steady, and the knuckles were quite white showing that he had already taken up the initial pull on the trigger. He was in a shocking temper, and his face was mottled red. Rubberneck, like the Kommandant, knew he was going to have a lot of explaining to do.

Shag Rees and Red Noble came out of the hut together, and when Rubberneck noticed them you could practically see his hackles rising. Red and Shag were his personal enemies. They had always given him trouble, and he'd sent them both to the cooler a couple of times. He rushed over as they were being searched, grabbed the shoulders of their coats, and pushed them around as he tried to tear the coats off.

Red and Shag both wrenched themselves away and swung defiantly out of his reach. A guard raised his rifle and squinted down the sights at Shag, and Rubberneck drew a bead on Red with his pistol. There was one of those long, deadly silences while the incident was on the verge of ending with a couple of shots, and then the barrels lowered slowly as the tension relaxed, and Red and Shag stripped in peace. The guard took their trousers and slung them aside, leaving them in their underpants.

Von Lindeiner had watched the incident, and his face went a shade richer in color.

"Cooler," he said curtly (funny how even the Kommandant used that word). Four guards marched Red and Shag off to the cells.

When the search was over, the prisoners stayed standing in the snow in three ranks, surrounded by guards. Some of them without coat or trousers were shivering. No one knew what was coming next, and there wasn't much humor left in the situation until Johnny Hutson, a fair-haired little Spitfire pilot from Kenya, relieved the atmosphere by making little mocking noises in his throat. Von Lindeiner saw and heard him.

"Cooler," he said tersely, with a face like thunder, and the guards marched Johnny off.

There was a friendly feud between Hutson and a young London bombardier, a tousle-headed kid of about nineteen, not long out of school. He couldn't hide a grin as Hutson was marched off, and Von Lindeiner saw him too.

"Cooler," he said again with the same black look, and two more guards marched Horace off; the grin now transferred to Hutson's face.

Von Lindeiner spoke to the prisoners near him. "If there are any more disturbances here," he said, "I will personally shoot two of you."

There were no more disturbances. Von Lindeiner meant it.

After a while, Eichacher brought out the identification photographs and checked all the men standing in the snow. Von Lindeiner left them standing there another two hours while they made a photographic check of everyone else in the compound to find out who was missing.

When they reported to Von Lindeiner that seventy-six people had escaped, he walked, frozen-faced, out of the compound. Shortly after, the 140 were marched down to the gate, and there they stopped again. Pieber remained with them, in charge, and looked reproachfully through his glasses at them.

"Ah, shentlemen, shentlemen!" he said. "You should not do this thing. It makes only trouble. The Kommandant is very cross; very angry indeed. I do not know yet what he will do with you. Ah, I would not like to be in the Kommandant's shoes."

Shaking a disapproving head, Pieber turned sorrowfully away.

The Kommandant didn't know what he was going to do with them either. They waited there another half-hour in the snow, and then a runner came in and spoke briefly to Pieber. The little Austrian turned to the shivering men.

"You can dismiss," he said briefly, and they turned and ran off to their huts where the rest of the camp was waiting impatiently to hear all about the night's doings.

Von Lindeiner had wanted to send them to the cooler, but there wasn't enough room.

☐ CHAPTER 18 ☐

SHORTLY after six o'clock that morning, the telephone from Sagan had called Oberregierungsrat Max Wielen out of his bed in Breslau. He was area chief of the Kriminalpolizei, and as soon as he realized the extent of the break, he ordered a Grossfahndung. That was the nationwide hue and cry, the highest search order in Germany.

The German radio broadcasted the news, and thousands of troops and auxiliaries turned out to search. Gestapo and Sicherheitspolizei worked through all trains checking papers, searched vehicles on the roads, patrolled the roads, checked hotels and houses and farms. The warnings went out to all the S.S., Army, and Luftwaffe troops in the neighborhood, and out from their homes for miles around came the old men and boys of the Landwehr and Landwacht (a sort of Home Guard) to watch over the fields and lanes. Far away in ports like Stettin and Danzig, the Kriegsmarine co-operated with the Gestapo and Polizei to prevent any escapees slipping across to Sweden as stowaways. Around the Czech, Swiss, Danish, and French borders the Grenzpolizei were alerted. For a hundred miles around Sagan itself the country was thick with searching Germans.

It developed into the greatest search in Germany during the war up to that time. Wielen, that morning, appointed Kriminal Kommissar Dr. Absalon to inquire fully into the circumstances of the break and furnish a report.

After getting out of the tunnel, Marshall and Valenta had walked cautiously through the woods for ten minutes until they emerged from the trees. Their direction had been good. In front of them was a narrow road and directly opposite, beyond crisscrossing railway lines shining dimly in the dark, they saw Sagan station. They walked up and down looking for the entrance to the subway which, they had been told, led under the tracks to the booking office and platforms. Unfortunately a shed had been built over the subway entrance as a shelter from the weather, and it was unrecognizable in the dark from the description they had.

For some time they searched for the subway which was right under their noses. A couple more dark shapes emerged from the woods and then two more. They couldn't find the subway either, and before long there were a dozen or so tramping up and down looking for it. A couple of times Marshall heard muffled curses and once, distinctly, an angry English voice asking where the hell the bloody subway was. By the grace of God no Germans heard.

In desperation Marshall and Valenta pushed open the door of the shed to see what was there. A couple of trains had come and gone already, and then they heard the air raid sirens. They couldn't see anything in the darkness of the shed, and while they were wondering what to do a German poked his head around the door and flashed a torch on them.

"What are you doing here?" he asked. "Don't you know the siren has gone and you must go to the shelter?"

Valenta mumbled something at him in German, and they brushed past out into the road again. There was only one train left that they could catch. It meant a dubious change of trains later on, and in any case the train might be held up by the air raid. If the escape were discovered early, the train was bound to be searched.

"It's not worth the risk," Valenta said. "Let's strike down on foot for Czechoslovakia. I know the way, and I can get help there fairly easily."

They turned back into the woods, heading for the road that skipped the western boundary of the camp, found the road, and followed it till they were out of the camp area. They tried then to walk parallel to it across the fields, but it was too slushy and they had to go back to the roads and take the risk of running into Germans.

Well before dawn they came to the Breslau *Autobahn* running about twelve miles south of the camp, crossed over it, and as dawn broke sheltered deep in some woods. They stayed there shivering with cold all day and too keyed up to sleep. At dusk they pushed on along a lane and walked through a small village. At the other end three men suddenly loomed out of the darkness, and before they quite realized it a shotgun was pointing at them.

Valenta tried to bluff it out, but they started firing questions at Marshall then. Marshall knew little German and tried to bluff it out as a French worker, but one of the Germans spoke better French and the game was up. The Germans were so obviously expecting to meet the escaped prisoners that they had no chance. The Germans marched them back to the village and phoned for police from Halbau. Marshall knew then there was no hope of bluffing any further and managed to tread his passes, maps, and compass into the snow.

An hour later a police car arrived and drove them to a small jail. They pushed them into a tiny cell about seven feet square, and there they found Humphries, a slim Australian called Paul Royle, and Shorty Armstrong, whom they had seen last the previous night in 104. All three had been caught in much the same circumstances. Jammed in the cell like sardines they found a little comfort in the common predicament. At least it was warm there in contrast to the weather outside. They chewed at their hard rations, talked for a while, and then slept, exhausted.

MAP SHOWING LOCATION OF SAGAN AND ESCAPE ROUTES

At dawn the cell door swung open and half a dozen tough-looking men in police uniforms called them out, pushed them roughly into a car, and drove them back to Sagan over the road they had walked. Not to the compound, but to the civil jail, where they were interrogated and pushed into a large cell full of three-tier bunks.

During Marshall's interrogation the phone rang in the little office, and he heard a guard who answered repeat in German into the mouthpiece, "Yes, yes. Six at Hirschberg, yes, and four at Danzig."

It wasn't hard to guess what it meant.

They found the big cell bug-ridden and cold. It was a little surprising not to be taken back to the camp cooler, and a vague disquiet was growing in them. The door opened again after a while, and in came Ogilvy, Chaz Hall, and two other escapees. Like Marshall and company, they had been picked up by patrols south of the autobahn and found the Germans too suspicious to be bluffed.

Three times more during the day the door opened and more escapees were shoved in. It was the same story. They had tried to walk across the fields, but the snow and slush had forced them back onto the roads and into the hands of the patrols. By dusk there were nineteen of them. The guards gave them each two slices of black bread for the day, but no blankets.

Wings Day and Tobolski found the booking office hall on Sagan Station half full of escapees. A couple of hours earlier they'd all been chatting in 104, and now they were walking around not recognizing each other. Day brushed shoulders with Kirby-Green and Kidder, who were traveling together, and the South Africans, Gouws and Stevens, and none of them even winked at each other.

In the train to Berlin, Day sat apart from Tobolski, but they joined up later and felt safer when they walked among the crowds in the Berlin streets. They had the address of a Dane living in Berlin, found him at his flat, and stayed there overnight. In the morning they didn't like the look of the Dane's German girl friend and spent the next two days in a bombed-out cellar. On the Monday they went to the Stettiner Bahnhof for a train to the Baltic port, and on the platform a man sidled up to Day, showed a police pass, and asked for his identity card.

Day showed it to him, feeling the sweat starting up all over him and the detective glanced casually, handed it back, and walked off. "Unteroffizier" Tobolski brazenly got his soldbuch stamped for leave at the R.T.O.'s office. They reached Stettin safely and after a day there made successful contact with some Frenchmen in a labor camp. The Frenchmen took them into their barracks and promised to find some Swedish sailors for them.

They were waiting there in the morning when four German police burst in, and the leader demanded at once, "Where are the Englishmen?"

Day and Tobolski tried bluff for a while, but five minutes later they were being marched off with hands in the air and guns in their backs.

The Dodger, traveling with Werner, accompanied the party of ten "workmen," including Pop Green, going by train to Hirschberg and then down to Czechoslovakia. All wearing cloth caps and dirty clothes, they got out of the train at dawn at a little station just before Hirschberg, and there they split up.

The Dodger and Werner set out to walk to Czechoslovakia, but it didn't take more than a couple of hours to see that the snow was going to beat them. They went to Hirschberg Station that night, had a little trouble getting their tickets, but collected them eventually and were sitting in the carriage waiting for the train to start when the police came through, looked very closely at their passes and said, "Komm mit."

Taken to Gestapo headquarters, they found half a dozen old friends, Jimmy James, Pop Green, and some of the Poles. The Gestapo had the Poles standing with their faces to the wall, forbidden to move. After interrogation, they handcuffed the Dodger and pushed him into a cell.

Plunkett, the map maker, and Dvorack lost their new freedom on the station at Klattau (Czechoslovakia) because they did not have the right type of leave pass. Danny Krol and Sydney Dowse were nabbed in a barn near Oels. The Gestapo caught Van Wyeermisch in Berlin.

Neely got to Stettin, where some French slave laborers hid him in a hut at the rear of a hospital while they tried to find him a ship to Sweden. They came back and told him that police were combing the whole town. Soon after that police descended on the hospital, and Neely got out the back way as they were coming in the front door. He got to the station, caught a train to Munich, and miraculously avoided all identification checks on the way, but they picked him up in Munich Station when he arrived.

Tim's passes were good enough for ordinary times, but in that enormous grossfahndung you needed more than good papers. The Germans rounded up several thousand people and threw them into jail. Some were innocent and later released. Many more were German deserters or wandering slave laborers. Some were criminals, fugitives from justice for a variety of reasons. The net that spread out from Sagan gathered them all in.

One by one the Sagan escapees were rounded up, and a fortnight after the break, out of the seventy-six who had got clear of the tunnel, only three were still free. The Germans never did find them. Two were already in England; the third was on his way.

☐ C H A P T E R 1 9 ☐

A T BERCHTESGADEN, on the Sunday morn-
ing, twenty-six hours after the break had been found, Hitler
received the first full Gestapo report on it and flew into one of
the rages that were becoming more frequent with him. Staying
at Berchtesgaden at the time were Himmler, Goering, and
Keitel. The Fuehrer called them into immediate conference
and ordered that no minutes were to be taken of the meeting.
There is not much doubt that by this time he knew what he
was going to do. He had reached the state of mind that could
deal with the escaping prisoner problem by one method only.

Keitel later reported that Hitler was "very excited" as he
told them what had happened. Himmler immediately blamed
Keitel for it. It would take, he said bitterly, 70,000 police and
God knows how many working hours to recapture the escapees.
Goering blamed Keitel, too, and Keitel in turn blamed Himm-
ler and Goering, and a heated three-cornered argument de-
veloped in front of the angry Hitler. Keitel said they were Air
Force camps and therefore Goering's ultimate responsibility.
He would not, he said, endure any more reproaches in the
presence of the Fuehrer.

Hitler squashed the argument.

"They are all to be shot on recapture," he said flatly.

As tactfully as he could, Goering protested—not, be it said,
on grounds of humanity, but of practical politics.

To shoot them all, he explained, would make it quite obvious that it was murder. Besides, there might be reprisals taken on German prisoners in Allied hands.

Hitler apparently saw the logic of this.

"In that case," he said, "more than half of them are to be shot."

Keitel and Himmler held a private conference afterward to plan the shootings, and later that day Keitel saw Generalmajor Von Graevenitz, his staff officer in charge of prisoners of war, and told him that more than half of the recaptured prisoners were to be shot.

Von Graevenitz, a regular Wehrmacht officer, was disturbed by the news. "We cannot just shoot these officers," he said, and the angry Keitel shouted at him, "The time has come for an example to be made, or we will not be able to cope with escapes. This ought to be such a shock that prisoners won't escape any more. Every prisoner must be told about it."

That night Himmler spoke to his second in command, Kaltenbrunner, in Berlin, and in the morning Kaltenbrunner issued the text of what has since become known as the "Sagan Order."

"The increase of escapes by officer prisoners of war is a menace to internal security. I am indignant about the inefficient security measures. As a deterrent the Fuehrer has ordered that more than half the escaped officers are to be shot. Therefore I order that Kriminalpolizei are to hand over for interrogation to the Gestapo more than half of the recaptured officers. After interrogation the officers are to be taken in the direction of their original camp and shot en route. The shootings will be explained by the fact that the recaptured officers were shot while trying to escape, or because they offered resistance, so that nothing can be proved later. The Gestapo will report the shootings to the Kriminalpolizei giving this reason. In the event of future escapes my decision will be awaited as to whether the same procedure is to be adopted. Prominent personalities will excepted. Their names will be reported to me and my decision awaited."

S.S.-General Mueller, Berlin Gestapo chief, and General Nebe, Kriminalpolizei chief, sent for Wielen, and that night they showed the Sagan Order to the Breslau police chief and sent him back with orders that Oberregierungsrat Scharpwinkel, Gestapo chief in Breslau, was to form an execution squad to dispose of the escapees caught in the area.

Scharpwinkel appointed one of his trusted lieutenants, Obersekretaer Lux, to head the squad, and he and Lux chose half a dozen men to help him.

In Berlin, General Nebe told Mertens, his secretary, to bring him the record cards of the recaptured prisoners. He sat at his desk looking at them and sorted them into two piles on his desk. Mertens remembers him looking at one card and saying, "Der muss dran glauben" ("He is for it") and putting the card on the bigger pile in front of him. Later, looking at another, he said, "He is so young. No." and he put it on the other pile.

Nebe marked the cards on the larger pile with red crosses. Mertens said he was grimly excited and behaved "uncontrollably."

Top secret teleprint messages went out to Gestapo bureaus which had reported recapture of some of the escaped prisoners. The first message said simply, "In five minutes a message will be coming over which is for the eyes of the senior official of the bureau only. No one else will be standing by the machine when it comes over."

A few minutes later the teleprinters tapped out the main

message. *It ordered the shooting of the officers being held, as laid down by the Sagan Order, and commanded absolute secrecy.*

They arrested Von Lindeiner on the Sunday morning, on Goering's orders. He was confined to his room. Pieber reported later in the compound that he had gone to bed with a heart attack. That same morning Von Lindeiner heard that some of the escaped prisoners had been lodged in Sagan Civil Jail. He rang Dr. Absalon and asked that they be returned to the camp. Absalon refused insultingly. He said he wouldn't take any orders from Von Lindeiner because Von Lindeiner had been relieved of his post.

About midnight on the Monday night the nineteen men huddled on the bug-ridden bunks in the big community cell at Sagan Jail heard tramping feet outside; the door swung open and in walked a collection of sinister-looking men who bashed them to their feet with tommyguns. The newcomers were all in civilian clothes, but it was a kind of uniform dress: they all wore heavy overcoats with belts and had black felt hats pulled down over their eyes. Marshall thought they looked like Hollywood's typical gangsters.

They prodded the nineteen outside and herded them into the back of a big covered-in truck which shortly moved off. Marshall thought they were being taken back to the camp, which was only a mile or so away, but the truck kept going, and he soon realized that they were on their way somewhere else. He thought it might be to another camp, and Valenta asked one of the guards who was sitting by the tailboard, nursing his tommygun and morosely surveying them. For answer he got a grunt and an ugly look. They could not see much outside the truck, and it was quite dark anyway so they just sat there quietly and not very happily.

It was nearly 3 A.M. when someone up by the tailboard said he thought he could see houses on each side, and soon he reported that they were running over a cobbled road and seemed to be in a largish town. The truck slowed and passed under what looked to be a stone arch, and a few yards further on it braked to a stop.

The guards piled out shouting "Raus! Raus!" and formed a cordon around them as they dropped one by one over the tailboard. In the darkness they could dimly see they were in a cobbled courtyard surrounded on all sides by stone walls about three stories high, pierced by little windows. There were bars over the windows. Evidently they were in a jail. Not so good!

At gunpoint, the guards herded them through a door, along gloomy stone corridors, and up a couple of flights of stairs. At the top they were pushed, four at a time, into tiny cells about six by nine feet. Three-quarters of the floor space in each cell was taken up by a wooden platform about a foot high. That was supposed to be the communal cell bed. Exhausted and hungry, the fours in each cell crowded together on the platforms for warmth and slept fitfully.

Crashing doors woke them at first light, and guards brought in their breakfast, a thin slice of black bread and a cup of ersatz mint tea, cold and horrible. No milk. No sugar. Funnily enough everyone was in fairly high spirits. They hadn't the faintest idea what was going to happen, and for the time being anyway, they didn't let it bother them.

They inspected the new quarters. Not much to see. Four bare stone walls of dirty white, a concrete floor, thick steel door, and high up in the walls a small window, heavily barred. Looking at the window they could see that the walls were nearly two feet thick. It wasn't very cold just then, and they relaxed on the wooden platforms and started yarning about their experiences since they crawled out of the tunnel. It was the first decent chance they'd had to talk, and in lighthearted

213

accounts of their adventures their spirits rose further and they passed an uneventful, though hungry, day.

There wasn't room in the tiny cells for the usual bucket that served as a latrine in Nazi prisons, but if they banged long enough on the door a guard came eventually and took them to a bucket down the corridor.

The corridor reminded Paul Royle of a submarine—it was narrow, dank, and gray with the forbidding steel doors inset at intervals. The only people they saw for a while were drab-uniformed warders carrying bunches of enormous keys for the old-fashioned locks. All of them were unfriendly.

Later on a doddering old German and a little Polish boy, a slave worker aged about fourteen, came around and perfunctorily cleaned the cells out. Marshall tried to get the boy to talk, but he didn't seem to understand and the only thing he said, with a sidelong glance toward the door, was "*Deutschland Kaput.*" Supper consisted of two slices of black bread and a bowl of watery soup. They felt just as hungry afterward.

Valenta was getting worried but trying not to show it. Only Marshall knew that Valenta had done intelligence work before he joined the R.A.F. Valenta knew the Nazis rather better than the others. None of them slept well that night.

In the morning guards several times entered the cells and took out one prisoner at a time. No one knew where, or why, and nerves were getting a little edgy. In the afternoon a guard came and took Paul Royle out, escorted him downstairs, out into the courtyard, under the archway, and into the street. It was the first time Royle had walked openly in daylight in a street for four years, and after the confinement of the cells he felt exhilarated just to be looking at people and houses. It seemed a big town, and the guard, who was friendly enough, told him it was Goerlitz, about forty miles south of Sagan and not far from the Czech border.

They walked half a mile, and the guard prodded him into a gray stone building about four stories high and took him up several flights of stairs and into an office where a villainous-looking interpreter with a strong American accent told him to stand up and answer questions. Behind a desk sat an elderly gray-haired man who put the queries through the interpreter.

The questions seemed harmless enough—"Where were you heading?" "What were your plans?" "Where is all your equipment . . . compass and maps?" "What sabotage directions did you receive?" "What information were you to collect on the way?"

Royle answered simply and as disarmingly as he could. He denied, with a faint smile, that he had had any sabotage directions or intentions to collect information. He had just been four years behind the wire, he said, and he was sick of it. He suggested that the interrogator might feel the same if the positions were reversed.

The interrogator seemed like some sort of civil police official. He did not seem particularly hostile, and after a while he said to the interpreter, "This man is obviously all right." Royle knew just enough German to understand the words and began to feel a little better. The guard took him out after a while and back to the jail, but this time he was put in a different cell.

As every man returned from his interrogation he was put in a different cell, where he found other prisoners whom he had not seen since the night of the break. Evidently there were more of the escapees held there than the nineteen from Sagan Jail.

The interrogations went on for four days. Marshall had a bad time. The men who questioned him were much more hostile than those who saw Royle. As soon as he was pushed into the interrogation room, a heavy-featured English-speaking German got up from a chair, walked heavily across the room, stopped six inches from him, stuck his face out till it was almost touching Marshall's, and said ominously, "You'll never see your wife and children again."

Not an encouraging start but so obviously meant to intimidate that Marshall became very much on his guard and decided to play dumb. The interrogator behind the desk was a brisk, businesslike man who shot his questions out curtly. Marshall replied innocently to the same innocuous questions that Royle had been asked, and then the interrogator started insisting on knowing what Marshall had done with his papers.

"Papers?" Marshall asked, stalling and playing dumb as hard as he could.

"The papers you got in the camp," the interrogator said dryly. "You got papers, didn't you?"

"Heavens yes," Marshall said. "The *Voelkischer Beobachter* —that's Goering's paper, isn't it?—the *Deutsche Allgemeine Zeitung* and the . . ."

"No," snapped the interpreter. "Forged papers and identity cards. Don't be stupid. What did you do with them?"

Marshall looked surprised.

"Did the others have them?" he asked. "Lord, I wish I'd had some. Where did they get them? How could they possibly have got hold of identity cards—" and he rattled on and on. He talked garrulously and aimlessly, misunderstanding some questions, deflecting others, and branching off onto new subjects, trying as hard as he could to give the impression of an amiable and voluble pinhead. It was the same when they asked him about maps. (He'd had several good detailed maps.)

"Map?" he said. "Yes, I had a map. I made it myself from a war map of Europe in the *Voelkischer Beobachter*. It wasn't very good. I think that's why I was caught . . ." and off he went again on a long monologue.

The same with his clothes. He was wearing one of Tommy Guest's suits, and it was one of Guest's best efforts, dyed dark

216

gray, and it had been topped off by a ski cap till they took his cap away.

"Of course you realize," said the interpreter, "you can be shot as a spy for wearing civilian clothes around Germany."

"Oh, this is only a uniform I changed about," Marshall said, beginning to feel uncomfortable. "See, I recut it, put boot polish on it, and changed the buttons."

"That's a civilian suit," the interpreter said.

Marshall denied it again and tried to show where he had altered it. "Bring in someone who knows about cloth, and they'll tell you it isn't a proper suit."

The interrogator pressed a button on his desk, and his stenographer walked through the door from an adjoining room. The brusque man behind the desk pointed to Marshall and spoke to her in German, telling her, apparently, to examine Marshall's clothes. She stood in front of Marshall diffidently rubbing the cloth of his coat between bony fingers and looking at the seams inside. She was a gaunt, unhappy-looking woman, nudging the forty mark, with untidy gray hair and long features like a tired horse.

Covered by her head from the interrogator, Marshall smiled into her eyes, and faintly surprised, she smiled back. Turning to the man behind the desk, she said they were not proper civilian clothes but—demonstrating with her fingers—had seams where one usually found them on uniforms. She left the room, and Marshall answered more questions, but his diarrhea of words exasperated the German so much that he slapped the desk with his hand and called the guard from outside, and Marshall was taken back to the jail.

After four days when everyone had been questioned, the prisoners were all depressed. They had no idea what was going to happen to them and could get no clues at all from the hostile wardens. Hunger was worrying them all the time, as they only got three or four thin slices of black bread a day and a little thin soup. By the fourth day there were hardly three words spoken an hour in any cell. There didn't seem to be anything more to say, and there was nothing to do except lie there and think about food and what might happen to them.

A warden caught one of them standing on someone's shoulders and looking out of the window. He hauled him roughly down and told them that the next man who looked out of the window would be shot. On the fourth afternoon, after all the sorting-out process of prisoners leaving one cell and being put back in another, Marshall found himself in the same cell as Royle, Ogilvy, and McDonald, a Scot with a patient and prematurely lined face.

In the morning they heard tramping along the corridor, and there was the sound of abrupt voices. Down the corridor cell doors were opening and there were sounds of shuffling feet as prisoners walked out. Ogilvy banged on the door till the guards came to take him to the latrine bucket, and on the way down he saw six of the prisoners being escorted out by several heavily armed men.

One of the prisoners was limping a little behind the others. It was Al Hake, and Ogilvy managed to whisper a few words to him. Hake said he had frostbitten feet. He thought they were going for another interrogation, and then the guards shouted angrily down the corridor and broke up the conversation.

"By God, they're plug-uglies," Ogilvy told the others when he got back to the cell. "Look like the same bunch that brought us from Sagan—same coats and black hats over their eyes. Must be Gestapo."

One of them risked a bullet by standing up and looking out of the window and saw the six, surrounded by the guards, standing in the courtyard below. He watched as they climbed into the back of a covered truck, followed by the guards, and then the truck moved off and rolled out through the archway.

The next morning the four in Marshall's cell heard more

tramping feet and shouting in the corridor and more cell doors opening. They heard another party shuffling down the corridor and, looking out of the window again, saw ten more of their prisoners below herded into a covered truck with guards. They sat around all day tensely waiting their turn, but no one came for them. That evening when the cell door opened and a warden brought in their cabbage water and bread Marshall saw a big "S" had been chalked on the door.

"Good show," he said. "S for *Sagan*. That must mean we're going back to the camp."

"Maybe it means S for *schiessen*" (shoot), said one of the others dryly, and there was a slightly hollow laugh.

That evening three Luftwaffe guards arrived in the jail and slept the night in the room opposite them. They told the four prisoners they were taking them back to Sagan in the morning. It was true. About 9 A.M., the cell door opened and the Luftwaffe guards escorted them down to the station and took them by train back to Sagan where they were pushed into the cooler for three weeks. This time it wasn't solitary confinement. The cooler was so full that everyone had company in his cell.

After a couple of days they found out who else was in the cooler—Rees, Noble, Baines, Hutson, Reavell Carter, Langlois, Trent, McBride, and several other naughty boys, but none of the sixteen whom they had seen taken away in trucks from Goerlitz Jail.

IT WAS curiously quiet in north compound for a week after the break. We woke up every morning waiting for reprisals, and none came. It was a faintly unnatural atmosphere as the days passed, and we wondered what was going to happen to us. And on the seventh day the Gestapo arrived to search the camp—about six of them, hard-faced citizens who walked into the compound and looked at us coldly.

They hadn't come across Air Force prisoners before, which probably accounts for their innocence. Presumably they'd only dealt with their own population and the nameless victims they collected in their dungeons—people too terrified and in no position to differ with them. We were, I suppose, privileged (if you could call it privilege). So long as we didn't stick a nose over the warning wire or make public reference to Hitler's ancestry, the Luftwaffe doled out the black bread and potatoes and didn't go around the compound squirting tommyguns just for the hell of it. We were still under the Luftwaffe and generally outside the orbit of the Gestapo, and Goering wanted it kept that way.

The Gestapo curtly brushed aside any help from the ferrets and said they'd do the searches their own way. They let it be known, according to Eichacher, that they didn't regard the ferrets as being either intelligent or efficient.

They dumped their coats and hats in the entrances of the

huts and prowled around the rooms, emerging now and then with some of the nails we'd pulled out of the walls or a lump of iron they didn't think we should have. These they piled beside their coats, and as they vanished again into the rooms one of the boys reached around the hut door and took away anything we particularly wanted to keep. I don't think it ever occurred to the Gestapo that anyone would do that to them.

It seemed to be so successful that he got a little more daring and swiped one of the Gestapo hats. A couple more people joined in the game, and the idea seemed to snowball. One of them, with more zeal than discretion, rummaged in the pocket of one of the Gestapo overcoats and rushed up to Canton a minute later, grinning all over his face. He pulled his hand out of his jacket where he had been holding it like Napoleon, and there he was holding a little automatic pistol.

Unbidden, a little squawk of horror came out of the onlookers' throats.

"For God's sake," said Conk, "put it back. Put it back. You're making it too hot. You'll start 'em shooting."

Nervously the man replaced the pistol, and luckily for him he wasn't spotted. The Gestapo went off eventually, taking nothing we had particularly wanted to keep but leaving behind in the "X" secret cupboards a hat, two scarves, some gloves, another torch, and some Gestapo papers. I imagine they were too embarrassed when they found out to do anything about it. Besides it would have caused German casualties. All the ferrets would have died, laughing.

They descended on the other compounds then, both British and American, and searched them, presumably more cautiously, but again finding nothing of importance. Lamentably they were faced with failure of their mission, an unthinkable disgrace; so, in Gestapo fashion, they decided to search their own people in the kommandantur.

And, behold! Success at last! They unearthed a little black-market organization involving—you'll never guess—Von Lindeiner and Von Masse. A Luftwaffe major who flew transport aircraft used to bring in choice wines and foods from Denmark, and they had a little store of the stuff under the kommandantur cookhouse. We heard that a German who wasn't in on the game spilt on them to the Gestapo. Von Lindeiner was removed for court-martial.

The Gestapo got three more victims in their stay. They could not understand how we had obtained eight hundred feet of electric cable for the lighting system in "Harry." Being Gestapo, they could think of only one thing. Someone had betrayed the Reich. They looked through the inventories of the camp electricians and found that eight hundred feet of cable had been lost. Too late for the electricians to protest that the cable had been stolen from them while their backs were turned. The Gestapo, soaked in suspicion for years, took the two electricians and also the chief electrician, who had been too scared to report the loss of the wire, and they shot all three.

A new Kommandant arrived. His name, we heard, was Oberst Braune, but we didn't see him in north compound. The expected reprisals came a couple of days later. He shut the camp theater, put on three appells a day, and refused to let us have Red Cross boxes or food tins. There seemed to be something wrong somewhere. These were only pinpricks. After thinking about it for a while we concluded that the new Kommandant wasn't going to extremes, probably, because his own personal reputation had not been affected by the break.

Rubberneck was still around, having successfully talked himself out of trouble. According to a voluble ferret, Rubberneck had claimed that we must have finished the tunnel months before and bided our time to break it. We couldn't have dug it recently because we couldn't have dispersed the sand. They had found none under the huts, and we couldn't have put it on the snow. It must have been dug at the same time as "Tom," said Rubberneck.

And how, inquired Dr. Absalon, could so many people get into Block 104 on the night of the break without being detected? Rubberneck said we must have dug small tunnels from near-by blocks leading into 104. To prove it, he put on several surprise searches of the near-by huts, which proved, of course, nothing but gave time for official wrath to subside.

After the unfortunate effects of blowing up "Tom," they didn't quite know for a while how to destroy "Harry," but settled it finally by pouring sewage from the honey wagons down the 104 end, sealing it with concrete, and then blowing up the other end. Rubberneck resumed his patrolling of the compound with a churlish glitter in his eye, though no one bothered very much about that except the other ferrets who became more prudent in their lead-swinging.

We heard that Marshall, Ogilvy, Royle, and McDonald had arrived in the cooler. Jennens saw Pop Green and Poynter going into the cooler too. Then eight more were reported in the cells, having returned, it was said, from a town south of Sagan called Goerlitz. Next we heard Neely was locked up there. That made fifteen returned out of the seventy-six who had got clear of the tunnel. It was puzzling; hard to believe that only ten had been caught, considering the tough conditions for the hardarsers. We assumed that some had been purged to other camps—perhaps to Kolditz Strafelager.

A fortnight after the break it seemed that things were more or less normal again. The thaw had come and people were pounding the circuit without their greatcoats, reveling in the crisp air. With spring we were expecting the invasion almost any moment, and invasion meant the end of the war. We were just beginning to understand that release, some day, might actually become a reality instead of a dream.

On a morning in early April, Pieber walked into the compound, went straight to Massey's room, and saluted politely. Would the Group Captain be good enough to wait on the new Kommandant in the kommandantur at 11 A.M., bringing his official interpreter.

"What does he want?" asked Massey. "Is he going to announce more reprisals against us?"

Pieber's face was unusually solemn as he answered.

"I cannot tell you, Group Captain Massey, but it is something very terrible."

That rumor spread round the compound. No one worried very much. There had been fifty rumors since the break, some of them much worse than this one, and anyway Pieber was an old woman!

Just before eleven o'clock, Massey was escorted out of the gate with his personal interpreter, Squadron Leader Wank Murray. They were kept waiting only a few moments in the kommandantur, and then they were shown into the Kommandant's office, a normal barrack room, but with a carpet, a leather chair, a large desk, and on the wall behind it the standard décor of Luftwaffe offices—photographs of Hitler and Goering.

Oberst Braune was standing behind his desk, a fairly tall man of about fifty with a lined, rather sad and patient face, fair, thinning hair and the Iron Cross, first class, on his left breast pocket. Usually, when the Kommandant and the Senior British Officer met officially, there was a formal handshake and the usual military courtesies. This time, no handshake. Braune gave a stiff, slight bow and indicated to the two officers that they were to sit on two chairs that had been placed by the desk. Simoleit and Pieber were standing beside the desk and looking at the carpet.

The Kommandant stood up very straight and spoke in German.

"I have been instructed by my higher authority to communi-

224

cate to you this report. . . ." He paused and Murray translated so far to Massey. Braune continued: "The Senior British Officer is to be informed that as a result of a tunnel from which seventy-six officers escaped from Stalag Luft III, north compound, forty-one of these officers have been shot while resisting arrest or attempting further escape after arrest."

Murray felt himself going red in the face. Unbelieving, he asked, "How many were shot?"

"Forty-one," the Kommandant replied. Murray slowly translated the passage to Massey.

Massey listened in silence and made almost no sign that he was hearing except that he stiffened slightly in his chair and the lines of his face tightened. At the finish he said briefly, "How many were shot?"

Wank answered, "Forty-one." He felt his face was bright crimson and the scene in the room seemed unreal.

There was a long heavy silence. It dragged on and on as they waited for Massey to do something, and Massey just sat there looking unseeing in front of him. The tension was nearly unbearable when he raised his eyes slowly and turned them on Murray.

"Ask him," he said, "how many were wounded."

Murray put the question to the Kommandant. The German looked uncertainly at a paper on his desk and then looked out of the window. He hesitated and then said, "My higher authority only permits me to read this report and not to answer any questions or give any further information."

Massey said doggedly, "Ask him again how many were wounded."

The Kommandant looked painfully uncomfortable. He looked out of the window and then down to his desk, trying to make up his mind, and after another hesitation he slowly said, "I think no one was wounded."

"No one wounded?" said Massey, his voice rising a little.

"Do you mean to tell me forty-one can be shot in those circumstances and that all were killed and no one was wounded?"

"I am to read you this report," the Kommandant said, "and that is all I can do."

Simoleit and Pieber had not taken their eyes off the carpet. Massey asked for the names of the dead.

"I cannot give them to you," Braune said. "I have not got them. I have only this report which I am to read to you."

"I would like to have the names as soon as it is possible to get them," said Massey.

"Yes, I will do that," the Kommandant answered, and then, after another little hesitation he added more quickly, holding a hand up, palm out in a slightly appealing way, "I must remind you that I am acting under orders and may only divulge what I am instructed to by my higher authority."

"What is this higher authority?" Massey asked.

Braune made a futile little gesture.

"Just higher authority," he said.

"I require to know what has happened to the bodies so that I can arrange for burial and the disposal of their effects," Massey said. "I demand that the Protecting Power also be informed."

The Kommandant said that this would be done. He would let the Senior British Officer have every possible scrap of information as soon as he received it, but reminded him again he was always limited in action by "higher authority."

He rose to his feet. "I think that is all, gentlemen." Stiffly the two British officers withdrew, and as they emerged into the fresh air again Massey said to Murray, "Don't mention this dreadful thing to anyone till I have released it in the compound."

Murray still felt his face was crimson. Neither man felt like speaking, and Massey's face was grimly set. On the way back to the barbed wire Pieber joined them. He seemed nervous and distressed, and said in a low voice, "Please do not think that the Luftwaffe had anything to do with this dreadful thing. We do not wish to be associated with it. It is terrible . . . terrible."

Pieber at times may have been a hypocrite, but he wasn't this time. He was a shaken man.

Half an hour later, back in the compound, Massey sent word around asking the senior officer in every room to report to the camp theater for an announcement. With the order came a rumor that "something dreadful" had happened. We were a little uneasy but it was only another rumor. We thought it meant reprisals were going to start in earnest—possibly we were going to lose Red Cross food parcels for a while. God knows that would be serious enough. German rations were just enough to ensure starvation in its most prolonged and unpleasant form.

About three hundred officers crowded into the theater for the announcement. Massey walked onto the stage, waited a few seconds while the rustling died down, and then spoke without preamble.

"Gentlemen, I have just come from a meeting with the Kommandant in which he told me the unbelievable, the shocking news that forty-one of the officers who escaped from the tunnel on the twenty-fourth of March have been shot."

There was a stunned silence. A lot of people felt suddenly sick.

Massey went on to describe the meeting briefly. He would announce the names of the victims as soon as they were available. Just now there was little more that he could say. There would be a memorial service on the coming Sunday.

Still in a stunned silence, we filed out of the theater, and within two minutes the news had spread to everyone in the compound. Horror lay over the camp. Mass murder was something new in the quiet backwater of prison camp, however unpleasant the life was. A lot of us wouldn't believe it. "I know the Huns are murderous bastards," said a man in my room, "but they've never been game so far to murder British or American people openly in mass, and I can't see their point in starting that sort of thing on relatively harmless prisoners."

It about summed up the feeling. I suppose if the truth be known we wouldn't believe it because we didn't want to believe it. The mind builds its own defenses. Most of us thought that the whole thing was a bluff, that the forty-one had been moved to another camp, and that we, believing they were dead, would be intimidated into stopping all escape activity. But there was no getting away from the fact that it had been officially announced. We held a memorial service, and every man in the compound sewed a little black diamond on his sleeve.

The Kommandant was afraid there might be some sort of demonstration or revolt and ordered all the guards to be more watchful than usual—more ruthless if they had to be. When some of us were a little slow getting into our hut at lock-up time, a sentry in a goon-box sent a spray of bullets over our heads and a couple more zipping around our feet, kicking up little spurts of dust.

The air raid siren went one afternoon, a lovely sound. We got more kick out of watching American Fortresses draw their vapor trails across the sky than we ever got out of a barrel of raisin wine. The Germans knew it and ordered that whenever the sirens went we must run into our huts and pull the black-out shutters across so we couldn't see anything. Some of us were a little slow getting inside when the siren went that afternoon, and one of the guards running in emptied his pistol magazine at us. He was a rotten shot, but several people sitting in their room in 109 jumped smartly out of the way when a couple of bullets plowed through their wooden wall. They

228

drew rings around the bullet holes with a pencil and labeled them, "Easter Eggs, Sagan, 1944."

A couple of minutes after that, a guard got an American sergeant standing innocently in the doorway of his hut in the next compound. The bullet went in his mouth and he died instantly. It was not exactly unprecedented for a guard to kill one of the boys, but it was an unfortunate time for another killing. Some of that nice insulation we had wrapped around our minds began to wear thin; the people who believed the forty-one were still alive grew fewer and fewer.

At dusk one day Eichacher pinned a piece of paper on the notice board. Someone passing looked at it casually and gave a shout. "Here are the names!" And in seconds there was a crowd around the board. For the benefit of those at the back a man yelled for silence and slowly read them out. There were little gasps and curses behind as people heard their friends named.

Someone said, "That isn't forty-one! It's forty-seven."

A dozen people checked his count. He was right. Forty-seven!

It was a terrible list. Roger Bushell was on it. That wasn't unexpected. The ever-courteous Tim Walenn was on it. So were Gordon Brettell, Henri Picard, Birkland, Casey, Willy Williams, Al Hake, Chaz Hall, Tom Kirby-Green, Johnny Stower, Valenta, and Humphries, who had been caught with Royle. Denys Street was on it, too. He was the son of the British Permanent Under-Secretary For Air. The Germans certainly hadn't been discriminating.

Faced with the names we got back that stunned horror. Some of them were only kids, a year or two out of school. People stood about talking it over almost in whispers. Some still wouldn't believe it wasn't a bluff. Germany had been the first nation, in 1929, to sign the Geneva Convention, which lays it down that escape attempts from prison camps are quite legitimate and are not to be punished harshly.

A couple of days later another list was pinned to the board. It was a short one, just including the names of three more who had been shot—Tobolski, Cookie Long, and Danny Krol. It brought the names up to the round figure of fifty. It was noted that, with the exception of two Czechs, every non-Briton who had escaped had been reported shot.

A few days later a group of prisoners who had been badly wounded when they were shot down were taken out of the compound for repatriation to England. Massey was among them. About two hours before they left the compound the Germans called for all the kit of the fifty and took it all away.

It must have been rather senseless bluff. They knew the repatriates would tell everything they knew of the shootings when they got home, and presumably the Germans thought that the demand for the kit of the fifty would indicate that they had not, after all, been shot but removed to another camp.

None of it seemed to make sense. We'd been worrying ourselves sick over it for weeks when the few escapees who had returned came out of the cooler and back into the compound. We pumped them for news, and they, dazed by our news, wouldn't believe the others were dead. Some of them had seen them taken from the cells at Goerlitz, presumably for another interrogation. They were perfectly all right then. It must be a bluff.

There didn't seem to be any common factor in the shootings. Why shoot some and send others back? Al Hake had had badly frostbitten feet and was in no condition to try to escape again. Yet he'd been shot. And no one was wounded. So they certainly hadn't been shot trying to escape again. We began to think once more it must be a bluff.

And then the Germans brought back the kit of the fifty

that they had taken on the morning the repatriates left. A couple of days after that, they brought in some of the personal belongings of the missing fifty—photographs, and things like that. Some of them were bloodstained.

A fortnight later it was all put beyond doubt. The Kommandant informed the new S.B.O., Group Captain Wilson, that there had been delivered to him the urns carrying the ashes of the fifty. No need to ask why they had been cremated. It destroys the evidence of the manner of death.

Engraved on each urn was the locality where death had occurred. Four were engraved "Danzig," and just four of the escapees had been making for Danzig. Four were marked "Hirschberg," two more with the name of a town near the French border. There were several from Leignitz and a lot from Breslau. Still we couldn't find any common factor in the shootings. The only clue was the round number of fifty. It was pretty clear they'd just taken fifty and shot them as an example. God knows that was logical enough under Hitler.

There was only one bright point in the whole affair. Bit by bit we pieced together information brought in by the tame guards and eventually established the fact that the rather staggering figure of 5,000,000 Germans had spent some of their time looking for the prisoners, and many thousands of them were on the job full time for weeks. That meant that the break was some sort of success, if one could overlook the heavy cost.

The Kommandant got us some stone and let a working party go to a near-by cemetery to build a vault for the urns. There was already a row of graves in that cemetery where other victims from the camp had been buried.

Fifty were dead. Fifteen were back with us. We wondered what had become of the other eleven.

IN JUNE a letter came in the prisoners' mail signed
with two prearranged fictitious names. Rocky Rockland and
Jens Muller had made it back to England, via Sweden.

They had got to Kustrin, near Frankfurt on Oder, the morning after the break and changed trains there. By evening they
were in Stettin. Everything went smoothly. They met some
Swedish sailors whose ship was about to sail for home, and
the sailors took them on board and hid them. The Germans
checked the ship before it sailed but did not find the stowaways. At dawn the next day they landed in Sweden, and a
few days later the R.A.F. flew them back to England. It was
the perfect escape.

Weeks later another letter arrived signed with another fictitious name. Bob Van Der Stok had made it too.

Van Der Stok, Number 18 out of the tunnel, had traveled
alone, wearing a dark-blue Australian Air Force greatcoat,
Dutch naval trousers and a beret. As he came out of the woods
by the station, a German soldier stopped him and asked him
curtly who he was and where he thought he was going. Before
the shaken Van Der Stok could answer, he went on, "Don't
you know there's an air raid on? You should be in a shelter."

"I know," Van Der Stok apologized, "but I am a Dutch
worker and do not know where the shelter is."

"Well, you'd better come with me," the soldier said. "You'll be all right. The police won't touch you because I'm an armed guard from the prison camp back there."

Van Der Stok went with him, feeling most peculiar, praying he wouldn't be recognized. The guard took him right into the station booking hall and left him with an amiable smile. He bought his ticket to Breslau, looked around and recognized several prisoners from the camp standing around. He thought it would be safer to get into conversation with a German and began talking to a girl standing near by. She shook him considerably by telling him she was a censor from the camp and on duty at the station watching for officers trying to escape.

After a while she called a German military policeman and asked him to question two men of whom she was suspicious. She pointed to Kirby-Green and Kidder. The policeman crossed to them, and they started talking fast in Spanish and waving their hands. After a while the policeman came back to the girl and said she needn't worry. They were only Spanish workers. Van Der Stok was sweating.

He was thankful the train to Breslau was so full that he could only just squeeze himself in. It meant the security police couldn't walk through it checking papers. By 4 A.M. he was in Breslau and, producing his papers at the booking office, bought a ticket all the way through to Holland. On the station he counted ten other escapees. There was no trouble going to Dresden where he changed trains, and at Halle he changed again to a through train for Holland. The journey took thirteen hours, and every four hours the Gestapo walked through checking the papers of every passenger. The funny thing was that the Germans, including the soldiers, had much more trouble than Van Der Stok. One poor little gefreiter who had one stamp missing from his pass was handed over to the military police.

At the Dutch border the Gestapo peered very closely at his papers but again he was completely unsuspected. He got

233

off at Utrecht and found some old friends who sheltered him. It was just thirty-six hours after he had left the tunnel.

He waited six weeks in Holland till the Dutch underground fathered him to the south of Holland and smuggled him into Belgium across the Maas in a skiff. On the other side they gave him a bicycle and he pedaled to Brussels, to a Dutch family, and lived with them another six weeks before the underground could get him on a train for Paris, traveling now as a Flemish employee of a big Belgian firm. It was just before the invasion and during an "alert" they stopped outside a station on the way. Just as well. A formation of American Fortresses pattern-bombed it and wiped it out.

He had been told to make for Toulouse, and at St. Lazaire Station in Paris, where he bought his ticket, they told him he must get it stamped at German control in the station.

He took it to the German who said, "You must have a special permit to go to Toulouse before I can stamp this."

"I've got a permit," Van Der Stok said. "Otherwise how could I have got my ticket?"

"Oh," said the German, "of course," and stamped it.

In Toulouse Van Der Stok found a group of guides who were taking refugees across the Pyrenees—for a price. He sold his watch for 10,000 francs, handed the money over, and was taken to a farm high up in the mountains. Three days later he walked to the rendezvous on a hill and down the road saw a German barrier with sentries and machine guns. Standing watching, he saw the car with his guide and three other men race toward the post, and as it got near, the men in the car opened up with Sten guns and shot their way through, killing all the sentries. A moment later they drove into machine-gun fire from another German post down the road, and the car stopped and burst into flames. No one got out.

At the farm there were now twenty-seven of them stranded —two Dutchmen, two American pilots, two Canadians and twenty-one German Jews. That night Van Der Stok made contact with a band of Maquis on a near-by hill. They provided another guide. The Maquis did not trust the refugees. On the way to the frontier the refugees walked in single file, four Maquis just behind them with Sten guns.

The Maquis stopped after a while and pointed to a saddle back in the mountains.

"Beyond that," they said, "is Spain. Good luck," and left them.

A few days later, Van Der Stok was in Madrid. The British Consul sent him on to Gibraltar, and he was flown back to England. It was just four months since he had crawled out of the tunnel.

So eight were still missing. It wasn't till after the war we found out what had happened to them. Plunkett and the two Czechs, Tonder and Dvorack, were sweating it out in Czech concentration camps. The Gestapo had arrested all of Tonder's relatives. Van Wyeermisch was held in another concentration camp. The Gestapo shot his father in Belgium.

Wings Day and Tobolski had been taken to the police chief in Stettin. He was an affable man and told them they had been caught through a young Frenchman in the labor camp where they had sheltered. The young Frenchman had got 1,000 marks for betraying them.

"That's a bloody dirty trick," said Wings, disgusted. "I'd like to wring his neck."

"Don't worry about that," said the police chief, who was a very practical man. "When we've no more use for him, we'll tip off his friends about him. They'll wring his neck for you."

Day and Tobolski were taken by train to Berlin, and there, on Stettiner Bahnhof, Tobolski was taken away and Wings didn't see him again.

They took Day to Kriminalpolizei headquarters and escorted him into an office where a thin-lipped, white-haired man covered in braid and badges (it was General Nebe) said to him, "You've been giving us a lot of trouble."

"It's my duty to escape," Wings said.

"Well, we're sending you where you won't give any more trouble."

Wings thought it was a polite way of telling him that he was to be shot, and did not feel very comfortable when he was taken out and put in a car. They drove for an hour and pulled up outside a high stone wall that encircled Sachsenhausen Concentration Camp north of Berlin. Day was pushed into a small compound close inside the wall, and there he found the Dodger, Dowse, and James. In the same compound were some Irish soldiers (always fighting), some Russian generals, Italian orderlies, and a British commando, Major Jack Churchill.

There were no ferrets in the compound. They had never been needed. No one had ever escaped from Sachsenhausen, except horizontally in a wooden box. Two weeks later, the five Britons started tunneling, without telling any of the others, because they were not sure they could trust them and there would have been an enormous row if the tunnel had been found.

They cut a trap under Dowse's bed and worked in the dark all the time as in the first tunnel at Dulag. No such luxuries as fat lamps at Sachsenhausen. The soil was firm, unlike the sandy stuff at Sagan, so they didn't have to shore it, which was just as well because there was nothing to shore it with. There were also, as far as they knew, no microphones buried around the wire, so they were able to make it shallow, running about six feet deep.

Appell was at 6 A.M., and one man went below immediately afterward and dug. The others dispersed the sand under the hut. The tunnel wouldn't have lasted a week at Sagan, but at Sachsenhausen, free of ferrets, they kept at it for four months until in August it was nearly a hundred feet long and they calculated they were outside the compound wire. Their security had been perfect. The other people in the little compound still didn't dream that the tunnel existed.

Then Day came across a sheet from a weeks-old German newspaper in the latrine, and his blood literally seemed to run cold as he read a story at the top of the page, a report of the fifty from Sagan being shot trying to escape again or avoid recapture.

The five of them held a grim little meeting in Dowse's room. It was not a long meeting, and the vote was to take a chance and carry on. Having taken the tunnel so far, they couldn't bear the thought of not using it. It was rather a courageous vote.

They waited for a suitable time, and early in September there was a moonless night with the added cover of a drizzle of rain. About 11 P.M. they surfaced outside the wire, helped each other over the nine-foot outer wall, and dispersed into the darkness.

Wings Day, the old campaigner, still had a little of his money left from the Sagan break. He had sewed it into his coat, and the Gestapo had not found it. One of the Irish soldiers in the compound had given him the address of some people in a town south of Berlin who might help him.

Day and Dowse were traveling together, and in the darkness they asked a man the way to the nearest railway station. Only then did they notice he was in police uniform. Suspiciously he asked them who they were, and they ran off into the darkness. At dawn they found the railway station and caught the first train to Berlin, changed trains there, and reached the town they were aiming for. That night they sheltered in the cellar of a bombed house, but someone must have seen them going in because some people surrounded it and then men came in with revolvers and the police arrived.

237

They spent a couple of nights handcuffed in a Berlin Gestapo jail waiting for the firing squad and thought the time had come when they were taken out and put in a car. For an hour they drove out of Berlin expecting all the time to stop, be taken out and shot, and they were considerably surprised when they pulled up at Sachsenhausen again. There each was chained to the concrete floor of a dungeon in solitary confinement. They spent nearly five months in unspeakable conditions. Churchill and James had been caught also and were in cells near them.

The Dodger had an extraordinary time. He had gone off on his own from Sachsenhausen, aiming for Luebeck, and jumped into a coal truck of a goods train trundling roughly in that direction. At dawn he jumped out of the coal truck miles from the danger area of Sachsenhausen and slept all day in a thicket by the banks of a stream. At night he found a near-by siding and was going to try "jumping the rattler" again when he was caught in the beam of a watchman's torch. Not waiting to answer the challenge, he vanished into the darkness and went back to his hide-out.

All the next day he walked northwest in pouring rain and just outside a village met two friendly French slave laborers who sheltered him in a barn for a week, bringing him food every day. On the seventh day they said an untrustworthy Pole had seen him and he must move. They took him to a near-by café used by slave laborers, where an old, stone-deaf German served them with gallons of beer, and they talked openly in front of him. The Frenchmen hid him in another barn, and he was seen by a Russian whom the Frenchmen didn't trust, so they took him out the next day and put him for the night in a rabbit hutch. Again an unreliable Russian came across him so the Frenchmen took him to a hayloft, and there he spent a week, bedded down in clover hay listening to the pigs underneath. Once or twice he saw the German farmer walking by with his shotgun under his arm. The Frenchmen brought him food every day, and the German farmer must have seen them.

On the seventh morning the Dodger awoke to find the farmer looking at him from behind the hollow end of a pistol. The local policeman came around shortly after. He had been a Luxemburger, and when he got the Dodger by himself he apologized for having to hold him. He had to arrest him, he said, or be shot himself, but made up for it as far as he could by feeding him on hot oatcakes made specially by his wife. He brought out the *German Police Gazette*, and in it the Dodger saw a picture of himself, an unlovely and villainous one taken over four years earlier when he had first been captured.

It was the adjutant of Sachsenhausen himself who arrived by car with guards and handcuffs to take him back. In a cell along the corridor from Day and the others, they chained him to the floor, and the months passed in wretchedness. The five men heard nothing of the war except for scraps the guards told them about the "wonderfully successful" German offensive in the Ardennes. They made it sound as though the war might go on forever.

◻ CHAPTER 22 ◻

On FEBRUARY 3, they came to the Dodger's cell, took the chain off his ankles, and led him outside. A young German officer helped him into a car, climbed in after him, and off they drove to Berlin. What followed had the air of a dream. The young officer took him into a shop and bought him a complete outfit of civilian clothes: suit, shirts, socks, shoes, hat—the lot. Then he took him to a flat, introduced him to the S.S. major, his wife and child who occupied it, and showed him into a delightfully furnished bedroom.

"This will be your room," said the young officer, and to the man they had chained in a dungeon, none of it was real.

"Tell me," the Dodger asked the young officer, "what is all this about?"

"You will find out in due course," said the officer. "Now change into your new clothes. You will feel much more comfortable."

"Look here. I'm an officer," the Dodger said. "Will you, as an officer, give me your word I can wear these things without compromising myself?"

"Yes," said the German decisively. "I do."

A few hours later a thickset man in civilian clothes arrived and greeted the Dodger warmly. Dr. Thost had been London correspondent for the *Voelkischer Beobachter* in 1938–1939. Now he was a fairly high official in the German Foreign Office.

He put the Dodger in a car and drove him off to the Adlon Hotel, Berlin's finest.

"Will you please tell me what this is all about?" asked the Dodger, blinking unbelievably at a sparkling chandelier in the foyer, one of the few parts of the hotel not bomb-damaged.

"You will know soon," Thost promised. He took him up to a private room and introduced him to a large, fleshy man with a booming voice and an expansive, enveloping smile.

"This is Dr. Schmidt," said Thost. "Dr. Schmidt is Herr Hitler's interpreter."

"Have a drink, my dear fellow," boomed Dr. Schmidt, spilling over with bonhomie. He handed the Dodger a glass.

The Dodger looked at it.

"Scotch whisky," boomed Schmidt. "Not much of it left, I'm afraid."

The Dodger looked cautiously at Dr. Schmidt—the same kind of look that is in a small boy's eyes when he gazes first, suspiciously, upon Santa Claus, not knowing what to expect.

"You are going home, my dear sir," said Dr. Schmidt, as if the news made him happy. "No doubt you will be seeing your kinsman Mr. Churchill when you arrive." And then, confidentially and solemnly, "I want you to remember three things. One . . . no unconditional surrender. Two . . . ethnographical boundaries, and three . . . the balance of power in Europe. For Britain's safety, it must be maintained." He nodded vaguely toward the east where the Russians were preparing their assault on Berlin. "You know what I mean."

And the Dodger at last understood.

Thost took him to lunch in a smart restaurant the next day and in the afternoon drove him to Dresden. They gave the Dodger his own room in a hotel there. He was taken to meet the chief of police, and at lunch the chief spoke graciously about the traditional bond between the British and the Germans. The Dodger met a lot more pleasant people who all

241

thought the same. You wouldn't have thought they'd chain a dog in a dungeon, or even, for that matter, shoot fifty British bunny rabbits.

Thost took the Dodger (grinning grimly to himself) to the circus, and they were watching the lady on the tightrope when the sirens went and the first of the three great air raids on Dresden started. In an hour the center of the city was a sheet of flame. Thost and the Dodger got out of the danger area, and Thost escorted him to an administration headquarters outside the city where an S.S. General greeted him warmly.

"Major Dodge," said the General. "I am so glad to see you are safe. I have been on the phone to Herr Himmler and you are going home."

At the headquarters he met Frau Von Kleist, wife of the field marshal who had been relieved of his post. The Dodger was able to get a few words with her alone.

"Why don't you people put up the white flag?" he asked.

"That's what my husband thinks too," she said. "But we can't. We're not allowed to."

Back in Dresden they found their hotel in ruins. Thost took him on a bus to Weimar, where they were bombed again but spent several days in the town. The Dodger toyed with the idea of escaping again but couldn't quite see what good it would do. On the other hand, staying with Thost, observing the country and the people, and getting back with Schmidt's message might be of some conceivable benefit.

At last they struck off southeast through Regensburg to Bayreuth, and there someone overheard them talking in English in an *estaminet.* Thost and the Dodger knew nothing about it until the police arrived, handcuffed them, and marched them off as spies. Thost, the high official, was livid with rage and almost speechless for a while until he got his voice back, and then the air was quivering with his protests, which the police stolidly ignored. They were thrown into a cell and spent two days waiting for execution. At night they could hear the American guns, and the Dodger, so patient since 1940, felt only bitterness. With freedom just by his fingertips it seemed so unfair that death should come like this from the little officials, when the German Foreign Office itself was bowing to him as a mediator.

Thost was sweating with fright and fury, and that was not without humor, but the most sardonic touch was the manner of their release. The local Gestapo freed them after a message had penetrated to Berlin and the answer had come back clearing the "spies."

Thost and the Dodger went on to Munich, stayed a day or two in a little hotel in the mountains to the south, and on April 25 reached the Swiss border at Lake Constance. That night the Dodger left Thost and walked up to the Swiss police at St. Marguerita. In a couple of days he was lunching in Berne with army intelligence officers, and within a week the R.A.F. landed him in England.

It was two days before V.E. Day that the Dodger dined with Churchill and the American Ambassador, John Winant, and told them of his adventures. When he got to the part about Schmidt and no unconditional surrender, Churchill took the cigar out of his mouth and grinned from ear to ear.

Chained to the dungeon floor at Sachsenhausen, Wings Day had passed the time by learning by heart a Hitler speech on a piece of latrine newspaper. In February, he and Dowse, James, and Jack Churchill were unchained and taken by train to Flossenberg Concentration Camp in the Harz Mountains. They heard the volleys of the execution squads there and saw the bodies of the victims being carried past. It was not a comforting sight, and they waited rather tensely for their own turn but no one came for them. After a fortnight they heard the approaching American guns, and just as release was beginning to seem possible the Germans took them out, loaded them into trucks, and drove them to the notorious Dachau, where they were locked in the hut that had been the camp brothel. Again they heard the rifles of the execution squads, and again they waited for their own turn.

They heard the American guns again, and just as it seemed once more that release might be on the way, they were taken to a camp up in the hills near Innsbruck. The strain of alternate hope and dread was tearing their nerves to pieces.

After a fortnight the Germans took them across the Brenner Pass to an Italian village. By now they were deep in Hitler's "Southern Redoubt," and with them were about fifty more important prisoners. It was uncomfortably clear that they were being held as hostages. Among them were Blum, Pastor Niemoeller, Schuschnigg, Schacht, the Dutch Minister of War, Greek generals, Italian generals, a nephew of Molotov, a son-in-law of the King of Italy, and a sprinkling of princelings.

Wings got away from the party, met an Austrian called Toni, and got him to drive him in his car to Bolzano. He contacted the Italian Resistance and continued on by car and foot toward the Allied Lines. He joined in the fighting in one town and took over the Gestapo headquarters in another. He commandeered another car, drove full tilt through the German lines, and with a bursting feeling of exhilaration reached a forward American patrol. It was his ninth escape since being shot down in 1939, and at last he had made it. It was one day before the Italian Front Armistice.

It was from Wings Day that the Allies learned about the colony of important prisoners up by the border. The Americans sent a column pelting up to the border and rescued them just in time. The Germans had had orders to shoot them.

And north compound?
About the time of the Hitler bomb plot in July, 1944,

"George" was creeping out under the theater toward the wire. "George" was "Harry's" successor, and Crump and Canton had cut a trap for it under a seat in the twelfth row of the theater. They were dispersing the sand under the floor, and a re-formed "X organization" was very active, though there was no definite policy, just yet, on mass escapes. We wanted to get "George" finished first, and then see what the situation was.

A few weeks later the contacts picked up a few hints from Pieber and one or two others that if Germany fell—and nothing was surer—the camp might be wiped out. After the shooting of the fifty that seemed logical enough. We had no illusions as to the popularity of the Allied Air Forces. Wilson, the S.B.O., formed the Klim Klub. "Klim" was the name of a milk powder in the food parcels, but the Klim Klub was the camp self-defense unit. Everyone was in it—the whole compound population being split up into sections, platoons, and companies. There were secret lectures and training, and a special commando company was to have the honor of having their heads blown off first as shock troops. I don't suppose there was much we could have done, but if the regrettable business of impromptu demise had to be faced, it was better to be doing something about it rather than be sitting on one's bottom waiting for it.

Over in the kommandantur, a German stenographer, disgusted at the shooting of the fifty, sent in a message by a tame guard that she had heard through her work that all prisoners who escaped henceforth were to be shot. A bony-faced Scot called McCulloch wanted to try it anyway, but "X" wouldn't let him. He argued and argued until, rubbing their chins dubiously, they agreed to let him try.

He got out hiding under a pile of empty tins in one of the garbage wagons but was back in the cooler a couple of hours later, still alive. Some good-tempered Wehrmacht soldiers had nabbed him down the road and brought him straight back to the camp. It didn't prove anything one way or the other. It was a question of what would have happened if the Gestapo had got hold of him.

By the time the snow came and finished escapes for the winter, "George" had reached just beyond the wire. It was kept there as a bolt-hole in case the rough-stuff started.

In the middle of January, the Russians started their winter offensive and the Ostfront came sweeping toward Sagan like a whirlwind. We were praying they would overrun the camp. They did, but we weren't there any more. The Germans marched us out on January 26 into a foot of snow and force-marched us more than sixty miles for days and nights to Spemberg, where they loaded us into cattle trucks. It was a fairly grim trip. We'd been on half-issue of food parcels for some months, and they gave us only one meal (barley soup) on the way.

There was one laugh on that march. Glemnitz was back with us for the march. He'd always guessed we had a radio and came tramping along the column of men and boomed affably, "Well, I suppose you've brought your radio with you. Who's carrying it? Who's got it, eh . . . you?" (pointing to one man) . . . "you?" (pointing to another) . . . "you?" (to a third).

And one or two of us who knew where the radio was felt there was still something to laugh at in life.

Pieber, that kind and prudent man, had parts of it in his attaché case in his car.

We were two days in the cattle trucks. There was just room to sit, but not to move, and after thirty-six hours they did give us each a cup of foul water drained off the engine. They let us out of the trucks near Bremen, and we marched to an old condemned camp and waited seven hours outside in the rain to be searched before we entered. A lot of the men collapsed at that point. About seventy-five were already missing—about half left at various places through illness and the rest just "missing," maybe escaped, maybe shot. Of the rest of us, 70 per cent were sick, and everyone had lost more weight, up to thirty pounds. We really hadn't had that much to spare, and most of us were looking a little bony.

The Allies crossed the Rhine and came surging up toward us, but again the rosy dreams of liberation didn't come off. They marched us out again, heading north. I've got to hand it to the Germans. They were really reluctant to let us go. This trip, though, was a picnic by comparison with the last one. A few people were shot by trigger-happy guards and a few more killed by strafing aircraft, but the weather was good and we traded Red Cross coffee for eggs and bread and stole bushels and bushels of potatoes.

We didn't know it at the time (just as well) but the guards had orders to execute all of us if we didn't reach the Elbe by a certain day. We didn't reach the Elbe by that day but at this late stage the guards were getting rather prudent about mass murders so they decided to overlook the order.

We were sheltering in barns up near Luebeck when we heard the barrage as the British First Army crossed the Elbe. Two days later, on May 2, we heard firing down the road and two tanks rumbled through the trees from the south. We didn't know whether they were Germans or British, and you could practically see the nerves sticking out of everyone's skin and vibrating like piano wire. The hatch of the front tank opened, and two Tommies stuck their heads out. We ran up to them screaming at the top of our voices.

I T WAS cold-blooded butchery and we are resolved
that the foul criminals shall be tracked down."
Anthony Eden,
House of Commons, May, 1944.

In August, 1945, Wing Commander Bowes, of the R.A.F.
Special Investigation Branch, flew to Germany to find out
what had happened to the missing fifty. There was no final
proof they had been murdered, though there didn't seem
much doubt about it. Bowes was to find out if they had, in
fact, been murdered, track down the people responsible, and
arrest them.

He was a good choice for the job, an ex-Scotland Yard detective with no frills about him, a square red face and a reputation for dogged toughness. Back in Victoria's day, they'd
have called him one of the Bulldog Breed. He didn't have
much to go on—the stories of the people who had come back
from Goerlitz, the bare German announcements of the deaths,
and the urns of ashes engraved with the places of cremation.
He naturally suspected the Gestapo, but there was no real
evidence to pin on them.

In Hamburg he formed six interrogation teams of four men
each, and they toured the length and breadth of Western-
occupied Germany questioning captured Germans, now held

248

in scores of thousands in the camps where they had imprisoned us. They couldn't get into the Russian Zone, or Poland —the Russians wouldn't let them in—and that was the big snag. Sagan lay now across the new Polish border that had moved forward to embrace German Silesia. So did Breslau. Goerlitz lay half in the new Poland and half in the Russian Zone. In those forbidden cities lay the keys to the mystery.

Day after day, week after week, and then month after month, the interrogators went from camp to camp in the British, American, and French zones, questioning and questioning. One by one, Germans of the Wehrmacht, the Luftwaffe, the Kriegsmarine, the S.S., the Gestapo, and all the other police forces were marched in front of them. A man might question 250 of them in a day but every time, day after day, with the same result—nothing known.

They concentrated particularly on the areas named on the urns and leafed doggedly through reams and reams of records. They questioned altogether 250,000 Germans. No result. Not the vestige of a clue. The murderers, whoever they were, had covered their tracks and the mystery seemed impenetrable. . . .

Until, in March, 1946, a message came from Prague. The Czechs were holding a Gestapo man named Kiowski who they thought knew something about Kirby-Green and Kidder. Bowes flew to Prague, taking with him another ex-Scotland Yard detective, Flight Lieutenant Lyon, who spoke German.

The Czechs were holding Kiowski in Pangratz Prison, which the Gestapo had used during the war. A Czech officer showed Bowes over it.

"This is the efficient part," he said as they came to a long corridor with thirty cell doors on one side and a single door on the other.

"No accused man who went through this single door ever came out again," said the Czech. Behind the door was a courtroom and across the back of the room stretched a thick curtain. He pulled the curtain aside and showed them where the execution gangs waited for the victims of the court. This was sudden death. There was a rail across it, like the rails in butcher shops, and a row of nooses was hanging down from it. As men were sentenced, they strung them up and slid the nooses along the rail through another curtain into a room full of cheap coffins.

In a corner of the execution chamber, there was a guillotine. "They used to lie them face-up on this," said the Czech.

Bowes found Kiowski in a cell by himself, a dry-lipped, nervous little man with black hair. The Czechs had proof of ten murders against him. Kiowski admitted he *did* know a little about Kirby-Green and Kidder. It was the first break in the entire case. He had been stationed at Zlin, said Kiowski, on the German-Czech border, on March 28, 1944, when two suspects were caught trying to cross the frontier into Czechoslovakia. Their names, he found out later, were Kirby-Green and Kidder. The local Gestapo chief, Hans Ziegler, interrogated them, and later that night a Gestapo agent called Knuppelberg arrived from area Gestapo headquarters at Brno with orders about the two prisoners.

Kiowski said he was duty driver that night, and about 2 A.M. in the morning Ziegler called him and another driver named Schwarzer to drive the two prisoners back to Sagan. Knuppelberg sat in the back of his car with the handcuffed Kidder, and a local Gestapo man called Zacharias sat in the other car with Kirby-Green, also handcuffed.

About forty miles along the road, some ten miles before Moravska Ostrava, Knuppelberg stopped the cars and they let the two prisoners get out to relieve themselves, removing the handcuffs. Kiowski said that as they got to the side of the road, both Kirby-Green and Kidder made a sudden dash into the darkness. Sitting in the car, he heard shots from Zacharias and Knuppelberg, and both fleeing prisoners fell dead.

Bowes was certain Kiowski was lying. He had always expected that when he found the murderers they would say that the prisoners had been killed trying to escape. He and Lyon straddled themselves on two chairs, rested their arms on the backs, and settled down to cross-question Kiowski. They kept at it for six straight hours till they were all hoarse and sweating, Kiowski still sticking to his story.

And then they caught him in a flat lie. Hours earlier, Kiowski had said his orders were to drive straight to Sagan without stopping. And then later, in answer to what seemed an innocent question, Kiowski described how he had fueled the cars before they drove off and told how much gas he had put in. It was only enough to get them to Moravska Ostrava (where there was a crematorium) and back to Zlin. Sagan lay another 140 miles further on. Bowes put his red face close to Kiowski and shouted the lie back at him, and Kiowski fainted.

They brought him around by pouring slivovitch down his throat, and then Kiowski told the truth.

Before they set out from Zlin, he said, he had asked Zacharias what was going to happen to the two prisoners, and Zacharias had pointed with his thumb downward. About ten miles from Moravska Ostrava, as he had said before, they had stopped the cars and let the two prisoners out to urinate. As they stood by the side of the road, Zacharias stood behind Kidder and Knuppelberg behind Kirby-Green, both with drawn pistols. Knuppelberg looked at Zacharias across the few feet of darkness and raised his arm, the prearranged signal. Both lifted their pistols and fired simultaneously, and then Zacharias fired a second shot to make sure. Kirby-Green and Kidder slid to the ground without a sound. Death was instantaneous. Knuppelberg drove on to Moravska Ostrava and got an ambulance to take the bodies to the crematorium.

The Czechs wouldn't let Bowes take Kiowski. They had too much on him themselves, and later they executed him.

Bowes and Lyon went to Zlin to start the search for the

others, and there they found that Ziegler had committed suicide when Germany collapsed. In the local jail, however, they found Frau Zacharias. They learned a lot about Zacharias from her. Hell hath no fury like a woman scorned. He was not, it seems, either a good man or a good husband. There was the case of the Czech typist to whom Zacharias had paid some attention, and when she began to get a little difficult he murdered her. And after that there was the little girl of seventeen, a displaced person and suspected spy. Zacharias took her out into the woods and later he sent a Russian slave laborer to bury the body.

"He is in Bremen now," said Frau Zacharias, and gave Bowes the address. Bowes sent a man flying to Bremen, and at the address the wife had given, he arrested Zacharias, a big, blond-haired man with thin lips and nostrils; a very tough character as he proved within twenty-four hours by escaping from American custody.

Bowes was seething. They searched half of Germany, but there was no trace of Zacharias till on the seventeenth day they intercepted a letter card addressed to a relative which said, "Uncle Erich is well and is leaving shortly on a trip."

Zacharias' Christian names were Herman, August, Erich. The letter card came from a town up near the border of the Russian Zone. Bowes drove full speed there with a team of police, and at dusk they surrounded the house from which the letter card had come. Bowes and Lyon rushed in the back and front doors with drawn pistols, and in the kitchen they found Zacharias eating supper. Beside him was his bag, ready packed. He was to leave in an hour to slip across the border into the Russian Zone, where there would have been no hope of finding him.

Bowes flew him back to England, where he escaped again but was once more recaptured. In London District Cage he denied knowing anything about the shootings until they slapped in front of him the evidence of his wife and Kiowski, and Zacharias looked up and shrugged.

"Well, I can only die once," he said, and confessed.

Bowes at last knew the Gestapo was definitely involved in the shootings. He flew to Brno to track down Knuppelberg, and there he heard that a Brno Gestapo official, S.S.-*Hauptsturmfuehrer* Franz Schauschutz had been in Zlin about the time of the murders.

He found in Brno a little café where the Gestapo used to drink at night, and the proprietor, spitting at the mention of his former clients, told Bowes that Schauschutz and Knuppelberg and others used to hold drunken parties there several times a week, bringing typists whom they usually stripped naked. Around the walls a local artist had captured the spirit of some of the gatherings with a series of murals of satyrs holding naked girls. Greatly daring, the artist had drawn on the satyrs the heads of the Gestapo men (who had thought it a great joke).

"This," said the proprietor, stabbing a dirty finger at one, "is Knuppelberg. And this," pointing to another, "is Schauschutz." He added bitterly. "They never paid a bill in five years."

Bowes photographed the heads. In what was left of the Brno police records he found Schauschutz's name and an address in a little town in Austria. He drove to the town and arrested Schauschutz there, recognizing him from the photograph of the drawing on the wall of the Brno café.

Schauschutz had apparently not been involved in the actual shooting, but he knew something of the aftermath. After the announcements of the shootings there had been a great outcry in England (Bowes knew that well enough). An alarmed Ribbentrop had demanded of Himmler that the shootings be adequately covered.

Schauschutz said that Gestapo headquarters in Berlin sent

for Knuppelberg, and there in Gestapo chief Mueller's Berlin office Knuppelberg saw a man called Scharpwinkel, who was Gestapo chief at Breslau, and Gestapo men from Karlsruhe, Munich, Strasbourg, Saarbruecken, Danzig, and Kiel. As Schauschutz spoke, the case was breaking wide open.

Mueller, said Schauschutz, roughly rebuked the Gestapo representatives present. Their reports of the shootings of the escaped Air Force prisoners were all unimaginatively the same. Without exception, they said the prisoners tried to escape while being allowed to urinate beside the road on the way back to Sagan. They were to go and prepare fresh reports, said Mueller, putting more variety and convincing detail into them. Schauschutz said that Knuppelberg came back to Brno and made out a new fake report, which was sent to Berlin.

Bowes sent his teams to the cities mentioned by Schauschutz and applied to Warsaw for a permit to go to Breslau himself.

On four of the urns no town name had been engraved but in the Kiel Crematorium record book one of Bowes' men found an entry showing that, on March 29, 1944, four people had been cremated there. The column where the names should have been showed four blanks. Otto Fahl, the old crematorium attendant, said he vaguely remembered the four. They were men. He understood that they had come from Flensburg, on the Danish border.

In Flensburg, Bowes found some of the old local Gestapo in British custody, and they told him that the four had been escaped airmen who had been collected from them by men from Kiel Gestapo, led by a Major Post.

Bowes tracked down Post and arrested him in a garage at Celle. He was a dark, strong-looking, arrogant man and said he knew nothing of four such men. Bowes and his teams picked up more of Kiel Gestapo—Kaehler, Oskar Schmidt, Franz Schmidt, Jackobs and others. Franz Schmidt was the first to crack, and he told the story.

Jimmy Catanach, the Australian, Christensen, a New Zealander, and two Norwegians, Espelid and Fugelsang, had been arrested at gun-point right on the Danish border and thrown into jail. Fritz Schmidt, chief of Kiel Gestapo, received a secret order from Mueller in Berlin that the four were to be shot. He called Post and several more reliable executioners and told them what they had to do. Then he shook hands with each man to bind him to secrecy under his Gestapo oath.

Post and the others drove to Flensburg, and Post put Catanach in his car. The other three traveled in the second car. Post drew a couple of miles ahead of the others and stopped by a field near Rotenhahn. He led Catanach behind the hedge and shot him in the back. Catanach died instantly. A couple of minutes later the other car drove up. The other three prisoners were pushed into the field. One of them saw Catanach's body and let out a shout, and the three of them scattered, running, but were shot down before they had gone ten paces.

Bowes' men gave Schmidt paper and a pen and sent him to his cell to write out his confession. When they went back they found he had taken his singlet off, stood on a chair, tied the end of his singlet to the cell ventilator, twisted the armholes around his neck and stepped off the chair. He was hanging, quite dead. He had written something on the paper they had given him—a note addressed to his daughter. It said, "Hitler was right," and told her not to forget her Nazi teachings.

The other Kiel prisoners talked freely and gladly about Post, telling Bowes that he was an insatiable sadist. One of them told how Post had built a slave-labor camp outside Kiel and suggested that a certain one of the huts should be pulled down. The British put German workmen on to pulling it down, and under the foundations they found 160 corpses of Post's victims.

Bowes finally got around through Warsaw to Breslau, Goerlitz, Hirschberg, and Sagan but from the Russians and the Poles met only obstructionism and was not able to see a single one of the local Gestapo whom they had in jails. A Polish officer trailed him wherever he went, and Bowes finally sat down next to his shadow in a café and bought him drinks till he was glassy-eyed, in which condition the Pole freely told Bowes he was regarded as a spy.

Curiously enough, a report came through from Moscow that Scharpwinkel was being held there. Captain Cornish of the British Army flew there, and the Russians took him to see Scharpwinkel, a dark, ruthless man whom the Russians persuaded to speak. Though Scharpwinkel himself was economical with the truth, the details he gave implicated Wielen, and Wielen was tracked down in Western Germany. Wielen implicated Scharpwinkel, and bit by bit the truth came out.

Scharpwinkel had gone with Lux and his murder gang to Goerlitz on March 30, 1944, and there they had interrogated some of the prisoners. After lunch they put six of them in a truck—Cross, Mike Casey, Wiley, Leigh, Pohé, and Al Hake —and drove off toward Sagan. Five miles past Halbau, Scharpwinkel ordered the truck to pull up, and Lux and his gunmen prodded the prisoners into the roadway. They escorted them about a hundred yards into the wood and there Scharpwinkel told them they were to be executed.

("I was surprised," Scharpwinkel said reflectively in Moscow, "that they took it so calmly.")

They were lined up, and Lux gave the order to fire. By the second salvo they were all dead. Lux told Scharpwinkel that the following day they would go to Hirschberg.

The next day Lux and his men took ten more from Goerlitz —Humphries, McGill, Swain, Hall, Pat Langford, Evans, Valenta, Kolanowski, Stewart, and Birkland. The urns containing the ashes of these men showed they were cremated at

Liegnitz. Either that day or the day after, Lux also took his men to Hirschberg, where they took Kiewnarski, Pawluk, Wernham, and Skanziklas and shot them.

On April 6, Lux took another six from Goerlitz—Grisman, Gunn, J. F. Williams, Milford, Street, and McGarr. They were cremated at Breslau. But it was not till April 13 that Lux took Cookie Long from Goerlitz. His urn shows that he was cremated at Breslau.

That brought Lux's murder total to twenty-seven, a figure to which Tobolski can probably be added, and also, perhaps, Danny Krol, who was caught with Dowse at Oels, in the Breslau area. He was last seen alive there, and his urn is marked "Breslau."

Gradually, through patient research into regional Gestapos, Bowes brought to light the details of most of the other shootings.

Willy Williams (Squadron Leader J. E. A. Williams), Johnny Bull, Kierath, and Mondschein were caught trying to cross the Czech border near Reichenberg, and after interrogation and several days in the cells they were taken away from Reichenberg at four o'clock on the morning of March 29, and not seen again. They were cremated that same day at Bruex. They certainly weren't killed trying to escape again. Baatz, the local Gestapo chief, had signed the order for their cremation the previous day. Stower also vanished from Reichenberg Jail.

Kriminalpolizei took Gouws and Stevens off a train south of Munich and, on the evening of March 28, three Gestapo men were ordered to shoot them and pledged to secrecy by handshake. They drove the two prisoners out of Munich in a car, stopped in open country, and told them they could get out to relieve themselves. As they stood by the side of the road, a Gestapo agent called Schneider shot both with a machine pistol. They were cremated at Munich. A year later, when the

American Army was approaching Munich, Weil, one of the shooting party, went to the crematorium and tried to rub their names out of the record book with a penknife.

Cochran was caught near Karlsruhe, and on March 31, he was taken out in a car toward Natzweiler and shot from behind in the woods by a Gestapo agent called Preiss. Tony Hayter was not caught for nearly two weeks and then police picked him up at Strasbourg on the French border. On April 6, two Strasbourg Gestapo men drove him out on the autobahn toward Breslau and shot him, as the others had done, by the side of the road.

Bushell and Scheidhauer had caught their train all right from Sagan. (Van Der Stok saw Bushell buying train tickets in Breslau station.) A day or two later they reached Saarbruecken and were waiting on the platform for a train down to Alsace when two security policemen questioned them. They showed their papers, which were almost perfect. Roger had some of the original passes. Scheidhauer spoke natural French, of course, and Roger spoke good French and faultless Bernese German. They had their stories word-perfect—they were Frenchmen who'd been working in Germany and were going home on leave. They answered perfectly questions about their homes and families, and at last the police seemed satisfied and handed the passes back.

As they were walking away one of them pulled an old trick. He swung around and shot a sudden question at Scheidhauer, and Scheidhauer, who had been speaking English in the compound for two years, involuntarily answered in English. The police had their pistols out in a second and took them away to Lerchesflur Prison.

During the next few days they were interrogated by the Kriminalpolizei, and as the alternative seemed to lie in being regarded as spies, they finally admitted they had escaped from Stalag Luft III. On the evening of March 28, Dr. Spann,

Gestapo chief in Saarbruecken, received a top secret teleprint order from General Mueller that the two prisoners were to be shot. Spann sent his triggerman, Emil Schulz, to collect them from the prison. Schulz handcuffed them behind their backs, and a Gestapo driver called Breithaupt drove him, Spann, and the two prisoners out along the autobahn toward Kaiserslautern.

A few miles out, Spann ordered the car to stop, and they took the handcuffs off the prisoners and told them they could get out and relieve themselves. By the side of the road, Spann and Schulz each fired two shots. Scheidhauer fell straight forward on his face and did not move. Bushell crumpled slowly onto his right side. They were cremated at Saarbruecken.

Schulz and Breithaupt were not popular in Saarbruecken. Bowes found some of their old colleagues in prison camps there, and they told him everything they knew, including the probable whereabouts of the two. A couple of days later, Schulz was arrested at his home in the French Zone, and about the same time they found Breithaupt hiding in a hut in a wood in the American Zone. Retribution had already caught up with Spann. In the closing days of the war he had been killed in an air raid on Linz.

Spann wasn't the only one beyond human justice. Fittingly enough General Nebe, who had selected the fifty victims and given their names to the Gestapo, had had his own name handed to the Gestapo. He had been imprudent enough to become implicated in the Hitler bomb plot of July, and his old friend, General Mueller, with whom he and Kaltenbrunner had lunch every day, hanged him.

Mueller did not grieve long. He died in the fighting when the Russians took Berlin. Kaltenbrunner died at Nuremberg with other top Nazis.

Lux died in the fighting in Breslau, and so did most of his murder gang. The rest vanished.

The Russians did not hand Scharpwinkel over. They reported that he had died in Moscow after an illness. (Bowes will bet a pound to a penny that the brilliant and ruthless Scharpwinkel is still in an official uniform either in Russia or the Russian Zone of Germany, training men in the job he knows so well for new masters.)

Bowes now knew what had happened in varying detail to forty-six of the fifty, and in custody he had eighteen men for trial. There were several more smaller fry he wanted in addition to those who had died, but they had scattered throughout Germany and covered their tracks.

The trial of the eighteen started on July 1, 1947, before No. 1 War Crimes Court in the old-fashioned gray courtroom of the Kurio Haus in Hamburg. The military judges, red-tabbed in khaki and in R.A.F. blue, sat in a row before a table on a raised dais at the head of the room, a major-general, an air commodore, three colonels, and two wing commanders. In the middle of them, to guide them on law, sat the wigged and black-gowned Advocate-General, C. L. Stirling, C.B.E., K.C., a tall spare man with pince-nez and a crisp, incisive voice.

On the other side of the room, the accused sat in two rows on benches in the large dock, and in front of them sat their black-gowned German counsel.

For fifty days—one for each murdered man—the damning evidence mounted against them, and on the fiftieth day the court convicted them all.

Grizzled, sixty-four-year-old Wielen was found guilty of taking part in the high-level conspiracy to murder the fifty and sentenced to life imprisonment.

Schulz and Breithaupt were convicted of murdering Bushell and Scheidhauer and sentenced to death.

Alfred Schimmel was convicted of the murder of Tony Hayter and sentenced to death.

Josef Gmeiner, Walter Herberg, Otto Preiss, and Heinrich Boschert were found guilty of the murder of Cochran. Death sentence.

Johannes Post and Hans Kahler were sentenced to death for the murder of Catanach, Christensen, Fugelsang, and Espelid; Arthur Denkman, their driver, got ten years for being an accessory.

Oskar Schmidt and Walter Jackobs were sentenced to death for the murders of Christensen, Espelid, and Fugelsang. Their driver, Wilhelm Struve, was sentenced to ten years for being an accessory.

Emil Weil, Eduard Geith, and Johan Schneider were found guilty of the murders of Gouws and Stevens and sentenced to death.

Zacharias was sentenced to death for the murders of Kidder and Kirby-Green.

Post was arrogant and sneering to the last. He must have realized that there could only be one way out for him. Most of the others became very subdued. Jackobs embraced religion.

Boschert's death sentence was later commuted to life imprisonment, but the other fourteen condemned men were hanged in Hamelin Jail, near Hamburg, on February 26, 1948.

Four of the murdered airmen were still unavenged—Tim Walenn, Henri Picard, Gordon Brettell, and Romas Marcinkus. Bowes had traced them to Danzig, where they had been aiming. Police had taken them off a train near Schneidemuehl and lodged them for a day in a near-by prison camp. A British sergeant-major in that camp had reported after the war that they had a plot to escape again, and as they were about to put it into execution, the Gestapo arrived and took them away.

That, Bowes assumed, would be Danzig Gestapo. He had sixty of the former Danzig and district Gestapo held behind barbed wire at Esteveger, near Danzig, and he cross-questioned them repeatedly but could not get a lead. Danzig Gestapo chief, Dr. Venediger, would be certain to know, but Venediger had vanished. And then one day in July, 1948, one of the prisoners called Achterberg asked to see him.

"I feel that a lot of quite innocent men are being held here," Achterberg said. "The man you want is called Burchhardt, and I think I can tell you where you might find him. His wife lives just north of Hamburg," and Achterberg mentioned an address in a little town.

He and the others told Bowes a lot about their old colleague Burchhardt, and none of it was very nice. Burchhardt, they said, was Danzig's most reliable executioner because he took such a pride and pleasure in his work. He had a record of many murders in the name of duty. His favorite method, according to his comrades, was to take his victims to his own room and flog them to death with a rhinoceros hide whip. They said he was such a huge, gorilla-like man that he could almost take a man's head off with his whip. Bowes wouldn't believe it at first, but so many of Burchhardt's old colleagues repeated the story so sincerely that he came to believe them.

"Be careful of Burchhardt," one of them said. "He will probably shoot first."

A party of armed men went to the address Achterberg had given and found Burchhardt's wife there, but no Burchhardt. They *did* find, though, that Burchhardt had made the same mistake as Zacharias.

"He's run away with his mistress," said the abandoned frau with fury. "I can tell you where you'll find him—in a town called Kempten in the American Zone. He calls himself Brandt now and is working as a carpenter. You'll probably find him with the woman, Toni Schatz."

They drove all day and reached Kempten, near the Swiss border, about midnight, and at one o'clock in the morning they raided Toni Schatz' flat. Fraulein Schatz was a shapely blonde who welcomed them with shrill fury in a short slip that barely camouflaged what it did not hide. At first she said she'd never heard of Brandt, or Burchhardt, but when they threatened to confront her with Frau Burchhardt herself she broke down and gave them the address of a flat not far away.

Leaving a guard with Toni so she could not give a warning, Bowes posted twenty men around the entrances to the flats where the girl said Burchhardt was. He roused the janitor and got the master key, and at 3 A.M. Bowes and Lyon softly let themselves in the door of a flat where the janitor said Herr Brandt lived.

The flat was in darkness, and they felt their way into the bedroom. When they were quietly in position standing with drawn pistols over a dark form asleep in the bed, Bowes flicked on the light. Burchhardt was awake in a second and jumped halfway up the wall with shock at seeing them. They found a loaded gun under his pillow. He was so huge they could not fit the handcuffs over his wrists.

"I hope," said Burchhardt, the unorthodox executioner, "that I'm going to get fair play."

Checking Burchhardt's story with the evidence of the Danzig Gestapo men held at Esteveger (they were talking freely now), Bowes found what had happened to the last four recaptured airmen. Burchhardt and a murder team had driven them to a wood outside Trampken about twelve miles from Danzig, and among the trees, seventy yards away from the road, they machine-gunned them and the four died instantly.

About the same time, Bowes caught up with Erwin Wieczorek, who had been with Lux's gang in Goerlitz, and Richard Haensel, Kriminalpolizei chief in Goerlitz. On October 11, 1948, these two and Burchhardt faced the War Crimes Court, again sitting in the gray, paneled courtroom of the Kurio Haus in Hamburg.

The trial lasted twenty days and Wieczorek was found guilty of being concerned in the murders of Cross, Casey, Leigh, Wiley, Pohé, and Hake and sentenced to death.

Haensel was acquitted on the grounds that it was not proved that he had taken a real part in the murder conspiracy.

Burchhardt was convicted of the murders of Walenn, Picard, Brettell, and Marcinkus, and sentenced to death.

Wieczorek and Burchhardt did not hang. Wieczorek's conviction was not confirmed by the British occupation authorities. He claimed that he had not been present when the men had been shot in the woods but had stayed behind tinkering with the engine of one of the cars parked on the autobahn. He was freed.

The death sentence on that trusty executioner Burchhardt was commuted to imprisonment for life. The authorities considered it was a little too long since the four murders (four years) to exact the full penalty. Life imprisonment is twenty-one years. Some say there will be an amnesty long before that, and I expect they are probably right.